Social Sector in India

Social Sector in India

Changing Paradigms in Uttar Pradesh

Edited by

S.K. Pant

Published under the auspices of
Govind Ballabh Pant Social Science Institute, Allahabad

RAWAT PUBLICATIONS
Jaipur • New Delhi • Bangalore • Mumbai

ISBN 81-7033-965-0

First published, 2005

Published by
Prem Rawat for **Rawat Publications**
Satyam Apts., Sector 3, Jawahar Nagar, Jaipur 302 004 (India)
Phone: 0141 265 1748 / 7006 Fax: 0141 265 1748
E-mail: info@rawatbooks.com
Website: www.rawatbooks.com

New Delhi Office
4858/24, Ansari Road, Daryaganj, New Delhi 110 002
Phone: 011-23263290

Also at Bangalore and Mumbai

Typeset by Rawat Computers, Jaipur
Printed at Chaman Enterprises, New Delhi

Contents

Foreword

India's experience with planning has rather been a mixed one. On the one hand, it has, no doubt, propelled the country into the frontiers of some spheres while on the other, it has met with glaring disappointment in many other areas as well. In addition, the failure of the planning to distribute the fruits of development evenly has accentuated the problems of marginalisation of the disadvantaged sections of the society, regional imbalances, poverty, malnutrition etc. Moreover, all this has been experienced at a time when a number of economic assistance programmes were being launched from time to time in different plan periods to address these issues. The economic angularities, instead of mitigating, have not only persisted, with the time, but have even grown and become more sharp, thereby, threatening the fruits of development on one hand and questioning the relevance and basis of planning on the other. All these efforts have brought home the very fact that economic development alone was neither sufficient nor capable of addressing the multi-dimensional problems of development. It has to be supplemented by strengthening the social sector. Emphasis on one, at the cost of other, would lead to disastrous consequences. The development experience of various nations all over world shows that the countries with rich human resources, consisting of healthy and educated people, with a sense of discipline, dedication and work culture, could ultimately gear the economy in the desired channels of growth. Thus, in order to provide sustainability to the overall process of growth, the development of social sector is a mandatory condition. Now, with the onset of new economic policy (NEP), in which increasing emphasis is being placed on liberalisation, privatisation and globalisation, the government expenditure on social sector is likely to be curtailed as has been reported in many of the studies by the scholars. Therefore, the real challenge before the government is not only to devise alternative means to provide adequate resources for this sector but also to provide conducive environment to develop it and to make it equally competitive.

G.B. Pant Social Science Institute, Allahabad, over the years, has been deeply involved in the development issues in general and of the state of Uttar Pradesh and its adjoining areas in particular. During all these times, it has brought out many books, monographs, project reports and research articles which have been well received by planners, research fraternity and the academia. We feel that it is our moral duty to highlight some of the social issues that have been studied and analysed by the faculty to a wider audience. Articles included in this volume have largely been drawn from the research projects that have been undertaken for various prestigious organisations and have focused on various crucial facets of the social sector. I am pretty sure that this book would be of special interest to planners, policy makers and research scholars. I take this opportunity to thank all the authors for contributing research articles despite their busy and demanding schedule. I am also thankful to my colleague S.K. Pant for willingly accepted the responsibility of editing the articles.

R.C. Tripathi
Director
G.B. Pant Social Science Institute, Allahabad

Introduction

S.K. Pant

India's tryst with planning, which began in the right earnest soon after attaining independence in the early fifties of the twentieth century, brought home many important but new lessons. The first and foremost being that economic development alone was not a sufficient condition to ensure all-round development. Though there has been a rise in per capita real income levels, however, the benefits of economic development have failed to reach the masses. The development experiences of various countries of the world, including Asian countries, revealed that the nations with rich human resources, consisting of healthy and educated people, with a sense of discipline, dedication and work culture, could ultimately gear the economy in the desired channels of growth. Thus, it became abundantly clear that economic development has not only to be matched but also supplemented with social development in order to provide the positive catalytic effect and sustenance to the overall process of development.

The failure of trickle down theory, along with other economic disappointments, precipitated in the marginalisation of a sizeable section of the population, which has also severely curtailed their ability to participate forcefully in the mainstream of planning process. The net outcome has been reflected in their stunted growth. All these socio-economic angularities, with the passage of time, have not only persisted but have also grown and become even more sharp, thereby, not only threatening to negate all the positive achievements attained so far but also questioning the rationale of planning. Besides this, the development process has also succeeded in creating many developed pockets, which were initially supposed to act as facilitators of development change by promoting the process of decentralised planning in other regionally backward areas. However, on the contrary, these pockets started attracting both the physical as well as non-physical resources thereby stifling the process to these less developed regions and also giving a severe jolt to the concept of balanced development.

With the onset of new economic policy (NEP) and increasing emphasis being placed on liberalisation, privatisation and globalisation (LPG), which are the main planks of market economy, the Indian economy appears to be at the crossroads. While, on the one hand, the growth and the performance of agricultural sector has been sluggish and dwindling, on the other hand, the industrial scenario has been marked by acquisitions, closures and takeovers by the multinationals, which has resulted in the retrenchment of large section of workers both in the skilled and unskilled categories. It has now become abundantly clear that without developing the social sector, the country cannot afford to compete with other developed nations of the world. Thus, the focus of the planning, which earlier was on the promotion of growth subsequently, shifted to empowerment of masses and finally to developing the social sector.

The present volume which is a compendium of nine research papers contributed by the faculty members of G.B. Pant Social Science Institute, Allahabad focuses on the how the various facets of social sector in the state of Uttar Pradesh have performed and undergone change with the passage of time. These articles have mainly been drawn from the projects they had pursued for various prestigious organisations like the Planning Commission, New Delhi; Landuse Board, Planning Department, Lucknow, National Council of Education Research and Training (NCERT), New Delhi; Directorate of Adult Education, UP etc. This volume is dedicated to Professor A.D. Pant, the first Director of the Institute, whose inspirational guidance, vision and encouragement have helped many of us to trek, understand and comprehend the subtle nuances and the difficult terrains of social science research.

The volume begins with a paper by Bhaskar Majumder who studies the public distribution system (PDS) in India with a focus on Allahabad. According to him, the PDS primarily aims at providing social protection to the vulnerable sections. The concept of PDS was evolved as a sequel to counter the frequent recurrence of famines during the British colonial rule in the country, which inflicted heavy causalities both in human and capital terms. The purpose of the study is to examine how social welfare is being promoted through protection of minimum necessary consumption of food for the vulnerable population in the country. The paper is divided into nine sections and each section is devoted to various facets of PDS, viz., the historical genesis of the scheme, its features and rationale, the administrative set-ups, objectives, methodology and finally the policy recommendations. The study strongly feels that in TDPS the targeting should take care of not only the exclusion of non-poor but also on covering the needy poor who have not been covered so far in the PDS network. It broadly covers 261 inhabited revenue villages and two town areas. The sample covers about 2 per cent of all the gram panchayats and 15 per cent of all the wards in two town areas of the district. In all, it covers a total of 1,400 households which were selected through stratified random sample technique. Accepting Rs. 11,000 per annum as the household income for defining the poverty level, the study shows that though the sample contained about 80 per cent of households falling in BPL (below poverty line) category, however, around 19 per cent of remaining households' income exceeded that level and were thus in the APL (above poverty line) category. There were more than 1 per cent of the beneficiaries who had remained cardless. Attempt has also been made to study the distribution of FPS (fair price shops) on the basis of distance from the beneficiaries houses and finds that about 14 per cent of the households did not have PDS facilities in their villages. The study also shows that about 5 per cent of the households were in possession of two ration cards and around 1 per cent also had three ration cards and this trend was more pronounced in the BPL category. Analysing the pattern of lifting and allotment of time and the gap between requirement and distribution of items in the PDS, the study finds that the level of lifting of items in the APL category was much lesser than the BPL category for items like wheat and rice. However, for kerosene, the level of lifting, as the percentage of allotment, was, on an average, over 96 per cent. The study further explains that though the PDS was meant to provide support to the vulnerable sections, its contribution in meeting the demand of the sample households has remained quite insignificant. It also shows that, item-wise, there was not much variation in the prices in the open market and the PDS. The study reveals that the overall awareness level among the beneficiaries regarding fair price shops, price information by price chart or by items was distressingly low, which also contributed to the poor performance of the PDS. In the end, the paper comes up with certain policy recommendations that aim at ensuring the regularity and allotment of distribution of items, making the upkeep of the records at FPS a mandatory practice, allotment of new FPS dealerships to local educated and unemployed youths, putting a blanket ban on criminal and illegal interference in the PDS network by outsiders, and toning up the village vigilance network.

According to Bimal Kumar, though the state of Uttar Pradesh continues to be predominantly agricultural, however, the area and proportion of urban population, of late, have steadily been increasing. There has been a continuous inward migration of people to cities in the hope of getting better economic opportunities, new jobs, education, etc., and all this was generating pollution beyond its tolerable limits. The situation is becoming an alarming one not because of rapid population growth but more due to failure of systematic planning. According to him, wherever the issues of urbanisation are taken up, they generally focus on problems pertaining only to metropolitan and big cities. The issues of smaller towns are generally overlooked. As a result, the policy framework, meant to regulate various dimensions of urbanisation, usually confines itself to discussing the peripheral urban problems rather than taking a comprehensive and holistic view.

The study covers two cities of the state of Uttar Pradesh, namely, Lucknow and Kanpur. Both of them have experienced high level of urbanisation and, consequently, large-scale conversion of agricultural land. The study has taken up only those villages where acquisition of land had taken place after 1980. Tracing the profile of the growth pattern and the impact on land use in these two cities, he cites different reasons for their expansion. In Kanpur, the major reason of expansion has been due to its emergence as a major commercial centre where trade and commerce and other services are the main occupations in which majority of the working population is engaged. However, Lucknow has experienced growth largely because of inward migration. Earlier, Lucknow had been famous for its household industries like chicken work, zardozi, gold lace etc., besides perfume and tobacco industries. However, during the last four decades, it has grown as an administrative-cum-commercial city. It has also witnessed rapid growth in the tertiary sector.

The paper also studies the impact of land acquisition on farmers and for this in all 348 farmers whose land had been acquired were selected. The caste composition of farmers shows that about 29 per cent were Scheduled Castes (SCs), 14 per cent belonged to Other Backward Castes (OBCs) and about 27 per cent were from the general castes. The acquisition of land was mainly for housing purpose, followed by setting up of industries. Most of the farmers from whom the land was acquired were small and marginal farmers and the average size of land acquired was less than two acres. As a result of land transfer, over 50 per cent of the cultivators have been forced to work as agricultural labourers, about 12 per cent have got service, over 17 per cent were engaged in business activities and about 4 per cent have so far remained unemployed. The study also shows that no one was given employment by the acquisition agency in lieu of the land acquired. In majority of the cases, the monthly income of affected families was less than Rs. 2,000 and the rate of compensation awarded to the affected families was quite meagre against which some families had filed petition in court and had duly won the case, but were not given the compensation amount, determined by the court, so far. The analysis also finds that majority of the farmers had spent the compensation amount either on the construction of house or on family marriages. No one had utilised it for augmenting their household income. On the basis of analysis, the study comes up with certain suggestions such as provision of detailed scheme for utilisation of land to be acquired also needs to be prepared along with the process of land acquisition, person from the affected family be provided employment by the acquiring agency, part of the appreciated value of acquisition land also needs to be paid to affected family, and necessary support and credit be given to the affected families so that they become beneficiaries of schemes which are specifically identified for them. Finally, the study also suggests a framework for maintaining urban-rural balance and strongly advocates for the convergence of administrative set-up at the state, region and block levels, provisions of providing basic infrastructural facilities to the acquired land, etc.

K.N. Bhatt, in his paper, analyses the standards of primary education in Uttar Pradesh. According to him, the basic objective of development process should be the removal of illiteracy, ill-health, social deprivation and above all expansion of individual freedom and elementary capabilities of the human beings. The nations all over the world have progressed largely on account of their well-developed structure of elementary education, which, in turn, promoted and facilitated the process of participatory development.

The paper is based on the findings of an empirical study conducted by G.B. Pant Social Science Institute, Allahabad in the year 1995-96 and highlights the academic achievements of the government schools in the three districts, viz., Allahabad, Ballia and Etawah of Uttar Pradesh. It primarily focuses on studying the academic standards of the students who have successfully completed the prescribed course of learning for class V in language and arithmetic in class II and examines, whether the exogenous factors like the caste, gender and location and heterogeneity affect their performance level, etc. The role of social environment and its influence on them has also been examined. The test papers used for assessing the performances of the students were developed by the NCERT, New Delhi and the data for the study were collected through a sample survey in each of the three districts. The study shows that the performance of students of both the classes in language as well as arithmetic subjects was quite poor in all the three sample districts. The achievement level of the students was scaled in five distinct categories, viz., those acquiring 0 marks, those acquiring below MLL (minimum learning level) i.e. less than 40 per cent, MLL i.e. 31 per cent and 59 per cent, near mastery i.e. between 60 per cent and 70 per cent and master grade between 80 per cent and 100 per cent. The analysis further reveals that the achievement levels of the students in language subject in both class II and primary levels was quite disappointing and hardly about 3 per cent of them in Allahabad, 7 per cent in Banda and 4 per cent in Etawah had attained the master grade and the majority of them did not even qualify the minimum literacy level grade. Likewise, in arithmetic also, none of the students in both classes could attain master grade and majority of them placed well below the MLL grade. It also shows that a majority of the dropout students had reverted back to the stage of complete illiteracy. This is attributed to factors like the urgency of household duties, compulsion of supplementing their family income, inability of the parents to meet the cost of their education and more importantly, the parental apathy towards education. The study also shows that almost all of them came from very poor families and in a majority of cases the parents were either illiterate or had scanty education as a result of which very few of the students received assistance from their families in their studies. The researcher feels that though the existing situation has been an outcome of several factors, however, through purposeful policy interventions, the performance could be enhanced and the areas that need toning were the regular inspection of the schools, improvement in the supervision and support services, enhancing the academic and professional competition to the teachers by organising regular on-the-job training and by providing adequate material inputs.

P.C. Upadhyaya and U. Kalpagam have studied the status of women's health in rural Uttar Pradesh and argue that there is a severe reproductive health crisis in the state. They feel that unless rural health infrastructure and health expenditure are not substantially improved, there is a very little chance of improving the productive and reproductive health status of rural women here. According to them, the health status should be understood in a broader perspective. It is largely the outcome of deprivations, which are of varied nature, viz., physical, economic, psychological, social and political. Deprivation, therefore, should be judged in terms of fulfilment of basic needs of which health care has an important place not only from the development aspect but also from the policy aspect as well. They have examined the status of rural women on the basis of some crucial indicators like life expectancy at birth, expectancy of life at the age of one, infant mortality rate, death rate, sex ratio, births attended by health professional and the women's control over reproductive decisions. Basing their analysis heavily on the secondary data from sources like the Human Development Report, NFHS, WHO, Planning Commission and census publications, they find that Uttar Pradesh was lagging behind the other states on almost all the critical indicators. According to them, rural women in the state have been very poor in health indicators largely on account of their inability or minimal role in the control over major health-related issues which have persisted largely on account of the dominance of patriarchal system in the family structure. Further, in their study of the health status of the Nuts, a recently settled semi-nomadic community, whose socio-cultural occupations are *fakiri*, acrobating, entertainment and ethno-medical practices, they have also found that the health status of their females was distressingly low. In the absence of registered medical practitioners, the birth of a child was taking place under the supervision of an elderly Nut woman who could be a mother-in-law or a sister-in-law or any other else from outside their community. On account of their reliance on traditional mode of therapeutics and prevalence of superstitions, the infant mortality rate among them was also found to be exceptionally high. Often deprived of food in the family, females faced a lot of gender bias also. The food deprivation often led to nutritional imbalances which had far-reaching impact on their reproductive and child bearing capacity. They conclude that the position of the Nut women was not satisfactory in their society. Deprived and neglected of their rights, they did not get opportunities of development. According to them, there is a need to re-orient the state's population policy which should go beyond target-specific approaches to a more comprehensive focus on reproductive health needs and services.

R.M. Tripathi has analysed the socio-economic and health problems of the aged people in Allahabad. According to him, aging is a natural process, which cannot be reversed. Of late, the proportion of senior citizens in the total population has been increasing rapidly in both the developed and developing worlds due to a number and factors like the advancement made in the field of medical sciences, better nourishment and improvement in the overall standard of public health institutions. While the developed world, on the one hand, has been taking a number of effective measures to cope up with the problem, the developing nations, on the other hand, have so far failed to address it adequately. The plans to support elderly people are highly inadequate as a result of which longevity for a majority of old people is taken as an adversity. The last years of their lives are full of hardships and loneliness. The study makes a detailed investigation on various aspects of the aged people, such as demographic structure, growth of elderly people along with its implications on wider perspectives in the urban setting of the city. In the investigation both the primary as well as secondary data have been used. While the secondary data was collected from sources like census reports, district gazetteers, district census handbooks, district statistical bulletins, etc., the primary data was collected largely through the structured questionnaire that contained relevant questions. The study also uses observational schedule to enable the study team to supplement the analysis.

Analysing the socio-economic conditions, he finds that the sample constituted a diverse and heterogeneous group, which differed from each other in many ways. A majority of them (over 64 per cent) were in the age group of 60-69 years and the average age of the sample was found to be about 65 years. The married aged comprised the largest group and about a quarter of them were widow or widower. The incidence of remarriage was not much reported after the separation, either through death or desertion. The study also shows that hardly 37 per cent of females were literate against 84 per cent in case of males. The sample comprised majority of the respondents (over 63 per cent) from the general castes while the proportion of OBCs and

SCs was worked out to be about 24 per cent and 9 per cent respectively. However, minority constituted only 4 per cent of the total. It also shows that the incidence of widowhood was highest amongst SCs, followed by OBCs and general castes. They attribute it to factors like practice of prohibition or non-acceptance of widow re-marriage in the Hindu caste system. Further, the study also reveals that about 13 per cent of the aged lived as wholly dependent on others while another quarter of them were partially dependent and were being supported either by their children or relatives. The dependency was more pronounced among the females because of their poor literacy status, lack of employment, lack of financial support, etc. They expect that with the spread of education among them, this trend would be reversed. The study further shows that a majority of them also owned the houses in which they lived. Commenting on the income level, the study uncovers that only about 87 per cent of the aged people were income holders which they were receiving through various pension schemes and only about 13 per cent of them had no secure income sources. The incidence of poverty was found to be highest among the SC and OBC groups while it was least among the general caste category. Analysing the health status and physical handicaps, it makes a distinction between illness and sickness. Accordingly, every living being may have disability of one kind or other, which surfaces with the advancement of age and is a natural process. The major factors contributing to the dependency were chronic and degenerative diseases or physical defects because they continue over a longer period with slow process of recovery. The major ailments among the aged were arthritis, muscular pain, blood pressure, etc., and a majority of them preferred allopathic treatment. About half of them received treatment from government doctors, i.e., from the government hospitals and other kinds of formal health centres. It was also found that the female patients generally preferred private doctors largely on account of their proximity or acquaintance and greater accessibility. The study shows that about half of the respondents had no complaints about the nature of arrangement that their family had made for their treatment. However, dissatisfaction prevailed mostly among the poor and economically dependent respondents. An overwhelming proportion of respondents received nursing from their families during illness. The elders, who lived alone, were left to find for themselves. It also unveils that there was a distinct variation in the type of persons who provided nursing to old persons. The male members, dependent more on their wives for nursing and care while females, by and large, were left to fend for themselves, largely because females were mostly widow and secondly nursing was considered to be a domestic task, which conventionally fell under the female's domain.

Sunit Singh and Vanita Somvanshi have studied how the community level participation ensures success of any development project. According to them, the role of community participation has now been well recognised that it has become a mandatory condition in all the development projects. However, despite of all these conditionalities and pre-requisites, the ground realities are quite different and there exists a wide gap between the spirit of the project, at the time of conception, and by the time it is implemented. As a result of which many a time the project even fails to take off.

Basing their assessment on the process and outcomes of the intervention activities that G.B. Pant Social Science Institute (hereinafter called the Institute), has been organising in one of the rural stations during the last eight years, the researchers feel that for success of the project, the identification of the problem has to be undertaken by the members of the community only and that too by consensus. Citing example of Asepur village, which had no girls' school before the experiment was initiated, the team of facilitators from the Institute organised a series of meetings and also facilitated opening of the community initiated girls' school without outside support, which has now been successfully running with over 150 students. The most striking feature of the experiment has been that the school's management has now been taken over by its alumni.

However, the success was not achieved in a day and for this the Institute had to adopt different and supplementary intervention strategies, such as process approach, convergence approach, agency approach etc. The basic focus of all these approaches was to sensitise the community and invoke its participation. The success of any programme lies only when it reaches the level of autonomy and self-sufficiency.

The paper is primarily divided into seven sections which, apart from highlighting the objective of the experiment, spells out the intervention approaches adopted, traces village profile and shares the outcomes of the experiment. In the course of implementation, the programme faced a lot of resistance from local people who had vested interests; however, through repeated rounds of talks and meetings, all doubts were cleared. The Institute not only encouraged the local villagers to come forward and stake their claim, but also facilitated their move by interacting with the government and district administration to support their cause.

The Institute, on its part, was keen to ensure the success of the programme and for this it devised many innovative strategies like invoking voluntary labour, encouraging partnership building, mobilisation of local resources, organising vocational training etc. The outcome of all years has been outstanding. It has succeeded in developing the local level of organisation with women as real stakeholders in the development of community school. Not only the target of 100 per cent enrolment of girls has been achieved but the performance of student has also been exceptional. The girls, who have acquired educational skill, have also taken the role of disseminating it to other deprived sections. Their literacy robustness has increased their horizon and they now envisage of attaining economic independence and financial security. The spin off effect of education on the community has been great; for instance, not only their awareness towards health, hygiene and environment has enhanced, but they have also gained confidence and have become assertive in managing the school. There has been a perceptible change in the attitude of parents who have now started valuing education, its relevance and validity. The community school has also succeeded in forging alliance with other organisations and institutions like the panchayats, education department, health department, local administration etc. This way it has succeeded in attaining backward and forward linkages in the area which is vital for sustainability of any project.

In the course of the study, it was also observed that for the success of any programme it is essential to have informal relationship with the community members without which the programme fails to sustain. Similarly, minimum social support at local level is also important to ensure effective implementation of any project. It was also felt that through local level strategies like inviting participation of voluntary labour, partnership building, and convergence and peaceful methods of resolving the conflicts are effective tools for mobilising the community support. Likewise, systematic documentation of policies and programmes that have been implemented in the area helps in keeping track of the level of progress achieved. Besides this, the administration cannot remain a passive player; it has to play a pro-active role in sustaining the momentum of the programme.

S.K. Pant studies the perception of urban poor in Allahabad towards educating their girl child. The urban poor have been identified as those sets of household who have migrated to city (urban areas) from rural areas in search of better economic opportunities. However, once they reach the urban settlement, they face a lot of hostilities. On account of their poor socio-economic and literacy status, they invariably fail to secure job in the city's urban formal sector where the remuneration and perks are high. They are ultimately drawn towards the city's informal sector. However, as the wage structure and service conditions are poor, the return they get fails to support their large families. So, in order to supplement their household income, they, at times, work at many places and often deploy their whole family, which includes their children or a female member. Education, in the process, is relegated to inferior position, as survival for them becomes the most crucial fact. While the males do various kinds of odd jobs, which include hawkers, venders, mechanics, helpers in roadside *dhabas*/restaurants, etc. The females either work independently or with urban households where they do various kinds of activities like cleansing of utensils, washing clothes or cooking and many a time even looking after younger siblings. It is their interaction with urban families that exposes them to a whole set of new urban culture, which they had not encountered before. It is expected that this exposure, on regular and sustained basis, is likely to influence their perception towards educating their children in general and girl child in particular. To what extent these urban poor households have been able to translate their perception into concrete action has been examined in this.

Two hundred families from the two slums, viz., Alopibagh and Mehdauri, were randomly selected from the list provided by DUDA (District Urban Development Agency). The households were classified into two groups on the basis of their nature of work. The first group consisted of those households who got the opportunity to work with urban families while the second group was of those households who were not associated with the urban families. The educational profile of the sample households shows that the sample contained an overwhelming proportion (over 63 per cent) of the households as illiterate while the proportion of households as literate and the those having technical qualifications was less than 1 per cent. The comparison of educational profile of households between the two slums shows that the incidence of illiteracy was higher in the Alopibagh and the highest proportion of illiterates was found among the OBC households, followed by the SCs. Likewise, the caste-wise enrolment shows that there has been a decline in the enrolment level of students as one moves from lower to higher classes and this dropout rate was highest among the students of SC category. The study, while analysing the gender-wise enrolment pattern, found that the dropout rate among the boys was much higher than that of the girls and it is attributed to factors like their role in supporting and supplementing household income, inability of the households to appreciate the importance of education etc. It further reveals that the involvement of households in their children's education was very disappointing as a majority of them were not concerned with any aspect of providing assistance to them, e.g., providing tuition, checking of home work, monitoring or even writing suggestions to schools etc. However, the study also shows that the households at Mehdauri slums were better involved in the education of their children which may be because of their involvement with the school activities there, while the indifferent attitude of parents in Alopibagh could be attributed to the fact that besides their low literacy status, the place also offered potential for a variety of petty economic activities where children could be engaged for earning quick money. So far as the distribution of resources in the sample schools is concerned the study shows that they were poorly equipped in matter of many articles pertaining to teaching and learning aids, such as books, blackboards, chalks, etc., which also contributed to their poor performance. It also shows that the schools at Alopibagh slums, though managed by district board, lacked in most of the resources. The analysis of the perception of households towards the benefits from education reveals that a sizeable proportion (over 47 per cent) accepted the importance of education in getting job or in becoming self-reliant or even in guarding against cheating, frauds and making them socially more conscious. It further shows that the inhabitants of Mehdauri slum were more sensitised towards the benefits of education than those of the Alopibagh slum. Regarding improving the performance of schools, the study shows that all were unanimous in accepting that the help of some professional organisations or the NGOs should be taken.

Besides this, by providing economic assistance to school children, and also free distribution of textbooks their performance could be substantially enhanced. The study reveals that a majority of the households (over 92 per cent) did not observe gender discrimination though they also accepted the prevalence of patriarchal practices in the society in which the male members got priority in many of the social functions. Elucidating the reason for discontinuation of education of their girl child, a majority of them stated the prevalence of traditional outlook of society that gave preference to early marriage and denounced late marriages, poverty and other economic hardships, deterioration of overall environment in and around their place of habitation etc. In the end, the study comes up with an array of suggestions that aim at improving the functioning of schools. Some of them target at improving the quality of education, such as toning up of monitoring mechanism, provision of uniforms, stationery, etc. Similarly, for promoting the female literacy, it recommends initiation of literacy programmes to be organised in collaboration with some professional organisations.

A.R. Mishra studies the socio-cultural lag and sectoral underdevelopment in Uttar Pradesh. He emphasised on the growth and role of cultural factors that exercised predominant influence in major parts of India and also acted as a catalyst to foster the road to progress. It was, according to him, quite paradoxical that the progressive seeds of social awakening, which were prevalent in Uttar Pradesh, did not sprout here but in other parts of the country, namely, Maharashtra and Punjab, where they heralded a new era of socio-economic and cultural transformation that later paved the way for the overall process of development of these states. In Bengal, the dialogue between Christianity and Hinduism was translated into sociological struggle between two visions, although Hinduism succeeded in asserting its identity mainly through the efforts of social reformers like Vivekananada, Raja Ram Mohan Roy, Ishwar Chandra Vidyasagar etc. The social reform movement in

Bengal initiated by these luminaries led to a mass awakening and within a few years, it succeeded in establishing various schools for girls, the results of which were surprisingly greater than expected. Likewise, in Maharashtra, Shivaji, under the moral influence of Ram Das, followed a pattern of land distribution that brought many marginalised sections into the mainstream of society. However, the Ram Das pattern of social justice also did not allow the growth of marginalisation for certain sections of society. In case of Punjab, which had experienced the growth of Sikhism, set in motion formation of a society that was based on egalitarian principles. However, later on, the conflict of the Sikh gurus with the Moghul power helped them strengthen the Sikh community and enthuse it with the martial art spirit. Banda Bairagi's crusade against big landlords in Punjab further brought significant material and psychological transformation among the peasants. In the latter stages, the contentious relationship between Arya Samaj and Sikh organisations prompted the Sikh community to move towards the Britishers. This provided an opportunity to them for making substantial investment in educational institutions. On the other hand, the Arya Samaj, too, mobilised various religious resources to make advances in the field of education and social reforms. Thus, the two forces—Hinduism and Sikhism—made rapid strides and ultimately laid a strong foundation for future development. In South India, the role of Christian missionaries in advancing the educational system was quite substantial. However, there was a different scenario in Uttar Pradesh. The policy followed by Akbar, to allow the landowning class to flourish, led Avadh become more a centre of luxury and ostentation rather than of learning and egality. After 1857, the British control over Avadh increased. The institutions founded by the Britishers for promotion of education were never appreciated by the masses. Even the landowning class, unlike in Bengal, showed little interest in such activities that were considered modern and progressive. The zamindars in Uttar Pradesh had their own surrogates. Whereas, the

Nirguna Bhakti had tremendous transformative role in Maharashtra and Punjab, in Uttar Pradesh, it was Saguna Bhakti as preached by Tulsidas in his Ramcharitmanas that came to capture the mind of the masses. The contexts and texts were separate and misutilised for compliance and apathy. The ruling caste/class found it most suitable to subserve its interests. It was at the end of the first quarter of the nineteenth century that social issues started being raised. Bhartendu Harishchandra was a leading figure of this period. Law became the most lucrative job and most of the leaders from Uttar Pradesh in this period such as Motilal Nehru, Jawaharlal Nehru, Ram Manohar Lohia, Govind Ballabh Pant and Narendra Deo were legal luminaries. The Congress also did not encourage peasant movements. Thus, in 1947, when India became independent, Uttar Pradesh was already lagging behind the other states. The initial gap in development and its concomitant effects are till date inhibitive to its development.

In the last paper on the migration, memory and social adjustment, Badri Narayan Tiwari traces the narration of pain conceived by site migration and social adjustment that haunts the memory in the Bhojpuri songs. According to him, it was the separation of migrants from their families that gave birth to a distinct folklore culture, which emerged as an expression of pain and anguish. It is also identified as the Bidesia folk culture and finds expression in many forms like *nautanki*, dramas, folk songs and folk paintings. Making a distinction between the words 'Videshi' and 'Bidesia', he points that though the later has been derived from the former, it has acquired multiple meaning and is now used more often as a metaphor rather than a word with a single meaning. Bhojpur region is identified not as a political unit but also as a cultural identity and the language spoken by the people there is called Bhojpuri. Recalling the history of migration, he observes the incidence of massive emigration that took place from this place in the nineteenth century and early twentieth century was primarily to European colonies that needed the migrants for their plantation work.

Earlier, in the seventeenth and eighteenth centuries, Bhojpur and Buxar were the places, which were used as the recruitment centres of sepoys by the Muslims and later by the Britishers. The sepoys of the Mughals, mill workers of the Kolkata, coolies of tea gardens of Assam and the milk sellers of Bombay were the main architects of transmitting Bhojpuri to other regions. Migration also took place in the form of indentured labour by the Britishers who, after suppressing the revolt, sent those people as a part of punishment to other parts of the world. Elaborating on multiple migration, the paper states that in Bhojpur, apart from external migration, which took the migrants to other parts of the country and even abroad, internal migration within the region was also taking place for quite sometime. The emigration was, generally, of semi-permanent nature. The young men who left maintained contact with their families through letters and paid occasional visits and in many cases hoped to come back to settle in the villages again. The magnitude of internal migration was also massive. Later, the introduction of steam ship and railways facilitated both types of migration and also provided a better networking of maintaining contact with their families. Though the process of migration had been going on for quite sometime, however, the migration during the colonial period was of different nature as it extended the danger of separation from the near and dear ones and to far off places and often resulted in snapping of many tender social relationships. This pain of separation later found its expression in the songs composed by emigrants consisting mainly of soldiers, jute mill workers and the labourers of the tea gardens. The paper also makes a distinction between Des, Durdes and Bides that finds an important place of Bhojpuri folk culture. Further, in Bidesia folk songs, the Batohi symbol became so popular that it later formed an important part in Bidesia folk culture. Thus, it could be said that Bhojpuri folk culture has a special tradition that reflects the history of emotions of bulk of the migrants and the émigrés. Though Bidesia folk tradition is also reflected in other folk songs like *poorvi*, *kajri*, *biraha*, etc., yet it maintains its distinct identity. All these folk songs depict sorrows and pains of the loved ones who have been left behind. Interestingly, these Bidesia folk songs are popular not only in the homeland of the migrants but also in the their far off destination points like Mauritius, Surinam, Trinidad, Fiji, etc.

Thus, to sum up, it could be said that development of social sector has been a painfully long process. It requires a lot of sustained investment over the years before its fruits become conspicuous unlike the economic development whose impact could be observed in the short run also. The plausible reason for this could be that in the social sector the internalisation of the exogenous social inputs on the people or masses takes a longer time to fructify. However, once social development sets in, then, the problem of development, its sustainability and other issues are automatically take care off. The perusal of papers clearly shows why the impact of the social programme has largely remained subdued or limited and rightly suggests various social interventions that need to be incorporated into the strategies to enhance their coverage and impact.

1

Public Distribution System in India

A Study of the District of Allahabad, Uttar Pradesh

Bhaskar Majumder

Man does not live by food alone, but food is the first indicator of survival of man. The food price index is one of the crucial determinants of aggregate food availability and individual entitlements. Generally, the successful arrest of increasing food prices helps in protecting the entitlements of vulnerable sections in the society (Dreze and Sen, 1989: 88). In India, generally, the people in the areas remote from food-related support by the government feel the impact of natural disasters frequently. If there occurs an increase in price following deficits in output and supply of essential commodities, it is the landless labourers, the marginal farmers, the unemployed and the underemployed, and the urban slum dwellers who will bear the brunt of it. The social objective of sharing the regional deficit in food output on a national basis remains absent. The public distribution system (PDS) aims at protecting the vulnerable sections of the society by encompassing them in the distribution network.

As a concept, social safety is as old as the existence of human beings as a social unit. In a broad sense, the purpose of social safety is to abolish want by guaranteeing every individual an adequate income at all times to meet his/her needs. The aim of social safety is to guarantee for each person a minimum level of living through a number of means (Savy, 1972: 2-3). These means include both supply-side and demand-side instruments that cover interventions of the government. The purpose of this paper is to examine how social welfare is promoted through protection of minimum necessary consumption of food of the vulnerable population in India. We examine this through government intervention in the market for foodgrains in India. The rest of the paper is structured into nine sections. In Section I, we spell out the history of PDS in India. In Section II, we narrate the features and rationale of targeted PDS in India. In Section III, we mention the objectives of the study, the methodology, the coverage and the sample. In Section IV, we describe the administrative set-up of the PDS in the district of Allahabad. In Section V, the allotment and lifting of items in PDS in the district of Allahabad has been explained. In Section VI, we calculate the gap between requirement and distribution of items and the gap between market price and FPS price of items at the district level. In Section VII, we take note of the awareness of the households as beneficiaries of PDS. In Section VIII, we offer residue observations in brief. Finally, in Section IX, we put forward policy recommendations.

I
PDS in India: The History

The history behind introduction of the PDS in India is rooted in famines and food scarcities during the entire period of British colonial rule in India. The first one was the Bengal famine of 1770. An estimated ten million people died in this famine that was essentially the consequence of plunder by the colonialists of the East India Company. Between 1860 and 1910, there occurred twenty major famines and scarcities. The last famine in British India was the Bengal famine of 1943 in which a half million lives were lost (Ghose, 1999: 355). The PDS in post-independence India essentially follows the 1943 famine and food scarcity during the Second World War.

The first Foodgrains Policy Committee, 1943 recommended only informal rationing in rural areas. By implication, free or open market in foodgrains was permitted in the rural areas, that is, the producing areas (Dandekar, 1994: 209). The Foodgrains Policy Committee, 1947 suggested progressive decontrol in the foodgrains sector following which a policy of gradual decontrol was announced by the government in November 1947. However, the expectation that decontrol would lead to dishoarding of stocks, increase in procurement and stability in prices did not materialise and prices rose fast. A reversion to controls was, therefore, decided upon in September 1948 (GoI, 1976, Part I: 145). By August 1949, the Government of India started receiving complaints on quality of foodgrains distributed, and appointed the Foodgrains Investigation Committee that submitted its report on 30th April, 1950 confirming the complaints (Dandekar, 1994: 212). In view of the persisting gap between the commitments of public distribution and the procurement, a Foodgrains Procurement Committee was appointed on 8th February, 1950, in pursuance of the recommendations of the All India Food Ministers' Conference, held in August 1949. The Foodgrains Procurement Committee of 1950 recommended monopoly procurement of foodgrains, abolition of the free market, imposition of complete statutory rationing in towns with a population of 50,000 and above and informal rationing elsewhere (GoI, 1976, Part I: 145). Since it was admitted by the Government of India that any scheme of decontrol would involve risks, hence on 8th July, 1952, the government issued the Foodgrains (Licensing and Procurement) Order, 1952. This order prohibited any individual from engaging in any business which involved purchase, sale or storage for sale of any foodgrains except under and in accordance with a licence issued by the state governments (Dandekar, 1994: 216). The Essential Commodities Act, 1955 entrusted the government with taking steps for regulation of production, supply, distribution and trade in essential commodities for securing equitable distribution (GoI, 1976, Part I: 167). Following the recommendations of the Foodgrains Prices Committee set up in 1964, there came an Agricultural Price Commission in January 1965.

The Essential Commodities Act that came into force in 1955 was meant to facilitate government regulation of trade and commerce. It empowered the public officials in enforcing the public distribution system. It, however, was not the first one for imposition of controls on trade and distribution. Of course, it was the first one in independent India. The British colonial government under the Defence of India Rules had implemented some control measures. Since 1946, there came legislation in the form of the Essential Supplies (Temporary Powers) Act, which was in fact replaced by the Essential Commodities Act of 1955 (Mooij, 1999: 193). The number of commodities declared essential under the Act rapidly increased from 10 in 1955 to 60 in 1992. In August 1992, it was decided to extend the Essential Commodities (Special Provisions) Act by another five years.

The prime objective of the Government of India's food security policy is to ensure availability of foodgrains to the people at an affordable price. The policy, thus aims at (i) ensuring adequacy or sufficiency in supply of foodgrains, and (ii) distributing foodgrains at an affordable price. To ensure these objectives, the availability of foodgrains is ensured through a network of Fair Price Shops (FPSs) licenced by the state/UT administrations where each such shop is envisaged to serve a population of 2,000. From over four lakh in March 1992, the number of FPSs rose to over 4.33 lakh as on 31st March, 1995. Most of these FPSs are in rural areas. In 1995, for example, the rural areas had the number of FPSs three times than that in the urban areas.

The procurement of foodgrains for distribution through PDS is maintained through domestic procurement rather than through imports. Probably, this was facilitated by the Green Revolution of the late 1960s. The PDS soon assumed the status of being the centerpiece in the anti-poverty programme. The plentiful supplies of foodgrains generated by the Green Revolution were matched by the ambitious target of extending the PDS to cover the entire population – both rural and urban (Rao, 2001: 82). Under this system, the price at which government procures foodgrains determines the price at which consumers receive foodgrains through the PDS. From the beginning, the Government of India made it clear that remunerative prices are to be a central feature of its policy towards agriculture. The concept of state trading was revived in January 1965 when, by the Act of Parliament, the Government of India set up the Food Corporation of India (FCI) and the Agricultural Prices Commission (now Commission for Agricultural Costs and Prices) in 1965. The post-1965 period, thus, brought about institutionalised arrangements and procedure for procurement, stocks, pricing, and distribution of foodgrains.

II
Targeted Public Distribution System: Features and Rationale

Following the recommendations of the Chief Ministers' Conference held in July 1996, an effort was made to streamline the PDS. Thus, the Targeted Public Distribution System (TPDS) was launched in June 1997. The PDS, as it was being implemented earlier, had been criticised for its urban bias and its failure to serve effectively the poorer sections of the population. The latent problem was that a sizeable number of marginalised people, in the absence of cash income that can be transformed into purchasing power, are excluded from the planning process because they do not constitute effective demand. This is true irrespective of the Green Revolution after the mid-sixties in India. Thus, the TPDS came to replace the erstwhile PDS from June 1997. This system divides the potential beneficiaries into families Below Poverty Line (BPL) and those Above Poverty Line (APL). Under the TPDS, the government is committed to issuing 10 kgs of foodgrains per month per BPL family at a price equal to half of the economic cost of FCI (GoI, 1999-2000: 79-80). The state governments were assigned the task to streamline the PDS by issuing special cards to BPL families and selling essential items under TPDS to them at specially subsidised prices, with better monitoring of the delivery system. The bifurcation of BPL and APL quotas of foodgrains into rice and wheat has been left to the states. In case of those states, which have not indicated the bifurcation, the average lifting of rice and wheat over the last ten years has been adopted on provisional basis. Following the TPDS guidelines, any requirement from states over and above TPDS quotas can be met subject to availability of foodgrains in the Central Pool and the rates equal to FCI's average economic cost (GoI, 1997-98: 72).

The essential features of the TPDS are the following:

- States to identify families below poverty line who would be issued 10 kg of foodgrains per month per family at prices less than the Central Issue Price(CIP).
- Population above poverty line (non-poor) now under PDS to continue to receive normal entitlement at the full CIP.
- The Centre should guarantee supply of foodgrains for the BPL at 10 kg per month per family to states. Additional quantities required by states would depend on the availability of stocks in the Central Pool.
- States will be free to add to the quantum, coverage and the subsidy from their own resources.
- Subsidised foodgrains will also be issued to all beneficiaries under the EAS/Jawahar Rozgar Yojana as per guidelines at the rate of 1 kg per man day for which food coupons would be issued to beneficiaries for exchanging at FPS (GoI, 1996-97: 77).

Rationale behind the TPDS

..the safest and most obvious way of guaranteeing the universal protection of entitlements is to provide direct and unconditional support to everyone without distinction...it does have the advantage of altogether bypassing the various difficulties which any form of selectivity in the provision of relief is bound to entail... Universal support can be a simple expression of ...right to food. However, the strategy of universal support has several disadvantages. It involves an administrative and logistic burden. In addition, universal support may require a commitment of resources that can be hard to obtain (Dreze and Sen, 1989: 104). The PDS, in post-independence India, cannot go to encompass all and offer benefits to all in terms of all essential commodities. "The need for reducing government expenditure under the stabilisation programme calls for a discriminatory approach in providing PDS benefits and hence should be targeted only to the vulnerable groups, since malnutrition is caused by an unequal distribution of food and misplaced consumer choices rather than inadequate supply" (Suryanarayana, 2000: 80). So comes the targeted system. The targeted system has the advantage that it can ensure the greatest economy of resources by withholding public support from less vulnerable groups. In addition, the targeted system can promote the redistribution of resources by concentrating public support exclusively on the most deprived groups. In India, targeting should take care of not only exclusion of the non-poor but also covering all the needy poor excluded at present from the PDS network.

III
The Study: Objectives, Methodology, Coverage, Sample

In this paper we study the extent to which TPDS has succeeded in providing essential commodities to the population living below poverty line. We will also see if the existing distributive set-up is efficient to run the PDS. For the purpose, we have chosen the Allahabad district purposively, it being one of the developed districts in eastern Uttar Pradesh. Eastern region is generally seen as the relatively underdeveloped region in the state.

The district of Allahabad has twenty development blocks, of which we have selected only four, that is, 20 per cent of the total blocks. We have chosen these blocks from the four administrative regions of the district, thereby taking care of the dispersal of the distribution facilities being administered by the state supply office. Besides, the blocks are selected by stratified sampling, the strata covering industrially developed, less developed and underdeveloped areas of the district.

The district of Allahabad has a total of 2,978 revenue villages, of which we have selected only 24, that is, 0.8 per cent of the total. The district has 11 towns, of which we have chosen only two for proper presentation of urban areas in the study. Though the percentage of towns selected is 18.2, by selection of two wards from each of the towns, the urban area being covered has been reduced. We have selected more of the median villages. This has been done by arrangement of villages by the size of population.

In each village, we have chosen 50 households by simple random sampling method, where in each village more than 50 per cent of the BPL (Below Poverty Line by card holding) families have been selected. In 24 villages, thus, we have covered 1,200 households. Of the two towns selected, we picked out two wards from each town, and a total of 50 households from each ward. Thus, 200 households as beneficiaries in the PDS have been selected from the urban area of the district. We have, thus, chosen 1,400 households as beneficiaries covering both rural and urban areas in Allahabad district, of which around 60 per cent of the households come from the BPL category.

In addition, we have studied one FPS in each village and one ward of each selected towns. Thus, we covered 28 FPSs for required information of the PDS in the district (see Box 1).

Box 1

Sampling Procedure

State of Uttar Pradesh

District Allahabad

It is one of the developed districts of eastern Uttar Pradesh. The district is divided into 6 tehsils, 20 community development blocks, 11 towns, 1,378 gram panchayats and 2,715 inhabited revenue villages.

Blocks/Towns

Four blocks have been selected by stratified purposive sampling method, which covers industrial, less developed and underdeveloped areas of district. We have also selected two towns, of which one is an industrial area and other is located on the border of another district, Mirzapur.

24 Revenue Villages and 4 Wards

All villages of the district are stratified into three groups by size of population:
(i) Between 500 and 999
(ii) Between 1,000 and 1,999
(iii) Between 2,000 and 4,999
Based on population criteria, these 24 villages have been selected. Also 4 wards have been covered from two selected towns.

1,400 Households

Selection of households within the villages has been done by simple random sampling method. Each sample unit has covered 50 households. More than 50 per cent of the families covered in sample villages/towns have been drawn from BPL families.

28 Fair Price Shops

Minimum one fair price shop has been covered in each sample village/ward.

Box 2 lists the tehsils, blocks/towns, villages/wards and gram/nagar panchayats in the district of Allahabad that we have covered in this study.

Box 2

Profile of Sample Villages/Wards within their Respective Blocks/Towns and Tehsils

Tehsils	*Blocks/ Towns*	*Villages/Wards*	*Gram/Nagar Panchayats*
Bara	Shankargarh	Janwan	Janwan
		Golhaiya	Golhaiya
		Garha	Garha
		Sheorajpur	Sheorajpur
		Benipur	Benipur
		Lohgara	Lohgara
Karchhana	Karchhana	Rithainya	Niria
		Semarha Uperhar	Semarha Uperhar
		Pach Dewra	Pach Dewra
		Dewri Kala	Dewari Kala
		Karchhana	Karchhana
		Bhatauli	Piparaon
Handia	Saidabad	Baragaon	Jalalpur
		Mahuwa Kothi	Chandopara
		Motiha	Barethi
		Jogapur	Mohua Dih
		Dusaoti	Mahua Dih
		Oasepur	Binda
Soraon	Kaurihar	Muzaffarpur Urf Bichhia	Muzaffarpur Urf Bichhia
		Fatehpur Kayasthan	Fatehpur Kayasthan
		Atrampur/Nawabganj	Atrampur
		Fatoopur Uperher	Fatoopur Uperher
		Kanjia	Kanjia
		Malak herher Uperher	Malak herher Uperher
Phulpur	Phulpur	Ward No. 3	Phulpur
		Ward No. 12	Phulpur
Meja	Bharatganj	Ward No. 1	Bharatganj
		Ward No. 12	Bharatganj

Source: NIC, Allahabad based on 1991 Census.

Sample Design

In the district of Allahabad, there are six tehsils, all of which have been covered in the study. Out of 20 blocks, the study has covered four, that is, 20 per cent. The study has covered 24 inhabited revenue villages, which is 0.9 per cent of total revenue villages in the district, and also two towns, which is 18.2 per cent of all the towns in the district. All the 24 villages have gram panchayats; the 24 gram panchayats, thus, covered constitute 1.7 per cent of all gram panchayats in the district. The four wards selected and studied constitute 15.4 per cent of all the 26 wards in two towns in the district (Table 1).

Table 1

Profile of Sample Villages/Wards, Allahabad District, 1998

Administrative Areas	*Selected*	*Total*
Tehsils	6 (100.0)	6 (100.0)
Blocks	4 (20.0)	20 (100.0)
Gram Panchayats	24 (1.7)	1,378 (100.0)
Inhabited Revenue Villages	24 (0.9)	2,715 (100.0)
Towns	2 (18.2)	11 (100.0)
Wards	4 (15.4)	26 (100.0)
(a) Phulpur	2 (14.3)	14 (100.0)
(b) Bharatganj	2 (16.7)	12 (100.0)

Source: District Statistical Handbook of Allahabad, 1998 and NIC, Allahabad.

We have selected the villages by size of population, considered in three categories: category I representing population size between 500 and 999, category II between 1,000 and 1,999 and category III 2,000 and 4,999. The sample (selected villages in number) represents 0.9 per cent of all villages in the district. But, the same sample represents 4.1 per cent in number when considered with respect to the total number of villages in the respective population categories. The sample villages in categories I, II, and III represent 21.10 per cent of all villages in the district in the said categories. Thus, selection of blocks out of total number of villages in categories I, II, and III bears a correspondence in terms of representation by number of blocks and villages selected.

We have purposively chosen 12 villages from category II, and six villages each from category I and category III. In the whole district, such selection would mean 1.8 per cent of the villages in category II out of total villages in category II understood as 100 per cent, while 0.7 per cent for category I out of total villages in category I understood as 100 per cent, and 1.9 per cent for category III out of total villages in category III also understood as 100 per cent. The sample proportions for categories I, II and III represent exactly the similar picture. If the number of villages in category II in the sample is taken as 100 per cent, then the 12 villages selected in this category represent 9.3 per cent. Similarly, if the number of villages in category I is taken as 100 per cent, then the six villages selected in this category represent 3.2 per cent, while in category III, this percentage is 9.4 (Table 2).

Table 2

Category-wise Distribution of Sample and Total Number of Villages in Allahabad District

Categories of Villages	*Total Sample*		*Total District*	
	Sample	*Total*	*Sample*	*Total*
I	6 (3.2)	186 (100.0)	6 (0.7)	804 (100.0)
II	12 (9.3)	129 (100.0)	12 (1.8)	673 (100.0)
III	6 (9.4)	64 (100.0)	6 (1.9)	319 (100.0)
Others	-	204	-	919
Total	24 (4.1)	583 (100.0)	24 (0.9)	2,715 (100.0)

Source: District Statistical Handbook of Allahabad, 1998 and NIC, Allahabad.

All the four blocks selected are represented by selection of six villages for each block chosen for the study in the district of

Allahabad. These four blocks are Shankargarh, Karchhana, Saidabad and Kaurihar. The six villages selected in Shankargarh represent 3.2 per cent of all villages in it; in Karchhana they represent 5 per cent of all villages in it; in Saidabad 3.8 per cent of all villages in it and in Kaurihar 4.9 per cent of all villages in it.

Depending on a number of factors in the respective categories, like the existence of gram panchayats, functioning FPSs etc., we have selected and surveyed the villages in the respective categories. Thus, equal number of villages, that is, two, does not represent each category in a particular block, but there is inter-category variation in the selection of villages. For example, for category III, which is large by size of population, in Shankargarh block there are only four villages, out of which we selected only one, while in the same category, in Saidabad, there are 26 villages and we selected two. Similarly, in Kaurihar, we selected two villages out of a total of 20 villages while in Karchhana, we selected one out of a total of 14 villages in this category. Since category II is constituted by the most representative villages by size of population (2,000-4,999), hence we selected three out of six villages in each block from this category, which is half of all villages selected from any block, and by summation, villages from category II represent half of all (24) villages selected for the study. The variation in number of villages, inter-block, thus rested on whether or not to take more villages from category I or category III, it is a variation between one closing village or two villages from each of the categories I and III (Table 3).

By distribution of households in the four blocks selected for the study, we find that the villages selected in Shankargarh have 21.7 per cent of all households in the sample, while for Karchhana it has 18.3 per cent, for Saidabad 26.6 per cent and for Kaurihar 33.4 per cent. By distribution of population, these selected villages in four blocks represent 21.1, 21.7, 24.1, and

Table 3

Profile of Selected Villages in Sample Blocks

Blocks	*Categories of Villages*						*Other Villages*	*Total Villages*	
	I		*II*		*III*				
	Selected	*Total*	*Selected*	*Total*	*Selected*	*Total*		*Selected*	*Total*
Shankargarh	2 (2.9)	68 (100.0)	3 (15.0)	20 (100.0)	1 (25.0)	4 (100.0)	93	6 (3.2)	185 (100.0)
Karchhana	2 (7.1)	28 (100.0)	3 (10.0)	43 (100.0)	1 (7.1)	14 (100.0)	34	6 (5.0)	119 (100.0)
Saidabad	1 (1.9)	52 (100.0)	3 (8.8)	34 (100.0)	2 (7.7)	26 (100.0)	44	6 (3.8)	156 (100.0)
Kaurihar	1 (2.6)	38 (100.0)	3 (9.4)	32 (100.0)	2 (10.0)	20 (100.0)	33	6 (4.9)	123 (100.0)
Total Sample	6 (3.2)	186 (100.0)	12 (9.3)	129 (100.0)	6 (9.3)	64 (100.0)	204	24 (4.1)	583 (100.0)
Total District	6 (0.7)	804 (100.0)	12 (1.8)	673 (100.0)	6 (1.9)	319 (100.0)	919	24 (0.9)	2,715 (100.0)

Notes: 1. Village categories based on total population of the villages (I = 500 to 999, II = 1,000 to 1,999 and III = 2,000 to 4,999, by population).

2. Due to not availability of census town data of 1991, categorisation of wards has not been done but weightage has been given to those wards where mostly BPL families reside.

3. Four wards have been selected from two towns, namely, Phulpur and Bharatganj, first one is an industrial area and the second one is located at a distance of 70 km from district headquarters and is located on the border of the district.

Source: District Statistical Handbook of Allahabad, 1998 and NIC of Allahabad.

33.1 per cent respectively of total population in all the sample blocks taken together. We, thus, have a one-to-one agreement between the distribution of number of households and the distribution of population by selection of six villages from each of the four blocks. The two distributions by number of households and population also show balanced representation block-wise besides a correspondence with villages selected by size of population categories, represented by I, II, and III.

Profile of Sample Households

Variations in the number of total households at village level follow variations in the size of population by which three categories of villages were selected. As a corollary, selection of identical number of sample households (50) for each village shows variation as a percentage of all households. Independent of the inter-village variations in the number of BPL households, we have selected sample BPL households in villages generally more than the number of selected APL households. The villages with more of APL households selected by percentage are also the villages where APL households stay more in number by percentage. The selection in general more of BPL households follows the objectives of the study.

The households studied in the rural region of four blocks taken together constitute 7.5 per cent of all households in those rural blocks. The households studied in the urban region of two towns taken together constitute 16.9 per cent of all households in those urban areas. As a whole, for rural and urban regions, by selection of households, it becomes 8.2 per cent of all households in the total sample region (rural and urban) (see Table 4).

The sample rural households comprise 0.1 per cent of all rural households in the district (universe) and the sample urban households constitute 0.06 per cent of all urban households in the district. As a whole, for rural and urban regions taken together, it becomes 0.1 per cent. In the sample households studied, BPL households selected constitute 15.9 per cent of all rural households in existence, whereas APL households selected constitute 4.3 per cent of all APL households in existence in rural region. BPL households selected in rural region as a percentage of all households (BPL and APL) comprise 58.7 per cent. For urban areas, BPL households selected constitute 35.8 per cent of all urban households in existence, whereas APL households selected comprise 9.6 per cent of all APL households in the urban areas of the district. The percentages for selected BPL and APL households for the whole selected sample (rural and urban) are 17.3 and 4.7 respectively.

Table 4

Village/Ward-wise Distribution of Households

Name of Village/ Ward	*Sample Households*			*Total Households*		
	BPL	*APL*	*Total*	*BPL*	*APL*	*Total*
Janwan	40	10	50	344 (53.7)	296	640
Golhaiya	32	18	50	155 (52.5)	140	295
Garha	41	9	50	496 (89.5)	58	554
Sheorajpur	32	18	50	302 (76.6)	92	394
Sidhtikar	37	13	50	366 (60.6)	238	604
Lohgara	38	12	50	325 (29.2)	787	1,112
Rithainya	16	34	50	60 (11.0)	485	545
Semraha Uperhar	30	20	50	50 (15.8)	266	316
Pach Dewra	27	23	50	52 (14.5)	307	359
Dewri Kala	34	16	50	110 (14.3)	659	769
Karchhana	26	24	50	95 (9.6)	895	990
Bhatauli	25	25	50	155 (9.6)	660	815
Baragaon	13	37	50	140 (30.4)	320	460
Mahuwa Kothi	35	15	50	211 (40.3)	312	523
Motiha	34	16	50	194 (40.9)	280	474
Jogapur	40	10	50	191 (41.4)	270	461
Osepur	30	20	50	339 (40.8)	492	831
Dusaoti	44	6	50	350 (53.8)	300	650
Muzaffarpur Urf Bichhia	5	45	50	77 (9.3)	750	827
Fatehpur Kayasthan	21	29	50	60 (11.4)	465	525
Atrampur/Nawabganj	33	17	50	90 (6.0)	1,412	1,502
Fatoopur Uperhar	25	25	50	52 (17.5)	245	297
Kanjia	24	26	50	122 (12.5)	850	972
Malak Herher Uperhar	23	27	50	88 (8.6)	939	1027
Ward No. 3 (Phulpur)	35	15	50	99 (27.6)	259	358
Ward No. 12 (Phulpur)*	24	26	50	17 (4.2)	389	406
Ward No. 1 (Bharatganj)	44	6	50	189 (91.7)	17	206
Ward No. 12 (Bharatganj)	15	35	50	25 (11.9)	185	210

* Sample figure is higher than total number of BPL, because some influential people got BPL cards and the record was not maintained by the Supply Office. Figures in parentheses show BPL households as percentage of total households.

Source: District Supply Office of Allahabad, September 2000.

Table 5

Distribution of Households Based on Sample and Universe

Block/Town	*Sample Households*						*Universe Households*					
	Selected			*Total*			*Sample*			*Total*		
	BPL	*APL*	*Total*	*BPL*	*APL*	*Total*	*BPL*	*APL*	*Total*	*BPL*	*APL*	*Total*
Shankargarh	220	80	300	1,988	1,611	3,599	220	80	300	15,184	16,798	31,982
	(11.1)	(5.0)	(8.3)	(100.0)	(100.0)	(100.0)	(1.4)	(0.5)	(0.9)	(100.0)	(100.0)	(100.0)
Karchhana	158	142	300	522	3,272	3,794	158	142	300	6,678	41,968	48,646
	(30.5)	(4.3)	(7.9)	(100.0)	(100.0)	(100.0)	(2.3)	(0.3)	(0.6)	(100.0)	(100.0)	(100.0)
Saidabad	196	104	300	1,425	1,874	3,399	196	104	300	21,417	30,127	51,544
	(13.8)	(5.5)	(8.8)	(100.0)	(100.0)	(100.0)	(0.9)	(0.3)	(0.6)	(100.0)	(100.0)	(100.0)
Kaurihar	131	169	300	489	4,661	5,150	131	169	300	5,690	39,398	45,088
	(26.8)	(3.6)	(5.8)	(100.0)	(100.0)	(100.0)	(2.3)	(0.4)	(0.7)	(100.0)	(100.0)	(100.0)
Total Rural	705	495	1,200	4,424	11,418	15,942	705	495	1,200	1,88,279	7,19,225	9,07,504
	(15.9)	(4.3)	(7.5)	(100.0)	(100.0)	(100.0)	(0.4)	(0.1)	(0.1)	(100.0)	(100.0)	(100.0)
Phulpur	59	41	100	116	648	764	59	41	100	590	4,012	4,602
	(50.9)	(6.3)	(13.1)	(100.0))	(100.0))	(100.0)	(10.0)	(1.0)	(2.2)	(100.0)	(100.0)	(100.0)
Bharatganj	59	41	100	214	202	416	59	41	100	685	3,253	3,938
	(27.6)	(20.3)	(24.0)	(100.0)	(100.0)	(100.0)	(8.6)	(1.3)	(2.5)	(100.0)	(100.0)	(100.0)
Total Urban	118	82	200	330	850	1180	118	82	200	11,112	2,99,109	3,10,221
	(35.8)	(9.6)	(16.9)	(100.0)	(100.0)	(100.0)	(1.1)	(0.02)	(0.06)	(100.0)	(100.0)	(100.0)
Grand Total	823	577	1,400	4,754	12,268	17,122	823	577	1,400	1,99,391	10,18,334	12,17,725
	(17.3)	(4.7)	(8.2)	(100.0)	(100.0)	(100.0)	(0.4)	(0.1)	(0.1)	(100.0)	(100.0)	(100.0)

Source: District Supply Office of Allahabad, November 2000.

There are inter-block variations in the selection of BPL households drawn from all BPL households in the respective blocks. The same is true for BPL households in urban areas selected from total urban BPL households. Of the total cardholders in rural areas, BPL households cover 57.8 per cent and APL households cover 41.2 per cent, the rest being covered by cardless households. The cardless households constitute 1 per cent of the sample households drawn in rural region of the district (see Table 5).

We got names of households in the list maintained by the State Supply Office, all supposedly with cards, but while in field we found cardless cases. There may be a number of reasons for non-availability of cards, like the possibility that cards were actually prepared but not allotted. The other possibility may be that cards were prepared, and allotted to wrong households, say, a few cards meant for BPL households actually allotted to the APL households. For the urban areas, BPL households constitute 59 per cent of the sample total, while APL households cover the rest. We did not find any case of cardless households in the urban areas chosen for the study. In totality, for both rural and urban areas studied, BPL families constitute 58 per cent while APL households comprise 41.2 per cent, cardless case as percentage of total (rural and urban) standing at 0.8 (see Table 6).

Table 6

Distribution of Sample Households

Category	*Rural*	*Urban*	*Total*
BPL	694 (57.8)	118 (59.0)	812 (58.0)
APL	495 (41.2))	82 (41.0)	577 (41.2)
Cardless	11 (1.0)	-	11 (0.8)
Total	1,200 (100.0)	200 (100.0)	1,400 (100.0)

Source: Field survey.

Profile of Population in the Sample

For distribution of cards by economic categories, BPL and APL, an income of Rs. 11,000 per annum per household has been accepted (as per the approval of the Eighth Plan, 1992-97, by the Planning Commission, Government of India) as the cut off line. Below this income level, households would be entitled to BPL cards, and above this, APL cards.

Of the total number of households (1,400) surveyed in 24 villages and two towns, we got 52.8 per cent with income less than Rs. 11,000 and 33 per cent with income less than Rs. 9,000 (the latter has been taken by the UP Supply Department, as the upper limit income for identification of BPL families, as per order no. 437/29-Khadya-Desc-I-I (9/97). Of the total households with income less than Rs. 11,000, while BPL cardholders constitute 79.56 per cent, APL cardholders constitute 19.07 per cent, the rest 1.37 per cent are cardless cases. Of the total population in the sample (7,073), the percentage of population below income category of Rs. 11,000 is 47.85 per cent. Of the total households (1,400), while BPL households by cardholding comprise 58 per cent, APL households comprise 41.21 per cent, the rest 0.78 per cent cardless cases. Of the total population (7,073), while BPL constitute 56.78 per cent, APL constitute 42.69 per cent, the rest 0.52 per cent are cardless cases. The households with income more than Rs. 11,000 per household per month enjoy BPL cards also. Of the total households with income above Rs. 11,000, BPL cardholding households constitute 33.88 per cent. Of the total households with BPL cards (812), households with income less than Rs. 11,000 are 72.41 per cent, implying that 27.59 per cent of households with income more than Rs. 11,000 held BPL cards. In other words, one-fourth of APL households by income category got entitlement to BPL cards (by error or by wrong decision or other administrative failure). What is more serious is that the income-poor households had to have APL cards. Of the total APL cards (577), such BPL families got 24.43 per cent. The APL households who got APL cards thus constitute three-fourths of what they should have received (see Table 7).

Table 7
Income-wise Distribution of Sample Households and Population at District Level

Block/Town	*Categories*	*Distance of FPS from Households*			*Total*
		In village or within 1 km	*Between 1 and 2 km*	*Above 2 km*	
Shankargarh	BPL	47	114	52	213
	APL	18	39	23	80
	Cardless	1	6	-	7
	Total	66 (22.0)	159 (53.0)	75 (25.0)	300 (100.0)
Karchhana	BPL	108	42	4	154
	APL	94	45	3	142
	Cardless	4	-	-	4
	Total	206 (68.7)	87 (29.0)	7 (2.3)	300 (100.0)
Saidabad	BPL	187	9	-	196
	APL	97	7	-	104
	Total	284 (94.7)	16 (5.3)	-	300 (100.0)
Kaurihar	BPL	91	40	-	131
	APL	97	71	1	169
	Total	188 (62.7)	111 (37.0)	1 (0.3)	300 (100.0)
Phulpur	BPL	57	2	-	59
	APL	40	1	-	41
	Total	97 (97.0)	3 (3.0)	-	100 (100.0)
Bharatganj	BPL	59	-	-	59
	APL	41	-	-	41
	Total	100 (100.0)	-	-	100 (100.0)
Total	BPL	549 (67.6)	207 (25.5)	56 (6.9)	812 (100.0)
	APL	387 (67.1)	163 (28.2)	27 (4.7)	577 (100.0)
	Cardless	5 (45.6)	6 (54.5)	-	11 (100.0)
	Total	941 (67.2)	376 (26.9)	82 (5.9)	1,400 (100.0)

Note: Figures in parentheses denote row percentages.

Source: Field survey.

There are inter-block and inter-town variations in distribution of cards - both BPL and APL - among respective income categories of population and households.

Distribution of Sample Households by Location and Number of Fair Price Shops at Village Level and Holding Pattern of Ration Cards

Location of FPSs

Of the total households (1,400) surveyed in 24 villages (in four blocks) and four wards (in two towns), 67.2 per cent get the FPS located within the village or within 1 km from the location (house) of the household. For 26.9 per cent of the households, the FPS is located at a distance of more than 1 km but less than 2 km. Only for 5.9 per cent of the households, the FPS is located at a distance of more than 2 km from the location (house) of the household.

Of the 1,400 households, 812 belong to the BPL category. Of these BPL households, 67.6 per cent get the FPS within the distance of the first category, 25.5 per cent get the FPS located by the second category, and 6.9 per cent in the third. For the APL households (577) the distribution of FPSs by location is similar, as it is for the BPL families. There are inter-block and inter-town variations in location of FPSs from the location (house) of the sample households.

Number of FPSs

Of the total households (1,400) surveyed, 13.7 per cent reported to have no FPS in their village, while 78.8 per cent have one FPS in the village. The distribution network of FPSs thus centres around one FPS per revenue village. Absence of FPS in a particular village does not imply that the households in that particular village do not have access to items distributable through the FPSs. The fact may be that these households are entitled to the essential items distributed through the FPSs in the adjoining village outside the geographic boundary of the village where they are settled. Only 7 per cent of the households reported to have two FPSs in a single village where they are settled. As low as 0.5 per cent of the households reported that they have as high as three FPSs in their localities. No block, constituting the rural region of the district, reported existence of three FPSs in any village. These high numbers by location of three FPSs, thus, is an urban phenomenon. In addition, of the households (98) reporting to have two FPSs in the locality, the percentage for urban areas is 69.38. Generally, more than one FPS in a particular village implies probably that, for kerosene there is another shop (owned by another licence holder).

Holding Pattern of Ration Cards among Households

Apart from 11 cardless cases, all the rest households surveyed own at least one ration card. We found households, inside both BPL and APL, who own more than one ration card. The BPL households who own two ration cards constitute 4.2 per cent of all BPL households (812), while APL households owning two ration cards constitute 6.1 per cent of the APL households (577). In total (BPL and APL), 4.9 per cent of the total households (1,400) have two ration cards. We also found households, inside both BPL and APL, who own three or more ration cards. In totality, such households (BPL and APL) constitute 0.8 per cent of the total households; for BPL households (812), it is 0.7 per cent while for APL households (577) it is 0.9 per cent. The BPL households owning two or more ration cards constitute 4.9 per cent of all BPL households while the APL households owning two or more ration cards constitute 6.9 per cent of all APL households. There are inter-block and inter-town variations in holding pattern of ration cards.

IV
Administrative Structure (Supply Office)

The district administrative set-up for the PDS works at three levels in descending order – tehsil, block and village. At the district level, the major responsibility regarding PDS is to ensure area-wise (tehsil) allotment and distribution of items at various levels in order to control the PDS all over the district. This is ensured jointly by Additional District Magistrate (Civil Supply) and District Supply Officer (DSO).

At the tehsil level, the Sub-Divisional Magistrate (SDM) is responsible for allotment of the licence for the FPSs and quota of items for each FPS. The SDM is supposed to control and ensure the distribution system up to the gram panchayat level. The Regional Food Officer (RFO), hierarchically just below the DSO, works parallel with the SDM to ensure FPS-wise allotment of items. The RFO issues the certificate for carrying and distribution of foodgrains and also verifying its control over the distribution system.

At the block level, the Block Development Officer (BDO) is assigned to ensure the proper functioning of the distribution network as guided by the SDM at the tehsil level. The Supply Inspector is the bottommost administrative unit/category who works at the village level to ensure the distribution of all items at gram panchayat level. He is supposed to check the FPS's stock of items, allotment of items, quality and price list of items, distribution of items per card etc. The FPS owner/dealer has a compulsion to draw the allotted items every month and distribute the drawn items to the cardholders attached to his FPS in prescribed quantity per head, unadulterated quality and at the price fixed for the said purpose. To have supervision and vigilance on the system at the village level, there is an elected panchayat, which can appoint and cancel the licence of any FPS dealer. The panchayat is also expected to form a vigilance committee for overall control over the distribution system. The village level workers are expected to play a constructive role in the open panchayat meetings for PDS (see Box 3).

Box 3

Administrative Set-Up of Supply Department, UP Government (Major Responsibilities of Officials)

District Allahabad

District Level

Additional District Magistrate (Civil Supplies)

Major Responsibilities

To ensure the area-wise (tehsil) allotment and distribution of items at various levels in order to control the PDS all over the district.

District Level

District Supply Officer

Tehsil Level

(Sub-Divisional Magistrate/Tehsildar)
To allot the licenses for the FPS and quota of items for each FPS. To control and ensure the distribution system at gram panchayat level.

City Area

(Regional Food Officer)
To ensure FPS-wise allotment of items. To Issue the certificate for carrying and distribution of foodgrains and verifying its control over the distribution system.

Tehsil Level

(Supply Inspector)
To ensure the distribution of all items at gram panchayat level. To check the FPS's stock, prescribed price and allotted quantity per card and unit actually distributed.

Block Level

(Block Development Officer)
To ensure the proper functioning of the distribution system as guided by the Sub-Divisional Magistrate at the tehsil level.

Village Level

(Fair Price Shopkeeper)
To draw the items every month and distribute those to all cardholders attached to the particular FPS in prescribed quality and price.

Village Level

(Village Level Worker)
To check and verify the stocks of FPS and ensure the distribution system at village level with the help of panchayats; to issue the certificate of distributed items, and also to issue new ration cards.

Role of Panchayat

Appointment and cancellation of FPS dealer with the help of open panchayat meeting. To form a vigilance committee for overall control over the distribution system at the village level. This includes checking the stock of items, prescribed price and allotted quality of items and to control the black marketing of items.

V
Allotment and Lifting of Items in PDS, District Allahabad, 1998-2001

For the Allahabad district we noticed lifting of items, rice, wheat, sugar, and kerosene, by the FPS dealers vis-à-vis allotment of these items for the period 1998-2001. While allotment and lifting of rice and wheat are specific to economic categories, i.e., BPL and APL, by cardholding, those of sugar and kerosene are general, that is, across categories.

In case of rice for BPL households in the district, lifting as percentage of allotment was 100 per cent for 1998-99 and 1999-2000, while it fell abruptly in 2000-01. For APL households, lifting of rice by the FPS dealers as percentage of allotment remained below 10 per cent for each of the years 1998-99 and 1999-2000, while it increased abruptly in 2000-01 (Table 8).

Table 8

Allotment and Lifting of Rice by FPS Dealers, District Allahabad, 1998-2001

(in quintals)

Year	*APL Households*			*BPL Households*		
	Allotment	*Lifting*	*Lifting as %age of Allotment*	*Allotment*	*Lifting*	*Lifting as %age of Allotment*
1998-99	23,560.0	2,328.0	9.8	21,180.0	21,180.0	100.0
1999-2000	77,520.0	7,883.8	10.2	75,850.0	75,850.0	100.0
2000-01	480.0	360.0	75.0	1,47,160.0	80,390.0	54.6

Source: District Supply Office.

For wheat we found declining a little the next year. Lifting of wheat for APL households as percentage of allotment remained moderate in 1998-99 as well as 2000-01, while it came down to a surprisingly low level at 2.5 per cent in 1999-2000. While, in general, absolute lifting of wheat by FPS dealers for APL households remains low as a trend, we find hardly any reason why allotment of wheat was raised for APL households at the district level. It was, thus, not reduced lifting by FPS dealers but increased allotment by supply authority that explains the very poor lifting as percentage of allotment of wheat for APL households (Table 9).

Table 9

Allotment and Lifting of Wheat by FPS Dealers, District Allahabad, 1998-2001

(in quintals)

Year	*APL Households*			*BPL Households*		
	Allotment	*Lifting*	*Lifting as %age of Allotment*	*Allotment*	*Lifting*	*Lifting as %age of Allotment*
1998-99	51,440.0	29,040.0	56.4	39,425.7	39,425.7	100.0
1999-2000	1,39,480.0	3,477.3	2.5	1,66,613.3	1,66,613.3	100.0
2000-01	3,000.0	2,100.0	70.0	3,32,136.0	2,78,982.2	84.0

Source: District Supply Office.

Lifting of sugar by FPS dealers for households, both BPL and APL, as percentage of allotment remained high and steady during the accounting period (Table 10).

Table 10

Allotment and Lifting of Sugar by FPS Dealers, District Allahabad, 1998-2001

(in quintals)

Year	*Allotment*	*Lifting*	*Lifting as %age of Allotment*
1998-99	2,31,708	2,22,416	96.0
1999-2000	2,18,640	2,18,640	100.0
2000-01	2,59,290	2,45,500	94.7

Source: District Supply Office.

For kerosene, lifting as percentage of allotment at the district level for households across categories came to be almost 100 per cent (Table 11).

Table 11
Allotment and Lifting of Kerosene by FPS Dealers, District Allahabad 1998-2001

(in kl.)

Year	*Allotment*	*Lifting*	*Lifting as %age of Allotment*
1998-99	47,278	47,067	99.5
1999-2000	47,296	46,752	98.8
2000-01	51,296	49,638	96.8

Source: District Supply Office.

VI
Gap between Requirement and Distribution of Items and between Market Price and FPS Price of Items at District Level

We now consider the consumption requirements of the households for the essential commodities distributed through the FPSs and what is actually distributed, so that we may derive the gap, if any, between these two. We see the gap item-wise and by economic categories, i.e., BPL and APL.

For rice, for BPL households, the percentage gap between requirement and that supplied by the FPS per family per month is 92.2. This means that only 7.8 per cent of the requirement of rice by BPL households is covered by distribution by FPS. For wheat, for BPL families, only 8.7 per cent of requirement per period per family is covered by distribution by FPS, the gap thus being 91.3 per cent between quantity required and quantity distributed through FPS. For sugar, for BPL families, the gap is 88.2 per cent, that is, 11.8 per cent of sugar required is supplied through FPS. For kerosene, for BPL families 77.3 per cent is covered by FPS. By absolute quantity supplied only 2.7 kg of rice per family per month is supplied through FPS for BPL households, while the required quantity is 34.5 kg. For wheat, for BPL households, only 3.8 kg is supplied through FPS while the required quantity is 43.5 kg. For sugar, the supplied quantity is 0.2 kg while the requirement is only 1.7 kg per family per month for BPL households.

The similar scenario holds good for APL households in terms of the gap between required quantity and received quantity, though the APL households are not entitled to rice and wheat at same prices as paid by BPL households. For cardless cases, the households somehow manage to get a little amount from the FPS, though generally they meet 95 per cent of demand for rice and wheat through the open market and 100 per cent for sugar. Surprisingly, the cardless households get 62.3 per cent of kerosene from the FPSs.

The high gap between quantity of essential items required and that distributed through FPSs shows the insignificant contribution of FPSs in meeting the consumption requirements of households. It also signals at the necessity for increased quantity to be supplied (for households) by the FPSs. What we observe is high requirement of rice and wheat, on average 35.1 kg and 44.6 kg respectively across BPL and APL households, as opposed to very low quantity of sugar required. On average, requirement of sugar per family per month is 2.6 kg for BPL and APL households taken together which is only 1.7 kg for BPL families. The major items in the consumption basket thus are rice and wheat, and more so for BPL households.

We now look at the price per unit of items the households pay in the open market and for distribution through FPSs. The open market price is the price on average as reported by the households and FPS price is the price actually charged on items by the FPS dealer. The gap between these two prices is always positive, but not very significant. For rice, for BPL households, the gap between the two is 10.2 per cent, absolute prices per kg being Rs. 7.12 and Rs. 6.46 on average. Likewise, for wheat, for BPL households, the gap between the two is only 1.4 per cent, while for sugar it is 28 per cent. The gap in price is very significant for kerosene, it is 39.5 per cent for BPL households, the absolute gap being Rs. 4 per litre.

Table 12

Gap between Requirement and Distribution of Items per month and Gap between Market Price and FPS Price of Items

Items	Category	Average Consumption of Items			Average Rate of Items		
		Requirement per family per month	Distributed by FPS per family per month	Gap between requirement and sup. by FPS	FPS price (in Rs.)	Market price (in Rs.)	Gap between market price and FPS price (in Rs.)
Rice (in kg)	BPL	34.5 (100.0)	2.7 (7.8)	31.8 (92.2)	6.46 (100.0)	7.12 (110.2)	0.66 (10.2)
	APL	36.3 (100.0)	0.4 (1.1)	35.9 (98.9)	6.77 (100.0)	7.29 (107.7)	0.52 (7.7)
	Cardless	26.8 (100.0)	1.3 (4.9)	25.5 (95.1)	6.25 (100.0)	7.63 (122.1)	1.38 (22.1)
	Total	35.1 (100.0)	1.7 (4.8)	33.4 (95.2)	6.22 (100.0)	7.19 (115.6)	0.97 (15.6)
Wheat (in kg)	BPL	43.5 (100.0)	3.8 (8.7)	39.7 (91.3)	5.03 (100.0)	5.10 (101.4)	0.07 (1.4)
	APL	46.2 (100.0)	0.5 (1.1)	45.7 (98.4)	5.15 (100.0)	5.13 (99.6)	-0.02 (-0.4)
	Cardless	40.9 (100.0)	1.8 (4.4)	39.1 (95.6)	5.16 (100.0)	5.18 (100.4)	0.02 (0.4)
	Total	44.6 (100.0)	2.4 (5.4)	42.2 (94.6)	5.05 (100.0)	5.11 (101.2)	0.06 (1.2)
Sugar (in kg)	BPL	1.7 (100.0)	0.2 (11.8)	1.5 (88.2)	13.59 (100.0)	17.40 (128.0)	3.81 (28.0)
	APL	3.8 (100.0)	0.3 (7.9)	3.5 (92.1)	13.58 (100.0)	17.50 (128.9)	3.92 (28.9)
	Cardless	0.3 (100.0)		0.3 (100.0)	13.75 (100.0)	17.33 (126.0)	3.58 (26.0)
	Total	2.6 (100.0)	0.2 (7.7)	2.4 (92.3)	13.59 (100.0)	17.43 (128.3)	3.84 (28.3)
Kerosene (in litres)	BPL	4.4 (100.0)	3.4 (77.3)	1.0 (22.7)	10.10 (100.0)	14.09 (139.5)	3.99 (39.5)
	APL	5.5 (100.0)	3.9 (70.9)	1.6 (29.1)	10.07 (100.0)	14.20 (141.0)	4.13 (41.0)
	Cardless	5.3 (100.0)	3.3 (62.3)	2.0 (37.7)	10.05 (100.0)	14.54 (144.7)	4.49 (44.7)
	Total	4.8 (100.0)	3.6 (75.0)	1.2 (25.0)	10.09 (100.0)	13.50 (133.8)	3.41 (33.8)

Source: Field survey.

For APL households, similarly, there is insignificant gap between market price and FPS price for rice and wheat. The gap is significant for sugar, i.e., 3.92 per cent. The prices paid by the APL households in the open market are always marginally higher than the prices paid for the same items by the BPL households. The quality of items bought by the respective households may explain this difference (see Table 12).

Item-wise Gap by Quantity Distribution to Households at Block Level

We now look at the gap between requirement and allotment of items for both BPL and APL households. For rice, the gap between required quantity by all households (BPL+APL+cardless) and received quantity from FPS is 33.4 kg per month which, in percentage terms, shows a gap of 95.2 per cent. For wheat, the gap is 94.6 per cent, for sugar it is 92.3 per cent, and for kerosene 25 per cent. Thus, the PDS has failed miserably in supplying essential items to the population across board, both BPL and APL, excepting kerosene.

For BPL households, required average consumption of rice is 34.5 kg per month per household, while the distributed quantity is only 2.7 kg, that is 7.8 per cent of the required quantity. Similarly, for wheat, average consumption requirement per household per month is 43.5 kg while the distributed quantity is 3.3 kg, that is, 8.7 per cent of the required quantity. For sugar, the required quantity per household per month is very meagre at 1.7 kg, of which, 11.8 per cent is distributed through the FPS. 77.3 per cent of consumption requirements for kerosene for BPL households is met through the FPSs.

APL households have a little higher requirement, per household per month, for all the items, viz., rice, wheat, sugar and kerosene, relative to the corresponding requirements of BPL households. For rice, wheat and kerosene they are marginally higher, while for sugar the requirement of APL households is double that of BPL households per household per period. Most of the requirements of APL households are met through open market, excepting kerosene. The APL households receive only 1.1 per cent of each of rice and wheat required from the FPSs, while they receive 7.9 per cent of sugar required for consumption per period, and 70.9 per cent of kerosene from the FPSs.

The cardless households do not receive sugar from the FPSs, but manage to get rice, wheat and kerosene from these shops. The quantities of rice, wheat and kerosene that these cardless households receive from the FPSs fall well below those received by the BPL cardholders. In any case, the cardless cases need to be taken care of by the administrative set-up meant for the PDS network in the district.

We have consistent information on consumption requirements of essential items by regional division of the district of Allahabad, as well as by selection of blocks and towns. For example, considering inter-block variations in consumption requirement of rice per household per month, we get the minimum at 34.5 kg for each of Karchhana and Kaurihar blocks and maximum at 36.7 kg for Shankargarh block. The range of variation in consumption requirement of rice for all (BPL + APL + cardless) thus is 2.2 kg per household per month, inter-block-wise. For wheat, the range of variation in requirement for all households blockwise is 6.2 kg per household per month, the maximum requirement being 47.9 kg for Saidabad block and the minimum being 41.7 kg for Kaurihar block. For sugar, the requirement for all households block-wise lies between 2.1 kg at minimum for each of Shankargarh and Kaurihar blocks and 2.9 kg at maximum for Karchhana block. The range of variation in consumption requirement of sugar (block-wise) per household per month, thus, is 0.8 kg. If we look at consumption requirement of essential items in urban areas, we find that for rice there is a wide variation between 20.6 kg for Bharatganj town and 36.4 kg for Phulpur town. For wheat also, the requirement in Phulpur is 46.5 kg, far more than the requirement in Bharatganj which is 34.4 kg per month per household.

In terms of consumption requirements for items by specific economic categories, there is consistency across blocks in the district. For example, for rice, the requirements of BPL households vary between the minimum at 34.5 kg for Karchhana and 37.4 kg for Shankargarh, a gap in inter-village requirement of rice for BPL households estimated at 2.9 kg. For wheat, for BPL households, the inter-block variation in consumption requirement is estimated at 5.6 kg, the maximum being 46.9 kg for Shankargarh and the minimum being 41.3 kg for Kaurihar. Thus, there exists a minimum requirement of BPL households for at least rice and wheat, which are very significant by quantity in the consumption basket. The average requirement of rice and wheat per BPL household per period can also be calculated.

For BPL households, the estimated range of variation among blocks in consumption requirement of sugar per household per month is 0.8 kg, the maximum at 2.1 kg for each of Shankargarh and Saidabad while the minimum is at 1.4 kg for Kaurihar. There, thus, exists minimum and average (with hypothetical maximum at given prices) requirement for sugar for BPL households for all the blocks taken together.

We have calculated the average requirements of items for BPL and APL households separately and together that may be taken as yardstick for consideration by the administrative division in the PDS network for supply through the FPSs. These average figures, that is, consumption requirements for each item, are approximations that aim at covering the average consumption requirements of households.

So far, for each block and town surveyed, the distribution of items on the average accounts for very insignificant percentage of requirements. The fact is that very low distribution rather than high requirement explain the large gap between requirement and distribution for the blocks, particularly for rice and wheat. Since requirement of kerosene is satisfied more or less equally across economic categories, BPL and APL, hence increased allotment of kerosene in FPSs is meant to offer benefits to both types of households.

Item-wise Price Differential between Open Market and FPSs at Block Level

Let us now point out the price differential item-wise between open market and FPS. For rice, the gap in price per unit between open market and FPS for all households, including BPL and APL, in all blocks and towns, that is, for the whole district on average, is Re. 0.97, which is 15.6 per cent of FPS price (Rs. 6.22 on an average). For wheat, the absolute gap is Re. 0.06, that is, 1.2 per cent of FPS price (Rs. 5.05 on an average). For sugar, the gap is Rs. 3.84, which is 28.3 per cent of FPS price (Rs. 13.59 on an average). For kerosene, the gap is Rs. 3.41, which is 33.8 per cent of FPS price (Rs. 10.09 on an average). This positive 'price gap' is more or less equally applicable for BPL and APL households in the district as a whole for rice, sugar and kerosene, but not for wheat. For wheat, for BPL households, the gap is 1.4 per cent of FPS price reported for BPL households (Rs. 5.03), it is negative at –0.4 per cent for APL households for whom the FPS price is recorded at Rs. 5.15. Open market rate for wheat differs insignificantly between BPL and APL households: for BPL households it is Rs. 5.10 per kg and for APL households, it is Rs. 5.13 per kg. For calculating the gap between open market price and FPS price, we have taken FPS price as base (with an index of 100). The prices we record are the prices reported by the households, the prices they pay while they buy the items (same quality) in the open market and from the FPS. Each of kerosene and sugar has approximately equal price for BPL and APL households as they receive these items from FPSs considered on average for the district as a whole. For sugar, the FPS price is Rs. 13.59 for BPL households and Rs. 13.58 for APL households. For kerosene, it is Rs. 10.10 for BPL households and Rs. 10.07 for APL households. There are, however, inter-regional (block-wise) variations in price gap item-wise. As reported by the beneficiaries, both BPL and APL households avail from the FPSs all the items, viz., rice, wheat, sugar, and kerosene, at same or similar prices. For example, while the average FPS price for rice is Rs. 6.46 for BPL households (average over blocks and towns), for APL households it is Rs. 6.77 higher by only Re. 0.31. For wheat, the reported average FPS price is Rs. 5.03 for BPL households and Rs. 5.15 for APL households higher for APL households by Rs. 0.12 only. For sugar, for BPL households, the reported average FPS price is Rs. 13.59, while for APL households, it is Rs. 13.58. For kerosene for BPL families it is Rs. 10.07 and for APL households, Rs. 10.05. The inter-regional (block-wise and town-wise) variations in reported FPS price per item is also not significant, considering over BPL and APL households. In other words, both BPL and APL households pay same or similar prices for essential items in all the blocks and towns. There is also not much variation in open market rates as bought by BPL and APL households of the items considered as reported by the respondents from households.

Required Expenditure by Households on Essential Commodities (at both Market Price and FPS Price)

To get market-based expenditure of households, we have multiplied actual quantity of the commodity required by (average) market price. This market price per unit of the item is based on the information provided by the households. To get FPS-based expenditure, we have multiplied actual quantity of the commodity required by FPS price. What we find is that for both BPL and APL households, FPS-based expenditure accounted for around 90 per cent of market-based expenditure. The expenditure by households has been calculated in rupee terms over all the items distributed, namely, wheat, rice, sugar and kerosene. We have calculated the annual expenditure of households, on the assumption of required quantity actually supplied (received by households), in the market and through

FPS. The implication is that at least 10 per cent of expenditure can be saved by households, both BPL and APL, if the required quantity is supplied through FPS. The price prevailing in the (open) market as responded by the households is by no means an overestimation, as reflected by the willingness of a major section of the households to buy from the open market.

The FPS price reported (as being paid by the households) is higher than the price fixed for distribution purposes. If we multiply the actual quantity of commodities supplied by the FPS by the (actually charged) price the households pay, we get (actual) expenditure of FPS items (quantities) bought by the households. This actual expenditure on FPS items constitutes 12.6 per cent of market-based expenditure for BPL households and 7.5 per cent for APL households. For both BPL and APL households taken together, actual expenditure on FPS items constitutes only 10 per cent of market-based expenditure. Thus, FPS-distributed items at FPS charged prices (prices higher than what is fixed) show not only a huge gap (90 per cent) between required expenditure on essential items (by consumption requirements of households) and expenditure incurred by households at FPS level, but also the scope for increased distribution of items.

While the market price (as reported by the households) is higher than the FPS price actually charged on households (the latter being higher than the FPS price fixed), for APL households market price is higher than the corresponding market price for BPL households. The reason may lie in quality differential of the same items bought in the open market.

Annual expenditure by BPL households on items actually supplied by FPSs and received by households shows higher percentage (12.6) of their market-based expenditure relative to the same of APL households (7.5). One interpretation could be that if all the required items were distributed through the FPSs at FPS prices, the possibility of saving (or income transfer) would be more for APL households; for BPL households, it is 87.4 per cent increase (100 – 12.6), while for APL households it is 92.5 per cent increase (100 – 7.5). This is where the question of targeting the BPL comes in terms of coverage by FPSs (Table 13).

Table 13

Required Expenditure (Annual Average) by Households on Essential Commodities (at both Market Price and FPS Price)

Categories	*Annual Expenditure on Commodities at Prices in FPS*[1]	*Required Expenditure on Essential Commodities*	
		At FPS Price[2]	*At Market Price*[2]
BPL	853.17 (12.6)	6,111.08 (90.5)	6,751.56 (100.0)
APL[3]	583.55 (7.5)	7,088.03 (91.4)	7,754.77 (100.0)
Cardless[4]	606.93 (10.1)	5,355.22 (89.5)	5,983.26 (100.0)
Total	740.81 (10.0)	6,264.80 (84.4)	7,421.66 (100.0)

Notes: 1. Annual expenditure on FPS has been calculated based on average monthly quantity of rice, wheat, sugar and kerosene drawn by households evaluated at average FPS prices.

2. The required expenditure has been calculated based on annual quantity of essential commodities required, evaluated at both FPS prices and market prices of rice, wheat, sugar and kerosene.

3. Rice and Wheat are not supposed to be distributed to APL households at same prices meant for BPL households but some APL households are reported to have taken these items in illegal manner.

4. These households have been found cardless during the field survey but they have taken some items from FPS dealers.

Source: Field survey.

VII

Awareness of the Households as Beneficiaries of PDS

Let us examine the awareness of the beneficiary households in terms of selected indicators like price charts at FPSs, the names of FPS dealers etc.

Price Chart at Fair Price Shops

Of all the households (1,400) surveyed in the district of Allahabad, as high as 61.4 per cent reported non-availability of 'price chart' in the FPSs, while 24.4 per cent reported availability of the chart. The rest of the households reported ignorance. The non-availability of price chart at FPS is cited more by BPL households, the latter seen as percentage of all BPL households reporting non-availability and seen also as percentage of all households reporting non-availability of price chart. The ignorance of the households reported regarding existence of price chart at FPS shows a higher percentage of APL relative to BPL, both calculated as percentages of their respective totals at the district level. The ignorance factor is much less for urban areas relative to the rural areas.

Price Information by Price Chart

Of all the households reporting availability of price chart (341), as low as 35.48 per cent confirmed availability of correct price information in the chart, which is only 8.6 per cent of all households (1,400). As high as 56.89 per cent of all households reporting availability of price chart negated existence of correct price chart, or informed existence of incorrect price chart. The households, who negated existence of correct price chart, constituted 13.9 per cent of all households (1,400). The households, who affirmed availability of price chart but expressed ignorance about the correctness of price information provided by the chart, are 7.62 per cent, which is 1.9 per cent of all households. The correctness of price information, even when the price chart is available in FPSs, thus, is questionable, as reported by the households of all categories, including BPL and APL. For urban (town) areas, the percentage of households in the category of confirmation in availability of correct information is higher, relative to those for the rural (block) areas.

Price Information by Items

Of all the households (1,400), only 0.6 per cent confirmed their correct knowledge about the FPS price of rice, 0.7 per cent of wheat, 1.4 per cent of sugar and 1.8 per cent of kerosene. The precise point is that most of the households, both BPL and APL, do not know the correct prices of items being distributed for them through the FPSs.

Names of FPS Dealers

Of all the households, as high as 91.9 per cent know the names of the FPS dealers. Category-wise, of the BPL households (812), as high as 91.3 per cent, and of the APL households (577) as high as 92.5 per cent know the names of the FPS dealers.

VIII
Other Observations in Brief

Because of the complex nature of the PDS, we had to encompass some of the problems that were not in the initial agenda for study. While in field, we encountered some issues, which we are offering in brief here.

- In almost all the villages, rice and wheat were not made available to the families owning ration cards. Even when these items arrived, a single day was fixed for distribution so that the income-poor (BPL) families were deprived. The simple reason is, apart from lack of timely information, the BPL families lack the power and time to collect money to buy the items abruptly announced for sale through the FPS.
- We found false/wrong entries in the cards for most of the BPL families, entries implying that all these families got all the items at scheduled rates (quantity and price).
- No cash memo was ever issued by any of the FPS owners.
- Even when the items were made available and the supply position was announced by the FPS dealer, the prices per unit of items were not displayed.
- One consequence of the above was that the benefits of price differential (sale price – scheduled PDS price) went in favour of the FPS dealer.
- Sugar was usually irregular in supply.

- Kerosene per head was distributed much less than what was allotted and that too at prices higher than the scheduled PDS rate.
- The section in higher socio-economic category derived almost all the benefits from irregular supply of items from the FPSs.
- We also found some villages where socially upper caste people continue to (mis)use the PDS by availing items much more than what is fixed per card.

IX
Policy Recommendations

Based on the facts that we collected for the district of Allahabad regarding the functioning of the PDS, and based on the observations that we gathered in our conversations with the beneficiaries, we offer our recommendations for improving the targeted PDS in India as under:

- Ensure regular distribution of rice, wheat and kerosene by exact quantity allotted at right price. Ensure withdrawal of rice and wheat by the FPS dealers for distribution among the households without any time lag.
- Ensure enhanced allotment of rice, wheat and kerosene per household per period so as to converge to the consumption requirements of the households per period for these items.
- Delete price differential for rice and wheat over BPL and APL categories and ensure quantity differential by allotting more of these items per household per period in favour of the BPL category.
- Ensure reduced price of kerosene per litre for all households, including BPL and APL, even if it costs more to the public exchequer.
- Ensure provision of purchase of rice, wheat and kerosene by instalments for that section of BPL households who cannot have disposable money as and when required to buy these items. Adopt a strategy of 'Due Slip' to be issued

by the FPS dealers to the targeted sections as such within the BPL category of households.

- Ensure allotment and distribution of sugar for BPL households at the prevailing price. Withdraw allotment of sugar for APL households. Announce 'special' distribution of sugar during festivals for both BPL and APL households.
- Raise the rate of commission on distribution of each of rice, wheat, sugar and kerosene per unit for the FPS dealers with immediate effect.
- Ensure release of quota to be withdrawn by the FPS dealer in a particular period (month) after subtracting 'undistributed items' of the preceding period (month). Set up a fact-finding committee, as and when necessary, to find out the reasons behind repetition of undistributed items accumulated over periods.
- Initiate time-bound inquiry for repetitive non-withdrawal of items by an FPS dealer instead of automatic cancellation of licence/quota of the dealer.
- Ensure compulsory maintenance of records for each of sale, stocks and ration card master register by the FPS dealers.
- Ensure allotment of new FPS dealership to local educated unemployed youth preferably from the socio-economically disadvantaged sections in the locality.
- Stop criminal/illegal interference in the PDS network at the local level.
- Ensure verification of ration cards at the local level, including issuing new cards, cancelling false cards etc.
- Ensure budget provision at Nigam/Regional Supply Office for allotment of quota to the FPS dealers, rather than asking the dealers to pay money in advance.
- Ensure public display of quantity of items distributed by the FPS dealers per period, and quantity of items remaining undistributed. The State Supply Department is being requested to provide necessary calendar to the FPS dealers for the said purpose.

- Ensure reduced number of FPSs for vigilance by a single Supply Inspector. The State Supply Department is expected to collect information from the 'Vigilance Committee' voluntarily formed by the consumers (households) at the village level regarding functioning of the PDS at the local level.
- In addition to strong vigilance by the panchayats and Supply Inspectors over visibility of correct price chart in the FPS, ensure 'secret and sudden' vigilance by RFO to check items in FPSs by quantity and quality and undistributed stocks. The vigilance by the RFO has to cover households also, both BPL and APL, at random in the concerned village.
- Ensure active and positive role of panchayats in an interactive manner with the State Supply Department/BDO etc., regarding preparation of correct schedule of cardholders, by BPL and APL, and hence make it transparent. Ensure training for panchayat members for convergence to perfect functioning of the system. Ensure active and positive role of panchayats for development of awareness of households regarding the 'right to food at fair price'. This requires an interactive frame among panchayats, NGOs, Supply Department and the media.
- Form an autonomous State Vigilance Committee to work as a complementary unit with the existing administrative network meant for the PDS.

Implementing the above measures in keeping with the objectives of TPDS requires a number of supplementary measures like:

(1) guarantee of social security through schemes like Employment Guarantee Scheme as in Maharashtra, Unemployment Allowance/Insurance etc. (ILO, 2000: 165, 167),

(2) Food for Work scheme, that can supplement PDS, and

(3) food coupon or food stamp system for the income-poor.

One of the objectives of the study is to examine the question of access of the income-poor to the essential commodities and thus examine the feasibility of the PDS to protect the poor. Since the measures mentioned above ensure direct and indirect income, including income transfer, to the socially and economically disadvantaged sections of the population, hence PDS, even if it is a supply-side measure, can protect the poor when supported by the measures that we suggested.

Acknowledgement

This paper is an offshoot of the project report on Public Distribution System that I submitted to the Planning Commission, Government of India, in November 2001. I am thankful to Prof. Ravi Srivastava for his helpful comments on the draft report. I am also grateful to Prof. Jean Dreze and Prof. Kripa Sankar for their comments on the final report. The staff that helped me in getting the report in shape are G.N. Jha, M.G. Gupta, A.K. Dwivedi and S.K. Jaiswal. The errors in interpretation of data lie with me.

References

Dandekar, V.M., 1994, *The Indian Economy*, 1947-92, Vol. I Sage Publications, New Delhi.

Dreze, J. and Sen, A., 1989, *Hunger and Public Action*, Clarendon Press, Oxford.

Ghose, Ajit Kumar, 1999, 'Food Supply and Starvation: A Study of Famines with Reference to the Indian Sub-Continent', in Dreze, Jean (ed.), *The Economics of Famine*, Edward Elgar Pub. Ltd., UK.

Government of India, 1996-97, *Economic Survey.*

Government of India, 1997-98, *Economic Survey.*

Government of India, 1999-2000, *Economic Survey.*

Government of India, Ministry of Agricultural and Irrigation, 1976, Report of the National Commission on Agriculture, Part I and Part II, New Delhi.

International Labor Office (ILO), 2000, *World Labor Report*, Geneva.

Mooij, Jos, 1999, *Food Policy and the Indian State: The Public Distribution System in South India*, Oxford University Press, Delhi.

Rao, V.M., 1996, 'Policy Research for Liberalized Agriculture: Some Illustrated Research Areas', *Indian Journal of Agricultural Economics*, Vol. 51, Nos. 1&2, January-June.

Savy, Robert, 1972, *Social Security in Agriculture and Rural Areas*, International Labour Office, Geneva.

Suryanarayana, M.H., 2000, Food Security and Calorie Adequacy Across States: Implications for Reform, in Krishnaji, N. and Krishnan, T.N. (eds.), *Public Support for Food Security: The Public Distribution System in India*, Sage Publications, New Delhi.

2

Urbanisation and Conversion of Agricultural Land for Non-Agricultural Purposes

Bimal Kumar

Though Uttar Pradesh (UP) continues to be predominantly rural, proportion of urban population and area is rising. Cities are generating and accumulating wealth. There is continuous influx to cities for education, jobs and greater economic opportunity. At the same time, cities are consuming natural resources at alarming rates. They also generate pollution beyond tolerable limits. These problems are more due to failure or lack of planning than rapid population growth.

While discussing urbanisation, debate is often focused on metropolitan and big cities, whereas the role of townships having population less than 20,000 is overlooked. The linkages between metropolis, medium towns and small towns and their role to improve agricultural performance and create employment linkages with local level economic activities is not paid due attention. As a result of this, the policy framework to regulate various dimensions of urbanisation generally confines itself narrowly to urban problems rather than taking a holistic view.

The area under urban land in UP is only 5.59 lakh hectares, which is merely 1.9 per cent of total area of the state, while 19.84 per cent population is settled in urban areas. This fact is also reflected in the density of population in urban areas, which is 4,937 persons per square kilometre, while density of population in the state as a whole is only 473 persons.

But area under urban land in UP is high only in few districts. Land under urban areas was found to be highest in Kanpur Nagar (28.89 per cent of total area of the Kanpur district) followed by Lucknow and Ghaziabad where the land under urban areas is accounted for 14.22 per cent and 10.96 per cent respectively of the total area of these districts. There were only two other districts, viz., Meerut and Bareilly, where this percentage of urban area was between 5 per cent and 10 per cent. In all other districts, urban area constituted less than 5 per cent of total area of districts.

As regards share of urban population to total population of the district, which is considered as an indicator of the level of urbanisation of the district, it was found that urban population consisted of 84.24 per cent in Kanpur Nagar, followed by 66.26 per cent in Lucknow, 50.26 per cent in Dehradun, 46.16 per cent in Ghaziabad and 40.38 per cent in Agra.

Methodology

Two cities, namely, Lucknow and Kanpur, were selected for the purpose of this study. The expansion of Lucknow and Kanpur cities has led to large-scale conversion of agricultural land. In recent years the area of Lucknow has particularly developed in all sides. Kanpur has also experienced major expansion in the western and southern sides. Therefore, three sites close to Lucknow and two sites close to Kanpur, where conversion of agricultural land for non-agricultural purposes has taken place at a very large scale, were selected for the study. Only such villages were covered under our study where land was acquired after 1980.

In Kanpur, the villages were selected from the southern and western sides. Incidentally, land of only four villages had been acquired in Kanpur. As such, all these four villages have been included in the sample.

In Lucknow, the acquisition of land has been carried out in around 40 villages. Out of these, a sample of 12 villages was drawn for inclusion in the sample. The selection was made from amongst affected villages of the following four areas of Lucknow: (i) eastern side; (ii) northwestern side; (iii) southern side; and (iv) area already within the city limits.

Table 1

Selected Villages, Number of Affected Cultivators and Number of Cultivators Selected under Study

Village	*No. of Cultivators whose land has been acquired*	*Sampled cultivators*
Lucknow		
Khurram Nagar	03	03
Adilnagar	07	07
Batha Sabauli	104	10
Shakurpur	191	10
Barauli Khalilabad	170	10
Utaratiya	715	20
Haibatnau Mabaiya	340	19
Kharika	434	10
Jiyamau	125	12
Jainabad	121	13
Khandak	526	27
Alipur (Dist. Barabanki)	94	13
Total	2,830	185
Kanpur		
Hanspur	127	23
Budhapur Machariya	138	27
Naubasta	02	02
Bara Sirohi	652	111
Total	919	163

Growth Pattern and Impact on Land Use

The process of urbanisation in UP shows a unique trend of its own. As stated above, for the purpose of our study, we selected two cities of Kanpur and Lucknow deliberately. The expansion of Kanpur owes to its position of being one of the oldest industrial towns of the country and indeed the first industrial town of the state. Lucknow, on the other hand, had been the citadel of old feudal civilisation and then became capital of United Provinces during pre-independence period and that of Uttar Pradesh, the most populous state of India, during the post-independence period.

Growth in Urban Area and Population

The Kanpur city owes its growth and expansion to industrialisation till around early seventies. However, there has been decline in industrial production and industrial employment since then. This phase also witnessed the closure of large-scale industries mainly the textile sector. However, small-scale units in diverse non-traditional areas were set up during this phase. The major reason for expansion of Kanpur during this phase could be attributed to its emergence as a major commercial centre in the region. Trade and commerce and other services are the main occupations in which the majority of working population of Kanpur is engaged.

On the other hand, Lucknow has grown basically because of migrants. According to 1971 and 1981 censuses the migrants constituted 33.26 per cent and 27.44 per cent of its population respectively. In the past, Lucknow had been famous for some of its household industries such as chikan work, kamdani, zardozi, gold lace weaving, metal and jewellery works besides perfume and tobacco industry. But, during the last four decades or so, the importance of Lucknow has grown as administrative-cum-commercial city. The number of workers in the tertiary sector has increased enormously during this period.

Lately, some non-planned development in industrial activity has taken place on Lucknow-Kanpur Highway route.

Since Lucknow is the centre of power, many industrial establishments have shifted their headquarters there. Some industries too have followed the suit. So, whereas trade and commerce followed industrialisation in Kanpur, in case of Lucknow, first trade and commerce flourished and then industrialisation is taking place around the city giving fillip to faster expansion of the city.

Table 2

Growth in Urban Area and Population in Lucknow and Kanpur

	Uttar Pradesh	*Lucknow*	*Kanpur (Nagar)*	*Kanpur (Dehat)*
Area in Km^2				
1961		135.53	196.66	
1971		133.90	300.90	
1981	4,560.40	168.00	327.02	
1991	5,603.10	359.51	307.66	35.94
Decadal Variation in Area				
1961-71		-1.21%	1.43%	
1971-81		25.46%	8.68%	
1981-91	22.86%	113.99%	5.07%	
Decadal Variation in Population				
1961-71	24.78%	24.14%	31.42%	
1971-81		23.79%	28.53%	
1981-91		65.66%	23.84%	31.28%

Sources: 1. District Census Handbook, Kanpur District for years 1961, 1971 and 1981.
2. Figures for 1991 have been quoted from Urbanisation in UP (Land Use Board, Department of Planning, Government of UP, Lucknow.

It could be seen from the above table that the area of Lucknow grew by 114 per cent during 1981-91 period, while the area under Kanpur urban agglomeration grew by only 5.07 per cent during the same period. Similarly, the growth rate of population during the decade 1981-91 was found to be 65.66 per cent for Lucknow and 31.28 per cent for Kanpur. The planned growth of urban areas of Lucknow and Kanpur are amazingly very large. This is evident from the proposed land use under the master plans of the two cities.

In Lucknow, a total of 13,643.75 acres of land are proposed to be acquired under the revised Master Plan. Out of this, 11,609.28 acres are to be acquired from the private owners. Besides this, 983.06 acres of land of Gram Sabhas and 1,051.41 acres of land of other departments are also proposed to be acquired under the Master Plan of Lucknow.

Table 3

Details of Land Proposed to be Acquired in Lucknow

	Land Area (in acres)
Land to be acquired from farmers	11,609.28
Gram Sabhas land	983.06
Nazul land (belonging to other departments)	1,051.41
Area planned to be acquired	13,643.75
Land not proposed to be acquired	474.09

Similarly, in Kanpur, the area of agricultural land, which is being included in the Master Plan of the city, is 20,821.00 hectares, which is 51.06 per cent of the total area of the expanded township as proposed in the Master Plan.

Besides the planned growth, urbanisation also leads to inclusion of many fringe areas under the urban expansion process. An additional area measuring 10 to 12 kilometres radius from the present boundary of Lucknow Development Authority and Kanpur Development Authority is gradually being engulfed under the urbanisation process of the cities, which is not part of the master plans of these cities. Land of these areas is being acquired by individuals, spurious housing cooperative societies and private builders.

A study by Remote Sensing Application Centre, UP on "Geographic Information System Applications Using High Resolution IRS-IC Data for Urban Land Use Mapping, Utility Modelling and Monitoring Urban Sprawl of the City of Lucknow" shows that whereas the Lucknow city area covered under Lucknow Development Authority is only 20,672 square kilometres, the urban sprawl covers an additional 504.93 square kilometres, out of which 375.87 square kilometres is cropped land.

A similar sprawl of Kanpur Nagar must be also in operation, but no authentic data of the same was available.

Table 4a

Proposed Land Use under Revised Master Plan of Lucknow, 2001

(in hectares)

Sl. No.	*Land Use*	*Proposed Area under Present Master Plan*	*Proposed Area under Revised Master Plan*
1.	Residential	7,105.7 (48.73)	15,923.8 (67.2)
2.	Commercial	377.4 (2.58)	936.2 (3.9)
3.	Residential-cum-Commercial	-	47.0 (0.2)
4.	Government/Semi-Government Offices	160.6 (1.10)	378.5 (1.7)
5.	Industrial	1,514.5 (10.39)	731.0 (3.1)
6.	Recreational/Park, Sports Complex, Garden, Orchards, etc.	1,630.0 (11.17)	1,868.5 (7.9)
7.	Public Utilities and Services	901.1 (6.19)	1,537.0 (6.5)
8.	Transportation	2,891.4 (19.84)	2,260.0 (9.5)
	Total	14,580.7 (100.00)	23,682.0 (100.0)

Note: Figures in parentheses indicate percentages.

Table 4b

Kanpur Land Use Pattern, 1989

Sl. No.	*Category*	*Area in Hectares*	*Percentage*
1.	Residential	5,044.48	12.37
2.	Commercial	127.32	0.31
3.	Residential-cum-Commercial	78.80	0.19
4.	Industrial	1,327.55	3.26
5.	Industrial-cum-Residential	18.56	0.05
6.	Warehouses	50.59	0.12
7.	Institutional-cum-Educational	557.63	1.37
8.	Instutitional-cum-Others	313.80	0.77
9.	Institutional-cum-Residential	136.14	0.33
10.	Recreational	332.14	0.81
11.	Urban Infrastructure	2,131.63	5.23
12.	Public Utility	4,326.54	10.61
13.	Water Bodies	1,299.67	3.19
14.	Agricultural Land	20,821.00	51.06
15.	Waste Land	2,450.11	6.00
16.	Others	1,763.92	4.33
	Total	40779.88	100.00

Source: Kanpur Master Plan, 1989.

Villages Covered under the Survey

Kanpur

In Kanpur land was reportedly acquired from four villages, out of which only one was located in the western side whereas other three in the southern side of city.

Bara Sirohi village is situated in the western side of the city. The village is about 10 kilometres further away in the west to IIT, Kanpur. Almost all the land of this village has been acquired. All the acquired land was fertile agricultural land, but their owners who were cultivators are now forced to earn through other works. A residential colony is being developed in the whole of acquired land of this village.

Three villages in the southern side of Kanpur, namely, Hanspur, Budhapur Machariya and Naubasta, have come under the acquisition plan. Almost all the land of these villages has been acquired. The acquired land has been put to two uses: one, development of residential colony by Kanpur Development Authority and two, setting up of a power sub-centre. The acquired land of these villages was very fertile and the cultivators were prosperous farmers. Even today, the productivity in adjoining areas is very high. But, those farmers who were affected due to acquisition of their land are now forced to work in non-agricultural activities.

Lucknow

In Lucknow, the land has been acquired in all the directions and, therefore, all the peripheral areas of Lucknow city are now becoming part of the city.

Northern Side

The main affected areas in the northern side of Lucknow are Sabauli, Batha, Adilnagar and Khurram Nagar. All the four villages, specially Batha and Sabauli, are predominantly SC/OBC areas. Their main occupation is casual labour even though in the past they were cultivators, specially vegetable growers. But, after the acquisition of land, they have no other work except wage labour. Compensation awarded against acquisition of their land was also less than the market value. Moreover, the money of compensation has generally been spent on various non-productive expenditures. In Sabauli, the rate of compensation was very low, i.e., Rs. 1.23 per square feet, while in other three villages it was awarded at the rate of Rs. 6 per square feet. In sum, they are living in poverty and even their educational level is also low.

Eastern Side

In the eastern side, the three affected villages covered under the survey were Alipur, Jainabad and Khandak. Alipur is part of Barabanki district adjoining Lucknow. Villagers of these areas were primarily agriculturists but their lands have been acquired for developing industrial area. Villagers were told at the time of acquisition that those households whose land was being acquired would be benefited as one member of their family would be provided job in these industries. But, even after a decade no one has got any job in these industries. Therefore, they are forced to work as wage labourers. The social composition of these villages showed that backward caste people were predominant in these villages. They have also been not given adequate compensation. The rate of compensation amount ranges between Rs. 16,000 and Rs. 20,000 per bigha, which is very low. Moreover, full amount of compensation has not been paid till the date of our investigation. Villagers were also assured that village development activities would be undertaken in these villages. But, in the name of development only, one *kharanja* (brick soling based) road had been constructed in Khandak village.

Southern Side

In the southern side five villages, namely, Kharika, Shakurpur, Haibatnau Mabaiya, Barauli Khalilabad and Utaratiya, were covered. Agricultural lands of these villages were very fertile and also availed good irrigation facility because of canals. Cultivation was the main occupation of residents of these villages. But, after the acquisition, most of them have been forced to work as wage labourers. Even those who have managed to save some land reported that the land left with them was not sufficient for their livelihood. However, villagers grow vegetables and sell it in the market in those small parcels of land, which left with them. Therefore, they looked to be slightly better off than those who had been rendered totally landless. Some villagers started their own small business. The rate of compensation was Rs. 9.30 per square feet in these villages.

Central Area

Jeeya Mau village comes in this area. It is situated at a distance of one-and-a-half kilometres from Hazaratganj – the posh market place of Lucknow – and is located in the middle of Lucknow city. Land of this village was also very fertile. Most of the land of this village have been acquired. The only exception is the land owned by a powerful farmer Md. Mazahar Ali. Farmers have been awarded compensation at the rate of Rs. 4.30 per square feet, while LDA has sold the same land to Sahara India at the rate of Rs. 4.00 per square feet. Some farmers moved to the court and the matter is still under litigation. Farmers had received only 40 per cent of the compensation amount and the remaining 60 per cent is still to be paid.

The following industries have been allotted land acquired from farmers in Lucknow:

1. Chinhat Industrial Area, promoted by UPSIDC, HIG 64/65
2. SFL Industry, Sahu Forging Ltd.
3. Suprabha Industry Ltd., Plot No. 2, UPSIDC Industrial Area
4. Central Food Technical Research Institute, UPSIDC Industrial Area, Deva Road, Chinhat
5. Spicer India Ltd.
6. Express Hi-Tech Pvt. Ltd.
7. RALCO, Agro Chemical Pvt. Ltd.
8. Triple-3 Aqua Minerale, Avadh Industries
9. ALPHA
10. एरोमेटिव केमिकल (चन्द्रलोक)
11. नेडा (वैकल्पिक ऊर्जा शोध एवं विकास केन्द्र)
12. Mother Land Dairy
13. Indo Class
14. UPTRON
15. TELCO

Major land has been acquired by the last two industries.

Impact on Farmers

We covered 185 farmers of Lucknow and 163 farmers of Kanpur in our survey. Thus, in all, 348 farmers whose land had been acquired were interviewed regarding various aspects related to acquisition. Out of these 348 farmers, 101 belonged to Scheduled Castes (Lucknow 60 + Kanpur 41), 153 to the category of OBCs (Lucknow 105 + Kanpur 48) and 94 to general castes (Lucknow 20 + Kanpur 74). Thus, whereas the number of upper caste farmers under acquisition proceedings was small in Lucknow, it was quite sizeable (45.4 per cent) in Kanpur (see Table 5).

Table 5

Cultivators: Caste, Gender and Age Group

		Lucknow				*Kanpur*			
		SC	*OBC*	*General*	*Total*	*SC*	*OBC*	*General*	*Total*
Male		59	98	16	173 (93.5)	40	47	73	160 (98.2)
Female		1	7	4	12 (6.5)	1	1	1	3 (1.8)
Age Group	Below 25	1	0	0	1 (0.5)	0	1	0	1 (0.6)
	25 to 34	10	0	1	11 (5.9)	1	3	1	5 (3.1)
	35 to 39	3	11	0	14 (7.6)	2	4	5	11 (6.7)
	40 to 44	8	23	6	37 (20.0)	6	6	13	25 (15.3)
	45 to 59	26	49	9	84 (45.4)	24	22	46	92 (56.4)
	60 and above	12	22	4	38 (20.5)	8	12	9	29 (17.8)
Total		60 (32.4)	105 (56.8)	20 (10.8)	185 (100)	41 (25.2)	48 (29.4)	74 (45.4)	163 (100)

Purpose of Acquisition

In Kanpur, all the 163 farmers land was acquired for housing and other related purposes. In Lucknow, 74.6 per cent land had been acquired for housing and other related purposes, whereas 25.4 per cent land had been acquired for setting up of industries (see Table 6).

Table 6

Purpose of Acquisition

Purpose	*Lucknow*				*Kanpur*			
	SC	*OBC*	*General*	*Total*	*SC*	*OBC*	*General*	*Total*
Housing and other related purposes	42	77	19	138 (74.6)	41	48	74	163 (100.0)
For industry	18	28	1	47 (25.4)	0	0	0	0
Total	60 (23.4)	105 (56.8)	20 (10.8)	185 (100.0)	41 (25.2)	48 (24.4)	74 (45.4)	163 (100.0)

Land Acquiring Agencies

In Kanpur, out of 163, the land of 122 farmers (i.e. 74.8 per cent) was acquired by Kanpur Development Authority whereas land of only 8 per cent farmers had been acquired by Awas Evam Vikas Parishad. Land of 17.2 per cent farmers in Kanpur had also been purchased by private industry owners. No land in Kanpur had been acquired for setting up public sector industries.

In contrast to Kanpur, in Lucknow, most of the land for developing housing colonies had been acquired by Awas Evam Vikas Parishad. It could be seen from Table 7 that the land of 103 farmers, out of 185, i.e., 55.7 per cent had been acquired by Awas Evam Vikas Parishad, while land of only 15.7 per cent farmers had been acquired by Lucknow Development Authority. Another distinguishing feature of Lucknow was that land of more than 28 per cent farmers had been acquired for setting up industries. Out of these, land of 14.1 per cent farmers had been acquired for setting up public sector industries, while the land of other 14.6 per cent farmers had been acquired by owners of private industries.

Table 7

Caste-wise Classification of Households whose Land was Acquired by Various Agencies

	Lucknow				*Kanpur*			
	SC	*OBC*	*General*	*Total*	*SC*	*OBC*	*General*	*Total*
LDA/KDA	7	16	6	29 (15.7)	36	45	41	122 (74.8)
Awas Evam Vikas Parishad	41	48	14	103 (55.7)	1	1	11	13 (8.0)
Government Industry	11	15	0	26 (14.1)	0	0	0	0
Private Industry	1	26	0	27 (14.6)	4	2	22	28 (17.2)
Total	60 (32.4)	105 (56.8)	20 (10.8)	185 (100.0)	41 (25.2)	48 (29.4)	74 (45.5)	163 (100.0)

Size of Land Acquired

Since most of the farmers were small and marginal farmers, the size of land acquired from them was, on an average, less than 2 acres.

In Lucknow, the size of land acquired from 56 farmers (i.e., 30.3 per cent) was less than one bigha, i.e., 0.63 acre, from 31 farmers it was between 1 and 2 bighas (i.e., 0.63 and 1.26 acres), and from 71 farmers (i.e., 38.4 per cent) it was between 2 and 3 bighas. Thus, in Lucknow, the size of land acquired from 158, out of 185 farmers, i.e., 75.5 per cent farmers was less than 3 bighas, i.e., less than 1.89 acres. Similarly, in Kanpur, the size of land acquired from 124 farmers, i.e., 76.1 per cent was less than 3 bighas, i.e., 1.89 acres (see Table 8).

Table 8
Size of Land Acquired

(in bigha)

	Lucknow				*Kanpur*			
	SC	*OBC*	*General*	*Total*	*SC*	*OBC*	*General*	*Total*
Below 1	29	21	6	56 (30.3)	4	0	4	8 (4.9)
1 to 2	9	21	1	31 (16.8)	24	26	38	88 (54.0)
2 to 3	15	45	11	71 (38.4)	5	8	15	28 (17.2)
3 to 5	3	15	0	21 (11.4)	4	5	7	16 (9.8)
5 to 10	1	3	2	6 (3.2)	4	6	4	14 (8.6)
Above 10	0	0	0	0	0	3	6	9 (5.5)
Total number of farmers	60 (32.4)	105 (56.8)	20 (10.8)	185 (100.0)	41 (25.2)	48 (29.4)	74 (45.4)	163 (100.0)

Note: 1 bigha = 0.63 acres.

Present Occupation of Cultivators

The acquisition of land has also made a far-reaching impact on the occupational structure of farmers. This is evident from Table 9, which shows their present occupation, after their land has been acquired.

In Lucknow, only 14.1 per cent of farmers whose land had been acquired continue to remain farmers. The rest, i.e., around 86 per cent have been forced to search jobs in other occupations. It could be further seen that 50.3 per cent farmers have been forced to work as labourers, 12.4 per cent have got service, 17.3 per cent are engaged in business, 2.2 per cent are working as domestic workers and 3.8 per cent are still unemployed.

Similarly, in Kanpur, only 11.7 per cent of those whose land has been acquired are continuing with cultivation work. That is, the acquisition of land has resulted in alienation of

Table 9
Occupation of Cultivators

	Lucknow				*Kanpur*			
	SC	*OBC*	*General*	*Total*	*SC*	*OBC*	*General*	*Total*
Cultivator	7	16	3	26 (14.1)	4	5	10	19 (11.7)
Labourer	37	52	4	93 (50.3)	24	22	13	59 (36.2)
Service	4	13	6	23 (12.4)	8	14	24	46 (28.2)
Business	8	20	4	32 (17.3)	4	7	15	26 (16.0)
Unemployed	4	3	0	7 (3.8)	1	0	12	13 (8.0)
Domestic work	0	1	3	4 (2.2)	0	0	0	0
Total	60 (32.4)	105 (56.8)	20 (10.8)	185 (100.0)	41 (25.2)	48 (29.4)	74 (45.4)	163 (100.0)

around 89 per cent farmers from cultivation work. The distribution of their new occupations to which they have shifted shows that 36.2 per cent have become labourers, 28.2 per cent have joined service, 16 per cent are engaged in business and 8 per cent of them have been rendered unemployed.

Thus, their present occupational status shows that acquisition of their land had adversely affected them. This negative impact has also resulted not only in lowering of their social status, but also in decline of their monthly income.

No farmer has reported receiving any other benefit or assistance from LDA/KDA or Awas Evam Vikas Parishad to provide them employment or even plots, even though there are such directives from the government.

Monthly Income

As is evident from Table 10 that the monthly income of affected families was found to be less than Rs. 2,000 in the majority of cases. In Lucknow, while the income of 74.5 per cent affected families was less than Rs. 2,000 per month, in Kanpur, the corresponding figure was 51.5 per cent.

Table 10

Monthly Income of Cultivators

(in Rs.)

	Lucknow				*Kanpur*			
	SC	*OBC*	*General*	*Total*	*SC*	*OBC*	*General*	*Total*
Below 1,000	9	6	1	16 (8.6)	6	6	10	22 (13.5)
1,001 to 1,500	33	54	3	90 (48.6)	22	17	9	48 (29.4)
1,501 to 2,000	10	21	1	32 (17.3)	1	6	7	14 (8.6)
2,001 to 3,000	3	14	8	25 (13.5)	9	11	22	42 (25.8)
3,001 to 5,000	5	9	6	20 (10.8)	3	6	22	31 (19.0)
5,001 and above	0	1	1	2 (1.1)	0	2	4	6 (3.7)
Total	60 (32.4)	105 (56.8)	20 (10.8)	185 (100.0)	41 (25.2)	48 (29.4)	74 (45.4)	163 (100.0)

The income distribution of affected families further shows that in Lucknow the income of 8.6 per cent families was less than Rs. 1,000 per month, that of 56 per cent it was between 1,000-2,000, 13.5 per cent belonged to the income category of Rs. 2,000-3,000 per month; and those who were earning more than Rs. 3,000 per month accounted for only around 12 per cent.

In Kanpur, 13.5 per cent affected families were earning less than Rs. 1,000 per month while the monthly income of 38 per cent families was in the range of Rs. 1,000-2,000 per month. The number of affected families in other income categories was as follows: between Rs. 2,000 and Rs. 3,000: 25.8 per cent; between Rs. 3,000 and Rs. 5,000: 19 per cent; and above Rs. 5,000: 3.7 per cent.

Compensation

The rate of compensation for acquired land in Lucknow was invariably lower than that in Kanpur. It could seen from Table 11 that in Lucknow the land of 21.1 per cent farmers was acquired at the rate of Rs. 10,000 to Rs. 16,000 per bigha and that of 63.8 per cent at Rs. 16,000 to Rs. 20,000 per bigha. Thus, the award lay between Rs. 10,000 and Rs. 20,000 per bigha for 85 per cent farmers in Lucknow. But, in case of Kanpur, the rate for 81 per cent farmers lay between Rs. 20,000 and Rs. 30,000 per bigha. However, the 15 per cent farmers received the compensation amount at the rate of Rs. 60,000 to Rs. 75,000 per bigha and 1.2 per cent at Rs. 11 lakh per bigha. This shows that only 16.2 per cent farmers in Kanpur received a substantial amount for their land. Otherwise, in Lucknow, as well as in Kanpur, the award was less than the market value of their land.

Table 11

Rate of Compensation for Acquired Land

(per bigha)

	Lucknow				*Kanpur*			
	SC	*OBC*	*General*	*Total*	*SC*	*OBC*	*General*	*Total*
Less than Rs. 4,000	7	3	6	16 (8.6)	2	0	2	4 (2.5)
Rs. 4,000 to 10,000	0	1	0	1 (0.5)	0	0	0	0
Rs. 10,000 to 16,000	21	17	1	39 (21.1)	0	0	0	0
Rs. 16,000 to 20,000	32	73	13	118 (63.8)	0	0	0	0
Rs. 20,000 to 25,000	0	1	0	1 (0.5)	1	1	19	21 (12.9)
Rs. 25,000 to 30,000	0	0	0	0	35	42	34	111 (68.1)
Rs. 60,000 to 75,000	0	0	0	0	3	5	17	25 (15.1)
Rs. 11 lakh	0	0	0	0	0	0	2	2 (1.2)
Not known	0	10	0	10 (5.4)	0	0	0	0
Total	60 (32.4)	105 (56.8)	20 (10.8)	185 (100.0)	41 (25.2)	48 (29.4)	74 (25.4)	163 (100.0)

A case in point is that of Naubasta of Kanpur. In Naubasta, the rate of compensation awarded was Rs. 65,000 per bigha. Challenging this, the two persons, namely, Sri Ram Khelawan Mishra (whose 18 bighas of land had been acquired) and Sri Munno Tiwari (whose 10 bighas of land had been acquired) moved to the High Court for raising the value of land to the level of current market value of land.

The High Court gave the decision in their favour and raised the value of acquired land to Rs. 11 lakh per bigha. The State Government filed an appeal against this order in the Supreme Court. The Supreme Court maintained the order of the High Court and upheld the value of compensation at Rs. 11 lakh per bigha. However, the two affected persons had not received the compensation till date.

There has been a lot of difference at which the land was acquired by LDA/KDA and the rate at which it was disposed of.

The market value of some of the areas in Lucknow was as follows:

(i) Jeeya Mau (Hazaratganj) - Rs. 300 to Rs. 400 per square feet.
(ii) Kursi Road (Aliganj) - Rs. 150 to Rs. 200 per square feet.
(iii) Chinhat Area - Rs. 45,000 to Rs. 75,000 per bigha.
(iv) Telibag - Rs. 150 to Rs. 250 per square feet.

In Jeeya Mau, Hazaratganj, LDA has sold land to Sahara India at the rate of Rs. 400 per square feet, whereas it was acquired at the rate of only Rs. 16 per square feet.

Amount of Compensation

The amount of compensation varied widely among the farmers. This was because of two reasons. One, the size of land acquired varied from less than 1 bigha to above 10 bighas. Secondly, the value of land assessed varied from less than Rs. 4,000 per bigha to Rs. 11 lakh per bigha. The distribution of amount of compensation received is shown in Table 12.

Table 12

Money Received After the Selling of Agricultural Land

(in Rs.)

	Lucknow				*Kanpur*			
	SC	*OBC*	*General*	*Total*	*SC*	*OBC*	*General*	*Total*
Below 10,000	4	1	0	5 (2.7)	0	2	3	5 (3.1)
10,001 to 20,000	3	5	0	8 (4.3)	9	1	6	16 (9.8)
20,001 to 50,000	8	30	0	38 (20.5)	16	20	21	57 (35.0)
50,001 to 75,000	4	10	1	15 (8.1)	6	8	9	23 (14.1)
75,001 to 1,00,000	1	6	1	8 (4.3)	3	10	7	20 (12.3)
1,00,001 to 1,50,000	12	7	2	21 (11.4)	1	3	6	10 (6.1)
1,50,001 to 2,00,000	12	10	1	23 (12.4)	5	3	4	12 (7.4)
2,00,001 to 3,00,000	2	6	2	10 (5.4)	1	3	11	12 (7.4)
Above 3,00,000	14	30	13	57 (30.8)	0	1	7	8 (4.9)
Total	60 (32.4)	105 (56.8)	20 (10.8)	185 (100.0)	41 (25.2)	48 (25.2)	74 (45.4)	163 (100.0)

It could be seen from the table that in Lucknow 20.5 per cent farmers received an amount between Rs. 20,000 and Rs. 50,000 as compensation, while 30 per cent received more than Rs. 3,00,000. The number of farmers who received other amounts was as follows: less than Rs. 20,000 – 7 per cent; between Rs. 50,000 and Rs. 1,00,000 – 12.4 per cent; between Rs. 1,00,000 and Rs. 2,00,000 – 22.8 per cent; and between Rs. 2,00,000 and Rs. 3,00,000 – 5.4 per cent.

Likewise, in Kanpur, 35 per cent farmers were paid the compensation amount between Rs. 20,000 and Rs. 50,000; 26.4 per cent between Rs. 50,000 and Rs. 1,00,000; and 13.5 per cent between Rs. 1,00,000 and Rs. 2,00,000. The number of farmers who received more than Rs. 2,00,000 was 12.3 per cent.

Utilisation of Amount Received

Land for farmers is not only a productive asset but also a perpetual source of livelihood. If a farmer is alienated from land, he must search an alternative source of income. In this respect, it was interesting to enquire whether the amount of compensation received was utilised to augment income or it was spent on other things.

The data (see Table 13) reveal that majority of farmers spent the amount of compensation either on construction of house or on marriages of their daughters. In Lucknow, the percentages of such farmers was 37.8 and 25.4 respectively. Thus, in totality, 63.2 per cent farmers of Lucknow spent the amount of compensation for these two purposes. Similarly, in Kanpur, 39.9 per cent farmers spent the amount of compensation on construction of house and 22.1 per cent on marriage of daughters, making a total of 62 per cent.

Table 13

Utilisation of Money Received After Selling the Land

	Lucknow				*Kanpur*			
	SC	*OBC*	*General*	*Total*	*SC*	*OBC*	*General*	*Total*
Construction of house	24	32	14	70 (37.8)	20	18	27	65 (39.9)
Marriage of daughters	17	30	0	47 (25.4)	13	13	10	36 (22.1)
Buy the tractor/auto rickshaw	9	8	3	20 (10.8)	2	3	4	9 (5.5)
Deposited in bank	2	5	2	9 (4.9)	2	10	7	19 (11.7)
Miscellaneous purposes	3	4	0	7 (3.8)	3	1	14	18 (11.0)
Not utilised	1	15	0	16 (8.6)	0	0	3	3 (1.8)
Other	4	11	1	16 (8.6)	1	3	9	13 (8.0)
Total	60 (32.4)	105 (56.8)	20 (10.8)	185 (100.0)	41 (25.2)	48 (29.4)	74 (45.4)	163 (100.0)

As regards investment on productive assets, only 10.8 per cent farmers of Lucknow and 5.5 per cent farmers of Kanpur spent the amount to purchase tractor or other transportation system such as auto-rickshaw. Some farmers, however, deposited the amount in banks. Number of such farmers was only 4.9 per cent in Lucknow and 11.7 per cent in Kanpur. The number of farmers, who spent the amount on other miscellaneous purposes, was 3.8 per cent in Lucknow and 11 per cent in Kanpur.

The amount of compensation was also used for some other purposes such as giving loans to others or on medicines etc. by around 8 per cent farmers in both the cities.

Thus, it would be wrong to say that the amount of compensation was utilised to regain the loss of income caused due to the acquisition of land.

Suggestions

(i) Land requirement norms should be evolved for expanding townships, and a detailed scheme for utilisation of land to be acquired should also be prepared.

(ii) If the livelihood of the families whose land has been acquired is affected, then the assistance for employment should also be provided by the acquiring agency. This assistance should be over and above the award of due compensation. Employment Guarantee Card should be provided to each affected family.

(iii) If the value of land appreciates after acquisition and the land acquiring agency reaps profit by allotting it to new users, then a part of profit should also be paid to the affected farmer.

(iv) Necessary support and credit should be provided to them so that they could take advantage of schemes which are specifically identified for them.

Framework for Urban-Rural Balance

1. Fix critical limits for density of population as well as area of urban settlements for each city.

2. Once an urban settlement reaches a stage where density of population or the area crosses the critical limit, following steps should be immediately taken up:
   (a) select markets/small townships which are 50 kilometres away from city limits and develop those townships with the facilities for (i) higher education, (ii) big hospitals with facilities for specialised treatments, (iii) sports and recreation centres, and (iv)setting up of business and industrial complexes;
   (b) provide all infrastructural (such as power, roads, communications etc.) facilities along with civic amenities;
   (c) develop a very efficient transport system from villages to these townships on the one hand and from these townships to big cities on the other; and
   (d) if an agricultural land of prime quality is being acquired with the approval of the state legislature or gaon sabha for urban development, (i) a levy must be imposed on such transfers, and (ii) 50 per cent of the final sale proceed be transferred for "agricultural development fund" of that area.

(3) Three-level planning-cum-administrative set-up comprising state, region and block be developed for future planned development. Districts could remain nodal units for maintaining law and order and administration of justice. Decentralise most of the administration to the block level. Block level plans be formulated instead of district level plans in the areas of health, education, manpower planning, irrigation, rural industrialisation, information and communication technology and for the energy sector. This could directly be linked with regional level planning-cum-administrative units.

(4) Plan dispersal of industries. Serious efforts should be made to develop industrial zones in least fertile and marginal lands.

(5) Housing schemes should be promoted, as far as possible, on barren and infertile lands.
(6) Fast transportation system and efficient communication network should be developed to link each and every village.

Appendix I

District-wise Urban Population, Level of Urbanisation and Urban Density in Uttar Pradesh, 1991

Sl. no.	Districts	Urban population	Urban area	Percentage of urban population to total population	Percentage of urban area to total area	Urban density
Hill Region						
1	Uttarkashi	17,261	17.13	7.2	0.21	1,006
2	Chamoli	40,540	74.13	9.91	0.81	547
3	Tehrigarhwal	32,895	55.91	5.67	1.26	588
4	Dehradun	5,15,480	198.37	50.26	6.42	2,593
5	Garhwal	81,812	67.68	11.89	1.24	1,199
6	Pithoragarh	42,113	34.80	7.43	0.39	1,210
7	Almora	53,507	37.65	6.39	0.67	1,421
8	Nainital	5,02,964	124.74	32.65	1.83	4,032
Western Region						
9	Saharanpur	5,89,652	51.66	25.53	1.40	1,414
10	Haridwar	3,48,142	64.58	30.96	2.73	5,391
11	Muzaffar Nagar	6,99,230	67.87	24.59	1.69	10,302
12	Bijnor	6,15,352	68.02	25.07	1.49	9,046
13	Meerut	12,76,577	245.27	37.02	6.27	5,204
14	Ghaziabad	12,48,260	283.93	46.16	10.96	4,396
15	Bulandsahar	5,92,795	122.94	20.80	1.93	4,822
16	Moradabad	11,39,469	174.76	27.65	2.47	6,520
17	Rampur	3,92,716	63.06	26.14	2.66	6,230
18	Badaun	4,31,305	138.57	17.61	2.68	3,112
19	Bareilly	9,29,465	219.09	32.78	5.32	4,242
20	Pilibhit	2,36,865	33.58	18.45	0.96	7,053
21	Shahjahapur	4,12,631	38.67	20.76	0.84	10,670
22	Aligarh	8,28,498	180.27	25.13	3.59	4,595

Contd...

Contd...

23	Mathura	4,55,251	68.23	23.57	1.70	6,672
24	Agra	11,11,086	179.80	40.38	4.46	6,179
25	Etah	3,75,258	42.31	16.71	0.95	8,869
26	Mainpuri	1,73,890	51.11	13.00	1.85	3,402
27	Farrukhabad	4,54,621	79.49	26.82	1.86	5,719
28	Etawah	3,33,701	49.81	15.70	1.15	6,699
29	Firozabad	4,07,560	51.98	26.58	2.20	7,840
Central Region						
30	Kanpur (rural)	1,22,043	35.94	5.71	0.70	3,396
31	Kanpur (city)	20,37,333	307.66	84.24	28.89	6,622
32	Fatehpur	1,88,013	79.08	9.90	1.90	2,377
33	Kheri	2,57,975	51.94	10.66	10.67	4,967
34	Sitapur	3,43,668	80.14	12.03	1.39	4,288
35	Hardoi	3,22,611	60.75	11.74	1.01	5,310
36	Unnao	2,99,298	54.05	13.60	1.18	5,537
37	Lucknow	10,59,339	359.51	62.66	14.22	4,815
38	Rae Bareily	209,912	71.64	9.03	1.55	2,929
39	Barabanki	224,878	55.82	9.28	1.04	4,903
Bundelkhand Region						
40	Jalaon	2,69,196	56.22	20.07	1.23	4,738
41	Jhansi	5,66,356	131.04	39.61	2.61	4,322
42	Lalitpur	1,05,548	20.64	14.03	0.41	5,114
43	Hamirpur	2,54,645	97.30	17.6	1.36	2,617
44	Banda	2,39,421	32.60	12.85	0.56	5,620

Appendix II

Growth in Number of Towns by Class in Uttar Pradesh since 1990

Size Class	*1901*	*1911*	*1921*	*1931*	*1941*	*1951*	*1961*	*1971*	*1981*	*1991*
I	7	7	7	8	12	16	17	22	30	41
II	11	10	12	11	11	12	16	20	36	46
III	20	17	18	29	40	42	52	67	86	130
IV	71	65	56	65	71	71	75	91	195	236
V	164	140	141	137	156	169	74	80	231	209
VI	185	181	210	182	144	153	10	13	81	40
Total	458	420	444	432	434	463	244	293	658	702

3

Primary Educational Standards in Uttar Pradesh

K.N. Bhatt

Recent work in economic growth theory has established that a 'residual' in development is impossible to be explained by physical capital alone. It has sharply brought out the contribution of education, experience and the human capital in the process of economic growth and development (Dreze and Gazdar, 1996). The notion of human development can be visualised as the process of widening people's choices and the level of well-being they attain. It must ensure for the people three essential choices: to lead long and healthy life, to acquire knowledge and to have access to resources needed for a decent standard of living (HDR, 1997). Thus, the central goal of human development can be taken as the expansion of human capabilities. It is with an explicit recognition of this basic end that debates on means and strategies can be adequately founded.

In the existing social reality of India, the basic objectives of the development process should be directed towards removal of illiteracy, ill-health and social deprivation to expand individual freedom and elementary capabilities of human beings. Basic education, good health and other human attainments are not only directly valuable as constituent elements of our basic capabilities, these capabilities can also help in generating better economic success, which in turn can contribute to enhancing the quality of human life even more. The components of a good quality life, including education, health and elementary freedom, have instrumental roles of immense value in making us more productive and helping us to generate more output and incomes. This will ensure participatory economic development and real social progress in the country (Myrdal, 1968). Our country can learn in this context from the experiences of the fast growing economies of the world, particularly of East Asia, where elementary education and labour skills have contributed enormously in the pace of development and economic expansion.

Thus, the role of elementary education in facilitating rapid and participatory process of development can hardly be overemphasised. It is the most crucial stage of learning and laying the foundation for personality, attitudes, habits, social confidence, learning skills and communicating capabilities among children. Several studies have shown that investment in primary education yields the highest rate of return to a nation and that it has a significant impact on the productivity and general well-being of the masses. The crucial role of primary education in strengthening of inherent individual potential has been accepted from the very beginning of the Constitution of India in which the Directive Principles of State Policy under Article 45 enjoin upon the state to provide free and compulsory education to all children up to the age of 14 years by 1960. This was reiterated in the National Policy of Education in 1968 and 1986. In pursuance of our constitutional commitment, the country has made some progress in quantitative terms. However, we have utterly failed in respect of overall coverage, equitable distribution and most of all in the quality of education that is being given through the primary schools (Census of India, 2001).

Primary Education Scenario in Uttar Pradesh

Comprising a large part of the country's population (166 million, 2001 census), the state of Uttar Pradesh is among one of the most backward states of India. In terms of Human Development Index, measuring life expectancy at birth, literacy levels and per capita income, the state is placed last among fourteen large states of India. It recorded a crude birth rate of 37 per thousand persons, infant mortality rate of 118 per 1,000 births, very high maternal mortality and very low gender ratio of 880 females per 1,000 males as per 1991 census. The state even today is far behind from the realisation of the constitutional goal of free and compulsory education for all children up to 14 years of age, which was envisaged to have been reached by 1960. The overall literacy rate remains at 57.36 per cent in the state against the national rate of 65.38 per cent. Male and female literacy rates are 70.23 per cent and 42.98 per cent compared to all-India averages of 75.85 per cent and 54.16 per cent respectively according to 2001 census (Sen, 1996).

Further, literacy figures show sharp variations between different caste, gender and region-specific population groups implying extremely low levels for disadvantaged groups. The figure for 7+ rural women literacy rate goes down to 19 per cent, it is at 8 per cent for SCs in rural areas and 8 per cent for whole rural population in the most educationally backward districts (Sen, 1996). It is reported that over 80 lakh children in the age group of 6-14 years do not attend school; about 28 lakh do not have access to full basic educational cycle, out of which 13 lakh are deprived of a primary school within their reach; and approximately 8,600 habitations do not have a primary school within walking distance (Tewari and Bhatt, 1996). At the root of these figures is an inefficient primary education system that usually enrols about 98 per cent of boys and 62 per cent girls, but loses approximately 40 per cent of the enrolled boys and 60 per cent of enrolled girls before they complete five years of education and acquire basic literacy skills. The learning achievements of those, who complete the five years of schooling, have also remained abysmally low.

The Scope of the Study

This paper is based on the findings of an empirical study conducted by G.B. Pant Social Science Institute, Allahabad during the year 1995-96. It highlights the state of academic achievements of the primary school students in Allahabad, Banda and Etawah districts of Uttar Pradesh and suggests the desired areas of policy interventions for its improvement. Some of the major research questions addressed in the study include: What are the academic standards of the students who successfully completed the prescribed course of learning for class IV in language and arithmetic? In what manner the exogenous factors like caste, sex and locational heterogeneity affect the average academic standards in primary schools? What other factors in the personal life of the students and their social environment affected the learning process and how relevant such factors were? To what extent the students have mastered a few basic competencies in literacy and numeracy expected at the end of class I? What are the causes, extent and the level of literacy retention among the dropouts in primary schools? What are the major areas of policy intervention needed for improving the general standards of academic achievements and reduce the level of variability in academic standards of the school children caused by the variation in their caste, sex and locational backgrounds? The Government of Uttar Pradesh under the 'Education for All' project sponsored the initial study with the funds received from the World Bank as a part of its multidimensional exercise to understand the real problems in the primary school system and initiate remedial measures.

Methodology

The data for the study was collected first hand through a sample survey of 135 randomly selected schools in Allahabad, Banda and Etawah districts of the state. To assess the levels of learning, primary school students studying in class II and class V, and dropout children, who withdrew from the school before completing primary schooling, were tested in language and mathematics. The test papers were developed by the NCERT for use in the countrywide survey on primary school attainments. Learning achievements of the sample students were graded in a five-point achievement scale as depicted in the following table:

Table 1

Scale for Learning Achievement Levels

Grade	*Percentage Score*
Zero	0
Below MLL	1-40
MLL	41-59
Near Mastery	60-79
Mastery	80-100

MLL = Minimum Level of Learning.

Information was also collected about important environmental factors, which affect the teaching/learning process in primary schools. These environmental factors relate to personal, social and the school environment of the primary school students in the state. In addition, a number of schedules were distributed among sample students, head teachers, other teachers, dropouts, etc., to elicit information about the functioning of the school system in the sample districts. The data were collected through a sample survey in each of the three districts. It provides useful descriptive information on the number of variables such as enrolment, attendance, dropout, school facilities, availability of education materials method of teaching, class work, home assignments, teaching and supervision process, which would interest the managers, planners and administrators in the state. The qualitative information collected through observational notes in the course of the survey provided insight into the relationship between the community and the school and was useful in understanding the social context in which the school functioned.

The primary school was the basic sampling unit for the survey. Selection of the sample schools was made from a consolidated list of primary schools in each district obtained from the Basic Siksha Adhikari (BSA). The list also included state recognised primary schools under private management. In all, 45 schools from each of the three districts (135 schools in total) were selected following the principles of simple random selection method. The schools to be surveyed were distributed between rural and urban strata in proposition of the ratio that existed between the primary schools in each district. In the final step the schools in the rural and urban samples were distributed among the wards and blocks in proportion to the number of primary schools in them. A well-trained team of a large number of field investigators, field supervisors, district supervisors, education experts and the project directors conducted the survey. In brief, the data of the study and relevant interpretational notes are presented in the paragraphs that follow.

Learning Achievements

The sample of class V students who were administered tests in language and mathematics consisted of 1,805 children of whom 745 belonged to Allahabad, 380 to Banda and 680 to Etawah. In class II, 1,633 students were tested, of which 602 came from Allahabad, 448 from Banda and 583 from Etawah. Similarly, out of a total sample of 408 dropout cases, 151 were in Allahabad, 153 in Banda and 104 in Etawah.

Analysis of the test scores of class V students in language reveals that about 58 per cent of the examinees in Allahabad, 49 per cent in Banda and 61 per cent in Etawah did not qualify for the MLL grade; 34 per cent in Allahabad, 35 per cent in Banda and 29 per cent in Etawah were placed in MLL grade; and only 7 per cent in Allahabad, 14 per cent in Banda and 8 per cent in Etawah reached near mastery grade. In mathematics test 79 per cent children in Allahabad, 60 per cent in Banda and 82 per cent in Etawah scored below MLL. The percentage of those reaching MLL remained only at 17 per cent, 30 per cent and 13 per cent for Allahabad, Banda and Etawah respectively. In Allahabad, 3 per cent, in Banda 7 per cent and in Etawah 4 per cent attained near mastery grade (Table 2).

Table 2

Achievement Levels of Class V Students in Language and Mathematics

Levels	*Allahabad*		*Banda*		*Etawah*	
	Language	*Maths*	*Language*	*Maths*	*Language*	*Maths*
Zero	0	3 (0.40)	1 (0.26)	3 (0.80)	0	7 (1.00)
Below MLL	431 (57.85)	587 (78.80)	186 (48.95)	229 (60.30)	417 (61.32)	558 (82.10)
MLL	256 (34.36)	130 (17.40)	132 (34.74)	115 (30.30)	195 (28.68)	85 (12.50)
Near Mastery	55 (7.38)	25 (3.40)	53 (13.95)	25 (6.60)	54 (7.94)	26 (3.80)
Mastery	5 (0.67)	0	8 (2.11)	8 (2.11)	14 (2.06)	4 (0.60)
Total	745 (100.00)	745 (100.00)	380 (100.00)	380 (100.00)	680 (100.00)	680 (100.00)

Note: Figures in parentheses denote column percentages.

Source: Data collected for the Baseline Study of Educational Standards in Primary Schools: A Study of Allahabad, Banda and Etawah Districts of Uttar Pradesh, G.B. Pant Social Science Institute, Allahabad, 1996.

Achievement level of class II students in language test revealed that 7 per cent in Allahabad, 4 per cent in Banda and 10 per cent in Etawah got zero marks and 27 per cent, 26 per cent and 35 per cent children for the sample districts respectively remained below MLL level in the test. Similarly, the test results in mathematics show the poorest performance of these children as about 74 per cent in Allahabad, 75 per cent in Banda and 83 per cent in Etawah scored either zero or remained below MLL. Only 26 per cent in Allahabad, 25 per cent in Banda and 17 per cent students in Etawah could qualify for MLL. None of the children in all three districts could achieve near mastery or mastery in the test (Table 3).

Table 3

Achievement Levels of Class II Students in Language and Mathematics

Levels	*Allahabad*		*Banda*		*Etawah*	
	Language	*Maths*	*Language*	*Maths*	*Language*	*Maths*
Zero	42 (7.00)	207 (34.40)	17 (3.80)	190 (42.40)	58 (9.90)	433 (74.30)
Below MLL	164 (27.20)	241 (40.00)	115 (25.70)	145 (32.40)	203 (34.80)	53 (9.10)
MLL	95 (15.80)	154 (25.60)	77 (17.20)	113 (25.20)	129 (22.10)	97 (16.60)
Near Mastery	118 (19.60)	0	85 (19.00)	0	62 (10.60)	0
Mastery	183 (30.40)	0	154 (34.40)	0	131 (22.50)	0
Total	602 (100.00)	602 (100.00)	448 (100.00)	448 (100.00)	583 (100.00)	583 (100.00)

Note: Figures in parentheses denote column percentages.

Source: As in Table 2.

Academic standard of the dropouts was also measured by their test scores in language and mathematics on five-point MLL scale as adopted in the case of class V and class II students. The result showed that 48 per cent in Allahabad, 54 per cent in Banda and 76 per cent in Etawah scored zero marks in the language test. This explains that these children had reverted to complete illiteracy by the time the test was conducted. Similarly, in mathematics, 52 per cent in Allahabad, 54 per cent in Banda and 63 per cent in Etawah secured zero marks and therefore reverted to complete ignorance in mathematical skills which they had acquired by attending school (Table 4).

Table 4

Achievement Levels of Dropout Students in Language and Mathematics

Levels	*Allahabad*		*Banda*		*Etawah*	
	Language	*Maths*	*Language*	*Maths*	*Language*	*Maths*
Zero	73 (48.30)	79 (52.30)	83 (54.20)	83 (54.20)	79 (76.00)	65 (62.50)
Below MLL	45 (29.80)	43 (28.50)	27 (18.00)	27 (17.60)	12 (11.50)	27 (26.00)
MLL	14 (9.30)	14 (9.30)	25 (16.30)	25 (17.20)	7 (6.70)	8 (7.70)
Near Mastery	11 (7.30)	6 (4.00	9 (5.90)	4 (2.60)	3 (2.90)	1 (1.00)
Mastery	8 (5.30)	9 (6.00)	9 (5.90)	12 (7.80)	3 (2.90)	3 (2.90)
Total	151 (100.00)	151 (100.00)	153 (100.00)	153 (100.00)	104 (100.00)	104 (100.00)

Note: Figures in parentheses denote column percentages.
Source: As in Table 3.

Reasons for School Desertion by Dropouts

The dropout students enumerated several reasons for the desertion of their school. One of the most important among these reasons in Allahabad was urgency of household duties, which was the main cause of 33 per cent dropout cases. About 24 per cent of the dropouts left school either due to the compulsion of supplementing their family income or due to illness; and 14 per cent dropped out due to the inability of the parents to meet the cost of their education or their unwillingness to send children to school. Similarly, in Banda, the most important cause was the parental apathy, which accounts for 70 per cent of the total school dropout cases. The next important urgencies were household duty and to earn a living. In Etawah, 36 per cent left school due to the urgency of household duties and 23 per cent deserted it due to their inability to afford expenses towards textbooks/notebooks (Table 5).

Table 5

Reasons for Discontinuance of Studies by Dropouts

Reasons	*Allahabad*	*Banda*	*Etawah*
Parents do not want	12 (7.90)	107 (69.90)	5 (4.80)
To assist in household work	49 (32.50)	12 (7.80)	37 (35.60)
To earn a living	18 (11.90)	12 (7.80)	9 (8.70)
To be trained in household enterprise	3 (2.00)	0	1 (1.00)
Could not afford textbooks/notebooks	10 (6.60)	0	24 (23.10)
Illness/not keeping well	18 (11.90)	1 (0.70)	13 (12.50)
To get married	11 (7.30)	1 (0.70)	8 (7.70)
Failure/did not learn anything	1 (0.70)	3 (2.00)	0
Teachers not cooperative	3 (2.00)	1 (0.70)	3 (2.90)
School too far	5 (3.30)	0	0
Others	15 (9.90)	1 (0.70)	4 (3.80)
Total	151 (100.00)	153 (100.00)	104 (100.00)

Note: Figures in parentheses denote column percentages.

Source: As in Table 4.

Personal, Family and Learning Background of the Students

All the class V students who were administered tests, were interviewed to record their personal family and learning background to understand the process of teaching/learning in primary schools in detail. The results of data analysis in this context show that nearly all the students in the sample came from very poor families. The male parent in majority of the cases worked as a wage earner in non-agricultural occupations. In most of the cases the parents of the students were either illiterate or scantily educated. The proportion of educated parents with academic standards of more than primary level in three sample districts varied from 47 to 53 per cent in case of fathers and 9 to 23 per cent only in case of mothers (Table 6).

Table 6

Distribution of Class V Sample Students by Level of Parental Education Status

Category	Allahabad		Banda		Etawah	
	Father	Mother	Father	Mother	Father	Mother
Illiterate	193 (25.90)	565 (75.80)	111 (29.20)	217 (71.30)	162 (23.80	375 (55.10)
Upto Primary	203 (27.30)	114 (15.30)	85 (22.40)	62 (16.30)	161 (23.70)	152 (22.40)
Above Primary	349 (46.80)	66 (8.90)	184 (48.40)	47 (12.40)	357 (52.50)	153 (22.50)
Total	745 (100.00)	745 (100.00)	380 (100.00)	380 (100.00)	680 (100.00)	680 (100.00)

Note: Figures in parentheses denote column percentages.

Source: As in Table 5.

Very few students received assistance from the family in completing their home assignments. About 60 to 64 per cent students did not get help from the family members in home work in all the three sample districts. Likewise, 90 per cent students in Allahabad, 99 per cent in Banda and 99 per cent in Etawah reported that their teacher did not come to the class regularly. In the absence of the teacher, most of the time the students were either left to their own or allowed to go out to play. The practice of giving homework was also reported to be quite infrequent as more than 55 per cent students complained that they were not given homework regularly. About 50 per cent respondents told that homework was seldom checked or corrected by their teachers. Similarly, about half of the students reported that monthly class tests are not held regularly and about 52 to 55 per cent said that the mistakes committed by them in the tests are never pointed out to them for correction in future (Table 7).

Table 7

Responses of the Class V Students on Other Important Factors Affecting Studies

(in %)

Factors	*Allahabad*	*Bonda*	*Etawah*
Proportion of students received assistance from family members in studies	41.07	36.32	37.65
Proportion of students reporting their teachers do not come regularly to class	89.80	99.20	99.30
Proportion of students reporting home work given by teachers regularly	43.76	43.16	37.71
Proportion of students reporting home work corrected by teachers regularly	55.17	43.16	51.76
Proportion of students reporting monthly class tests organised regularly	44.60	50.80	49.00
Proportion of students reporting regular feedback to students on class tests by teachers	46.40	47.70	45.00
Total Students	745	380	680

Source: As in Table 6.

Teachers

The sample consisted of 426 teachers, out of which 132 came from Allahabad, 124 from Banda and 170 from Etawah. More than 15 per cent of the teachers in primary schools in Allahabad, 18 per cent in Banda and 13 per cent in Etawah were found untrained. The proportion of teachers who reported their educational qualification upto high school were 27 per cent in Allahabad, 31 per cent in Banda and 23 per cent in Etawah. Similarly, 57 per cent teachers in Allahabad, 74 per cent in Banda and 69 per cent in Etawah had not taken advantage of the in-service training programmes organised by the department. This clearly indicates towards the lack of enthusiasm among them to improve their teaching skills.

Sub-Deputy Inspector (SDI) of schools is considered to be a friend, philosopher and guide to the primary teachers to help them not only in the academic matters but also in their routine service matters. The study results, however, suggest that 65 per cent of the sample teachers in Allahabad, 57 per cent in Banda and 80 per cent in Etawah were not happy with the role of SDIs. Similar dissatisfaction was expressed by the majority of teachers with the guidance and assistance they received from their head teacher. Another interesting finding of the study that came into light was about 58 per cent of teachers in Allahabad, 56 per cent in Banda and 32 per cent in Etawah were found engaged in teaching more than one class at a time (Table 8).

Table 8

Information Pertaining to Teachers

(in %)

Particulars		*Allahabad*	*Banda*	*Etawah*
Professional training of teachers	Trained	84.80	82.30	87.10
	Untrained	15.20	17.70	12.90
Educational qualification of teachers	Up to High School	26.50	30.70	23.10
	Intermediate	39.40	37.90	45.90
	Graduates	34.10	31.40	31.00
Teachers having undergone in-service training	Yes	43.10	25.60	31.30
	No	56.90	74.40	68.70
Level of help provided by SDIs to teachers	Very Helpful	06.90	08.50	02.70
	Somewhat Helpful	28.40	34.20	17.30
	Not Helpful	64.70	57.30	80.00
Level of help provided by head teachers to fellow teachers	Very Helpful	22.40	23.90	29.30
	Somewhat Helpful	17.20	20.50	19.30
	Not Helpful	60.40	55.60	51.4-0
Teacher engaged in multi-grade teaching	Engaged	57.80	56.40	32.00
	Not Engaged	42.20	43.60	68.00
Total Students		132	124	170

Source: As in Table 7.

Schools

As noted earlier, in all, 135 schools (45 schools in each sample district) were included in the sample. Most of these sample schools looked as a deserted and lone building, amidst dirt and squalor with stray animals freely roaming around in all the sample districts. Less than 1 per cent of such schools were found with enclosed compounds. About 98 per cent schools in Allahabad, 96 per cent in Banda and 93 per cent in Etawah needed additional classrooms ranging from 1 to 6 to be able to provide a roof over the heads of their students. Despite the 'Operation Blackboard' programme, sample schools did not have all the items supposed to have been provided to them in adequate quantity. About 91 per cent of the schools in Allahabad, 71 per cent in Banda and 64 per cent in Etawah district did not have mats for all students to sit on them. Likewise, 36 per cent schools in Allahabad, 42 per cent in Banda and 22 per cent in Etawah did not have blackboards for all classes. Similarly, in Allahabad, 76 per cent, in Banda 84 per cent and in Etawah 82 per cent schools did not provide chalk sticks and dusters to all their classes. More than half of the sample schools lacked safe drinking water facility and more than 90 per cent did not have electric connections and separate toilet facility for girls (Table 9).

Table 9

Some Important Data Pertaining to Schools

(in per cent)

Particulars	*Allahabad*	*Banda*	*Etawah*
Schools requiring additional classrooms (no. of rooms varying from 1-6)	97.80	95.60	93.30
Schools having no adequate mats for all students	91.10	71.10	64.40
Schools having no blackboards for all classes	35.60	42.20	22.20
Schools having no chalk-sticks/dusters for all classes	73.60	84.40	82.20
Schools having no safe drinking water facility	65.40	49.90	53.30
Schools without separate toilets facility for girls	91.10	91.10	88.90
Schools without playground	40.00	51.10	46.70
Schools without electric connection	95.60	93.30	91.10
Total Students	45	45	45

Source: As in Table 8.

Areas for Policy Intervention

The foregoing analysis reveals that the level of academic achievements of students in primary schools of the sample districts in Uttar Pradesh is depressingly low, particularly in mathematics. Similarly, the lack of material facilities, dilapidated and isolated school buildings, unqualified and demotivated lot of teachers and unconcerned educational managers and planners appear to be responsible for making the general environment of teaching and learning processes in primary school system of the state an uninteresting and uninspiring activity. Though the existing situation is an outcome of several factors, the main areas in which purposeful policy interventions could be helpful in bringing out improvements are: inspection, supervision and support services; academic and professional competence of teachers; and adequacy of material inputs.

Despite a large army of officials engaged for teacher supervision and support services, the primary schools are visited the least; classroom performance of the teachers is never inspected; they are hardly provided any academic guidance, even the head teachers rarely do so. The village community shows virtually no interest in the affairs of the school. Majority of the teachers have not undergone in-service training to improve their teaching performance which was observed to be of very low standard, particularly so in the teaching of mathematics and science. The inadequacy of basic facilities, teaching-learning materials and lack of motivation among teachers appears to be due to indifferent supervision system and lack of community's interest in school to a large extent. The primary school appeared deserted and forlorn because of the lack of enclosed compounds and absence of supervised sports and extra-curricular activities in the schools after school hours. This is so because teachers have neither been given residential facilities nor motivated to reside in the neighbourhood of the schools to organise these activities. The academic standards of the children and the teaching-learning environment of the primary schools could be substantially raised through purposeful policy interventions in these areas. The state government will have to immediately come forward to decide its educational and developmental priorities.

The persistent backwardness of elementary education system not only limits the freedom and well-being of the people but also sustains high levels of mortality and fertility rates, brings in mass poverty and relative deprivation of weaker sections, particularly women. The low level of basic educational development also severely restricts the goal of economic development and deprives the people from taking advantage of the social and economic opportunities offered by the process of economic reforms and globalisation. When the majority of population (as noticed in case of the state) who cannot read, write, count or follow written words and are unable to take advantage of the process of modernisation, socio-economic disparities are bound to widen further and deprive people of even bare minimum necessities (UP BEP, 1995). To save the nearly collapsing system of primary education in Uttar Pradesh, radical corrective measures will have to be taken urgently. The state needs not only to make qualitative improvement in elementary education and enhance the learning achievements of the students in schools, but also ensure quantitative expansion of the system to make the facility available to those who are deprived of it. The system of basic education in the state should be used as an instrument of social change; ensure well-being and freedom of the people; and bring in a participatory process of economic and social development.

References

Dreze, Jean and Haris Gazdar (1996), "Uttar Pradesh the Burden of Inertia" in Jean Dreze and A.K. Sen (eds.), *Indian Development: Some Regional Perspectives*, Oxford University Press, New Delhi, p. 42.

Human Development Report (1997), UNDP, Oxford University Press, New York, p. 14.

Myrdal, Gunnar (1968), *Asian Drama: An Inquiry into the Poverty of Nations*, Vol. III, Kalyani Publishers, New Delhi, p. 1540.

Provisional Population Totals, Paper-1, 2001, Census of India, Series-10, Director of Census Operation, Uttar Pradesh.

Sen, Amartya (1996), "Radical Needs and Moderate Reforms" in Jean Dreze and A.K. Sen (eds), *Indian Development: Some Regional Perspectives*, Oxford University Press, New Delhi, pp.2-7.

Tewari, G.C. and K.N. Bhatt (1996), Baseline Study of Educational Standards in Primary Schools: A Study of Allahabad, Banda and Etawah Districts of Uttar Pradesh, Project Report, G.B. Pant Social Science Institute, Allahabad, pp. 1-2.

UP Basic Education Project (1995), *Education for All*, State Project Office, Lucknow, p. 28.

4

Women's Health Status in Rural Uttar Pradesh

P.C. Upadhyaya and U. Kalpagam

Deprivation leads to the absence of well-being, and it could be of varied nature such as physical, economic, psychological, social and political. Physical deprivation could be just the lack of food and poor nutrition making up malnourished bodies, and such deprivation is often caused by economic deprivation arising on account of lack of adequate purchasing power. Uttar Pradesh is recognised as one among the 'Bimaru' states of India. The Bimaru states like Bihar, Madhya Pradesh, Rajasthan and Uttar Pradesh are having the worst human development profile in the country (HDR, 1999). In Uttar Pradesh, it is well known that people who live below the poverty line are at least 8 per cent of the total population of the world (World Bank Report, 2002).

Deprivation should also be judged in terms of fulfilment of basic needs, of which health and health care has its importance not only from developmental aspect of the problem but its planning aspect as well, since Article 25 of the Universal Declaration of Human Rights guarantees the right of everyone to a standard of living adequate for the health and well-being of himself/herself and his/her family including food, clothing, housing and medical care. Health is an important indicator of well-being.

Both health deprivation and gender disparities in health status in rural Uttar Pradesh are significant. Among the poor population of the state, a significant number of women are facing deprived, marginalised and isolated existence due to social, economic and cultural factors of deprivation in the state. They are also not getting access to public health interventions and government sponsored health care facilities in an easy and equal manner. Such types of deprivation are caused by factors that are related to various economic, social and/or political arenas of human life. The role and condition of poverty plays a great role in making a significant number of the population, mostly women, suffer ill-being and poor health conditions.

Generally, in India, the Sanskrit sloka *Yatra Naryastu Pujyante Ramante Tatra Devata* (which means, where the women are respected, there the Gods reside indicating the 'well-being' of the society) is popular since ancient times (Upadhyaya, 1999). Yet, the stark conditions of female deprivation and gender disparities suggest that it is necessary to undertake a deeper analysis of the view, to understand the nature and causes of deprivation as related to women's health in India. Such realities show that deprivation and well-being are opposite to each other in nature, concept and theme. If well-being is associated with "respect for women", the contrary must be true for their ill-being. This opens various grounds for discussion about issues such as gender empowerment, patriarchal power, sexual and caste identities, prevalent notions of masculinity and femininity, social norms and myths and how these impinge on the development efforts of the state.

Here, in this paper, we examine the status of rural women's health in rural Uttar Pradesh and argue that there is a severe reproductive health crisis in the state. We rely heavily for the statistical data on the National Human Development

Report (2002), published by the Planning Commission, Government of India. The paper explores the causes for the poor health status of rural women and shows that while rural health infrastructure and health expenditure by the state needs to be improved, these alone are not entirely responsible for rural women's health status. The health status of rural women is a reflection of the poor status of rural women in general and gender power relations among other social relations of power that are at work. If the productive and reproductive status of rural women has to be improved, both state and civil society initiatives are necessary.

Health Deprivation and Gender Disparity in Rural Uttar Pradesh

Expectation of life at birth in Uttar Pradesh (UP) went up from 50.2 for males in 1981-85 to 57.1 in 1992-96. For females, it increased from 46.9 to 55.4 over the same period. There is no denying the fact that these are marked improvements. Yet, they fall short of the national average and the gap in female life expectancy levels between UP and the national average is still large. Life expectancy for males at the all-India level was 58.9 in 1992-96, while for females it was 59.8. Also, let us note that while in general female life expectancy is higher than male, in UP, it is lower than male life expectancy.

Even Bihar has a higher life expectancy at birth for both males and females - 59.7 for males and 57.5 for females - in 1992-96, and for the males the Bihar level is higher than the national average. Madhya Pradesh was the only state that had a lower expectation of life at birth than UP in 1992-96 remaining at 53.9 for males and 53.4 for females. Life expectancy at birth for males in Orissa was 56.4 and hence lower than UP but the female level was higher than UP by 0.4 year. Kerala records the highest expectation of life at birth at 70.3 for males and 74.9 for females. Not only are life expectancies much higher but the female life expectancy at birth in Kerala is higher than males by

4.6 years. Excepting Bihar, UP, Madhya Pradesh, Rajasthan and Orissa, in all the other states, the female life expectancy at birth is higher than males. A lower female life expectancy at birth suggests severe disadvantages for females.

Now, let us compare the expectation of life at age one. This is in general higher than life expectancy at birth, for the risks of survival are high in the 0-1 age group. Male life expectancy at age one in rural UP increased from 58.3 years in 1981-85 to 62.2 years in 1992-96, while female life expectancy at this age increased from 55.2 years in 1981-85 to 60.8 years in 1992-96. Clearly, these are much higher than life expectancy at birth. Yet UP's life expectancies still fall short of the national average, this shortfall is especially marked for female life expectancies. While the All-India female life expectancy at age one in 1992-96 was 64.4 years, in UP it was only 60.8 years. Only Madhya Pradesh had a slightly lower life expectancy than UP. Once again, Kerala topped with 74.9 years in female life expectancy at age one.

In 1991, the percentage of persons not expected to survive beyond age 40 based on SRS data in UP was 20.8 among males and 26.5 among females. The only other state with higher risks was Madhya Pradesh where those not expected to survive beyond age 40 were 25.1 per cent among males and 29.3 per cent among females. UP's performance can be said to be improving over the period 1981 to 1991, especially given the fact that in 1981, 36.6 per cent of females in rural UP were not expected to survive beyond age 40. Even so, the figures of 26.5 per cent in 1991 is still high compared with rural Kerala where only 4.5 per cent of females were not expected to survive beyond age 40. Even for the country as a whole it is indeed disturbing to note that nearly a fifth of both male and female population in rural areas were not expected to survive beyond the age of 40. In urban areas, the situation is much better in general though not so much in UP and Madhya Pradesh.

Infant Mortality Rate (IMR) in UP (combined), which was as high as 131 per thousand among males in 1981, came down to 98 in 1991, and for the female it declined from 128 in 1981 to 104 in 1991. UP's IMR is much higher than the national average of 74 for males and 79 for females in 1991. Only Madhya Pradesh, Orissa and Arunachal Pradesh along with UP recorded female IMR above 100 in 1991. IMR in rural UP that was 139 in 1981 came down to 104 in 1991. It is still much higher than the national average of 84 in 1991, although not as bad as Madhya Pradesh with a rural IMR of 142 and Orissa with 130. UP's situation is still a cause for concern, and given that female IMR in 1991 in the state (rural and urban combined) was higher than male, we can expect female IMR for rural UP to be higher as well.

It is this high IMR, coupled with the high maternal mortality rate, which signifies women's severe health deprivation in UP. Maternal mortality rate in UP is the highest in the country, at the level of 707 per 100,000 live births in the age group 15-49 years. Although Madhya Pradesh had a high IMR, its maternal mortality rate at 498 is still far lower than UP. Rajasthan followed UP with a maternal mortality rate of 670. Bihar is much better than UP as its maternal mortality rate is 452. For the country, as a whole, the maternal mortality rate is 407. So we can see how far UP deviates from the national average. It is necessary to draw out the implications of this.

Table 1 below presents age-specific mortality, both for UP and all-India in 1981 and 1991. It can be observed that mortality rate in all groups, viz., under 5, 5-9 and 0-4, in UP and the country as a whole has decreased. Also female mortality rates for all groups are in general higher than male mortality rates which once again emphasise the demographic disadvantages of women arising in the context of social prejudices and social inequalities. Only under 5 mortality for females in 1991 is lower than the male mortality rate, which is an exception. Mortality rates in all age groups in UP are higher than the country levels and quite substantially so.

Table 1
Age-Specific Mortality Rates

Age-group	*Uttar Pradesh*		*India*	
	1981	*1991*	*1981*	*1991*
Under 5 years				
M	174	135	147	91
F	208	132	157	101
0-4 years				
M	56.3	35.5	43.1	28.1
F	73.1	41.0	48.0	30.2
5-9 years				
M	5.7	3.2	4.1	2.8
F	7.2	4.1	5.0	3.2

Source: National Human Development Report 2001, Planning Commission, GoI, March 2002.

Death Rate

In 1981, the number of deaths per 1,000 population in rural UP was 16.2 for males and 18.4 for females. It declined steadily and in 1997 it was 10.4 for males 11.1 for females. The decline in death rates for both males and females over the years is indeed remarkable though still higher than that of the national average. In general, female death rates are lower than male death rates but not in the states of UP, Bihar, Haryana and Rajasthan. Madhya Pradesh, Orissa and UP are the only three states where female death rate in 1997 has been above 11 per thousand, while in Assam and Bihar it is above 10 per 1,000. Clearly, despite the improvement in terms of decline in death rate over time, UP still does relatively badly and the high female death rates corroborate the other data such as maternal mortality rate to suggest that rural women's health in UP is a cause for concern. Barring a few north-eastern states and UTs, Kerala has the lowest female death rate of 5 per thousand, which is less than half the death rate in UP.

Sex Ratio

Perhaps on account of the decline in the death rate, it is heartening to note that the declining sex ratio in UP made an upturn in 2001. Rural sex ratio that was 893 in 1981 declined to 884 in 1991 and then increased to 904 at the 2001 census. But it is still far below the national average of 946 at 2001 and is lower than that of rural Bihar, MP and Rajasthan. But, the upswing is indeed noteworthy.

The estimated sex ratio at birth in 1981 in rural UP was 971 and in 1991 it was 943. Clearly, the decline between 1981 to 1991 can in part be on account of sex-selective abortions. But, the fact that the sex ratio at birth both in 1981 and 1991 was higher than the overall sex ratio in 1981 and 1991 indicates that chances of female survival are lower and females are at a greater risk even after birth. In general, there is need for concern about the declining sex ratio at birth in UP and the rest of the country as well. If we examine the sex ratio in the age group 0-4 years in rural UP, we observe that it decreased from 960 in 1981 to 947 in 1991 and it is estimated to be 916 (overall) in 2001. Clearly, there is cause for concern both about sex-selective abortions as well as neglect of female infants in UP if sex ratio in the age group 0-4 years in rural UP is declining.

Even urban sex ratio in 0-4 age group declined in UP from 986 in 1981 to 942 in 1991. The declining pattern holds good at the all-India level as well. Even Kerala that has occupied the pride of place on most other indicators shows a declining sex ratio in the 0-4 age group – the combined sex ratio declined from 975 in 1981 to 951 in 1991 and is estimated to be 963 in 2001. It is a little heartening to note that sex ratio in the age group 5-9 years in rural UP increased from 863 in 1981 to 889 in 1991, but it was still much below the national average of 939. Clearly, then, the problem so far as we can conclude lies in the increased survival risks in the infant groups, particularly neglect of female children, sex-selective abortions and greater risks for adult women in their reproductive years in rural UP.

Anthropometric measures such as the Body Mass Index indicate that in 1998-99 women in UP were close to the national average and the data is in no way as surprising as the BMI data for Arunachal Pradesh which is just 10.7 per cent or Sikkim with 11.2 per cent. It is a cause for worry that a little over half the female population and nearly three quarters of all children suffer from some kind of anaemia. The percentage of such women in rural India is 53.9, whereas the corresponding figure for rural UP is 49.4 per cent. Levels of anaemia among women in the north-eastern states as well as West Bengal, Orissa and Bihar were above 60 per cent in 1998-99. Among women of the scheduled castes and scheduled tribes these were even higher as 51.9 per cent of SC women in UP suffer from anaemia. It is more among the illiterate than literate women. While among illiterate women it was 50.6 per cent, among literate women it was 43 per cent.

Childbirths attended by Health Professionals

According to the NFHS data, only 17.2 per cent of women in UP had their childbearing attended by health professionals in 1992-93, which by 1998-99 increased to 23 per cent. Only 7.9 per cent of SC women in the state had their childbirth attended by health professionals. Even, in urban areas of the state, a little more than half (52.3 per cent) of childbirths are attended by health professionals, while the rural scenario is alarming as only 17.5 per cent of rural childbirths are attended by health professional according to the NFHS data for 1998-99. No doubt, the situation has improved because in 1992-93 only 11.6 per cent of childbirths in rural UP were attended by health professionals.

It is shocking to note that rural UP among all states had the lowest percentage of births attended by health professionals both in 1992-93 and in 1998-99. Compare UP's figure of 17.5 per cent with Kerala's figure of 92.8 per cent rural births being attended by health professionals. It is distressing to note that in 1992-93, only 7.9 per cent of SC births in UP were attended by health professionals. Even Bihar, Madhya Pradesh and

Rajasthan had higher percentages of SC births attended by health professionals (Bihar 18.8 per cent, Madhya Pradesh 32.5 per cent and Rajasthan 15.3 per cent). Compare once again UP's 7.9 per cent of SC births attended by professionals with Kerala's 96.9 per cent of SC births attended by professionals.

Clearly herein lies the main problem as regards women's health deprivation which is particularly severe among SC women – unattended births in rural UP in over 80 per cent of the cases. Childbirth, of course, need not be medicalised for it is a natural process but in the context of widespread poverty, malnutrition and illiteracy, unattended births are the cause of high maternal mortality.

The NFHS also provides data on the births delivered in medical institutions. In 1992-93, only 6.5 per cent of births in rural UP were delivered in medical institutions compared to the national average of 16 per cent. In Kerala, on the other hand, 85.4 per cent of rural births were delivered in medical institutions. In 1998-99, 11.7 per cent of rural births in UP were delivered in medical institutions against the national average of 24.6, whereas in Kerala, this time, this figure was 91.5 per cent.

The type of medical attention received is also revealing. Based on the NSS 52nd round (July 1995-June 1996) survey, it was found that 50.4 per cent in rural UP received no attention. Of the rest, only 7 per cent received attention from a doctor (either government or private), while 27.5 per cent received attention from nurses/midwives. And, 12.6 per cent of mothers received some other kind of medical attention at childbirth. For the country, as a whole, 15 per cent of rural births received medical attention from doctors; the figure is surprisingly low. Nearly 82 per cent of rural births in Kerala, on the other hand, are attended by doctors. The issue is not only whether mothers receive medical attention or not but also the kind of attention they receive. In rural Punjab, only 1.9 per cent of births do not receive any medical attention and the reach of doctors is also only around 17.10 per cent. But, the spread of nurses/ midwives, especially outside of the government sector, is as high as 66.3 per cent. In all, 76.4 per cent of births in rural Punjab are attended by nurses/midwives. So we have here two alternative approaches. The Kerala approach with a very high doctor outreach and the Punjab approach with an equally high nurse/midwife outreach to attend to rural births. Even if the Kerala approach proves costly and so remains an infeasible proposition in the short to medium run, UP should explore the possibilities of adopting the Punjab approach.

The fact that a high percentage of births in rural UP does not receive any medical attention also results in a low percentage of these receiving two or more doses of TT vaccination during pregnancy. According to the NFHS data for 1992-93 only 32.4 percentage received two or more doses of TT vaccination during pregnancy in rural UP. In Kerala, on the other hand, 88.9 per cent received the vaccination and for the country as a whole 47.7 per cent received it. Rajasthan and Bihar fared even poorly than UP. UP improved its performance on TT vaccination, as in 1998-99 NFHS 46.5 per cent in rural UP received two or more doses of TT vaccination during pregnancy. Despite the improvement UP had the lowest percentage among all states. Even Rajasthan and Bihar that had far lower levels than UP in 1992-93, improved their performance so much as to leave UP behind. In rural Rajasthan 47.4 per cent and in rural Bihar 55.9 per cent are vaccinated. This shows poor health care considerations for pregnant women in rural UP, no doubt reflected in the high maternal mortality rate.

Such a lack of concern for pregnant women's health is also reflected in the way infants/children are taken care of. The percentage of fully vaccinated children aged 12-23 months in rural UP according to the NFHS data for 1992-93 was 17.4 per cent against the national average of 30.9. Fully vaccinated children refer to those who have received BCG, measles and three doses DPT and polio vaccine. Even Kerala that had so far been a top performer on most other counts, floundered on children's vaccination as only 54 per cent of children aged 12-23 months were fully vaccinated in rural Kerala in 1992-93. In 1998-99, the percentage of fully vaccinated children in rural UP was 19.2 per cent – an increase of only 1.8 per cent over the six-year period. The country average increased by 5.7 per cent to 36.6 per cent. Kerala increased its coverage of vaccination from 54 per cent to 77.9 per cent in 1998-99, only to be beaten by rural Himachal Pradesh with a vaccination coverage of 83.7 per cent. Rural Bihar had the lowest vaccination coverage for children both in 1992-93 and 1998-99 being only 9.1 and 9.4 per cent in the two years respectively. This raises an interesting issue of child neglect vis-à-vis neglect of women in rural Bihar. For rural Bihar had been able to increase its vaccination coverage of pregnant women from 26.4 per cent in 1992-93 to 55.9 per cent in 1998-99. But children's vaccination was not considered important in rural Bihar. Why is it mothers in rural Bihar who had themselves availed of vaccination benefits failed to provide the same benefit to their children? Or is it because governmental measures received encouragement for one and not the other? Needless to say, in general, a higher percentage of male children are fully vaccinated than female children.

If we look at the data on children aged 12-23 months not vaccinated, we note that the percentage decreased from 46.1 in 1992-93 to 31.9 per cent in 1998-99 in rural UP, thus showing signs of improvement. Despite the improvement, UP's non-coverage of vaccination is still far higher than the national average of 16.7 per cent. Barring Assam, UP records the highest percentage of non-coverage. A comparison of UP's performance with rural Tamilnadu, where only 0.4 per cent of children are not vaccinated, points out starkly where it stands. Once again, non-coverage is relatively more among female children than among male children. In UP, as a whole, whereas 27.5 per cent male children were not vaccinated in 1998-99, the corresponding figure for females was 31.5 per cent.

We will explore in a preliminary manner as to the causes for such a poor concern for women's health in rural UP. Are the causes to be located in poor health infrastructure, or are there other reasons? Let us look at the available health infrastructure. Using the 1991 census data, the Bulletin of Rural Health Statistics in India (June 2000, GoI) presented data on population covered by Rural Health Care Infrastructure. Each PHC in rural UP covered a population of 29,282 while the country average was 27,364. Many other states too recorded a higher population per rural PHC such as Andhra Pradesh with 29,719 but their health indicators are much better than UP. Each sub-centre in rural UP covered a population of 5,533 – a figure higher than the country average of 4,579.

The population per bed in rural UP is 2,593 compared to the national average of 1,498. This is very high and states like Bihar, Madhya Pradesh, Haryana, Orissa and Rajasthan have even higher population per bed, the highest being Madhya Pradesh with 3,770. Kerala has a population per bed ratio of 391 only. If we are to conclude about the state of rural health infrastructure in UP, we would state that while hospitalisation and in-patient treatment facilities are poor, the coverage of population by PHCs and sub-centres is no worse than many other states of the country. The question is therefore not just of availability of health infrastructure. There is certainly a case to make for that as well. But, the crucial question is whether what is available is also being used. Are women accessing what is available and if not why needs to be posed and answered as well.

One of the indicators of women's health concern as well as her role and status in the family is in terms of control over reproductive decisions. Often, this is reflected in whether couples use family planning methods, as the use of it minimises the risks of unwanted pregnancies that affect women's health and causes anxiety and stress. The NFHS data on Couple Protection Rate (CPR) indicates that in 1992-93, in rural UP, only 16.7 per cent of the couples were protected at the time of the survey while the national average was 36.9 per cent. After Nagaland, UP had the lowest CPR in 1992-93. In 1998-99, CPR in rural UP increased to 23.9 per cent while the national average increased to 44.7 per cent. In 1998-99, UP had the lowest CPR after rural in Bihar where 22.9 per cent of couples were protected. Himachal Pradesh had the highest CPR of 67 per cent, followed by West Bengal (64.5 per cent) and Punjab (64.4 per cent).

Low CPRs are likely to result in high fertility rates. Total Fertility Rate (TFR) is defined as the number of children a woman would have if hypothetically she lived through her reproductive years (i.e., 15 to 49) experiencing the age-specific fertility rates prevailing in the population during a given period. The TFR for rural UP that was 6.1 in 1980-82 declined to 5.5 in 1990-92 and then to 5.1 in 1995-97. Even with the decline, UP's TFR at 5.1 is the highest in the country and higher than the national average of 3.7. UP's TFR has always been the highest except in 1990-92, when Tripura's TFR was 5.9.

These facts, in a sense, sum it all. Rural women in UP fare poorly on health indicators and suffer greater deprivation mainly on account of lack of control over their reproductive roles suggesting a high degree of patriarchal dominance in the family structures. The discounting of women's bodies and health appears to be deeply ingrained in rural lifestyles and culture. If this is the overall macro dimension of rural women's health status in UP, there must be significant micro variabilities. Even the limited data we had on SCs suggest that SC women fare even worse than others. The nature and degree of patriarchy could vary between castes and communities and across occupational groups as well. There is therefore a great need to understand how caste and gender factors interplay to produce poor outcomes on rural women's health care concerns. But, the broad contours of the story are clear enough. Women's bodies and lives are significantly devalued in rural Uttar Pradesh. Frequent and repeated childbirths on account of low adoption of family planning methods, signifying perhaps patriarchal dominance, unattended births, high maternal mortality, low vaccination coverage etc. suggest an overwhelming callousness towards women's bodies, their lives and their health. Coupled with poor sanitation practices, non-availability of water, dependence on handpumps, kutcha houses etc., rural women's reproductive health in UP is in a severe crisis.

It is an evasive argument to say that rural women's illiteracy is the cause for all this. In many other states, women's illiteracy has not hampered them in seeking some form of medical attention at childbirth, although on other matters like adoption of family planning methods illiteracy may become a barrier. The limited data we have examined does not throw light on myriad other problems affecting women's health in rural UP. Women suffer from malnutrition and a host of reproductive health and other health problems. Induced and unsafe abortions, excessive menstrual bleeding, uterine problems, back pain, rheumatism and arthritis, sexually transmitted diseases, cataract problems, non-diagnosis and lack of treatment for varieties of cancer afflicting women, especially breast cancer and cervical cancer, problems caused by sterilisation, improper insertion of IUD implants, calcium deficiency and osteoporosis, pregnancy on account of rape, HIV infections etc. are quite common. We know that these and other afflictions affect many women and often go unnoticed and uncared for. Often women's lack of control over reproductive matters is also accompanied by a high incidence of domestic violence.

Rural women's reproductive roles and productive roles are mutually reinforcing. Poor health of women resulting from a disempowered status affects rural women's ability to work both on-farm and off-farm and lack of employment and low incomes affect their ability to take care of their health. Rural women in UP are very vulnerable on the employment front both on account of lack of employment opportunities as well as poor health and nutrition. Lack of regular employment opportunities has resulted in a swelling of marginal workers. While the proportion of marginal workers in rural UP was 40 per cent in 1991, it increased to 63 per cent in 2002. This implies that rural women work more in conjunction with their domestic and childrearing duties at subsistence activities just to eke out a living, which means that their health goes uncared for. At such low levels of income, wages and assetlessness, it is not possible for them to spend on improving their nutritional and health status.

Mukhopadhyaya and Savitri (1998:20) have noted quite astutely that "for majority of women in rural Uttar Pradesh, patriarchy operates through numerous social practices and norms that limits such options. Gender discrimination manifests itself through unequal access to nutrition, health care, education for early childhood, early marriage and childbearing, female sexuality is strictly controlled by a myriad of social constraints and professed norms for womanly behaviour while marital rape is sometimes unheard of in the Indian Penal Code. Choice in the matters of sexuality is something that the average Indian woman can barely exercise. The ground reality of poverty and lack of access to resources is added to this scenario constraining the limits of the choice set even further."

Health Problems of Underprivileged Women

Thus far we have been discussing the condition of rural women as though they constituted a homogenous group. But we do know that the Indian rural scenario is marked by the existence of numerous underprivileged groups who are discriminated and occupy the lower rungs of social hierarchy. They suffer not only economic deprivation but social deprivation as well. According to the World Health Organisation (WHO) the definition of the underprivileged as those who are deprived through some form of social, cultural and economic discrimination of some of the fundamental human rights, that theoretically belong to all members of a civil society. The underprivileged groups are those sections of a population who are discriminated in social hierarchy and also economically and culturally marginalised as the Scheduled Castes, Scheduled Tribes and Other Backward Classes and other categories according to the criteria defined.

The underprivileged are those who are denied the enjoyment of normal privileges or the rights of a society due to low levels of socio-economic status. They get fewer opportunities to improve their life only because of sheer poverty and a low level of living and they suffer from agony of malnutrition and high incidence of morbidity and mortality rates. According to Hasan (1967), two types of social and cultural factors affect the health of any community. The first is that which directly affects the health of the community because certain customs, practices, beliefs, values and religious taboos etc. create an environment that helps in the spread of certain diseases, and secondly the factors that indirectly affect the health of the community as they are related to the problem of medical care available to the sick and invalid.

The problems with which the underprivileged are besieged are vulnerability, poverty, risk of hunger, risk of undernutrition and poor health. The state of being underprivileged could be measured in terms of low levels of living as reflected in inadequacy of food and nutrients, low level of income and expenditure, lack of awareness, ignorance and illiteracy, lack of assets, casual nature of employment, tied and low paid labour and occupational engagement in informal sectors both in rural and urban areas of the state. They are socially and economically backward and deprived of their access to social infrastructure and services, they generally suffer from poor and high incidence of diseases (Vishwakarma, 1991). Among all these sections, it is seen that women are more vulnerable and they generally are more prone to diseases due to their illiteracy, ignorance and unawareness of the situation.

The caste structure in India has for centuries tied up certain castes with certain occupations, whose nexus is dissolving rather slowly under the impact of economic development. Under such caste-occupation nexus, certain castes were classified as 'clean occupational castes' and others as 'unclean occupational castes'. This division had to do more with the nature of tasks that groups of people performed which also in many ways contributed to unhygienic and unsanitary conditions of living. Thus, according to the 1931 census, which was the last census at which caste data was collected, the castes of Julaha (weavers), Darzi (tailors), Qassab (butchers), Nai or Hajjam (barbers), Mirasi (musicians), Manihar (bangle sellers) etc. were classified as 'clean castes' while Bhangi (sweepers) and Chamars (leather tanners) were classified as 'unclean castes'. Occupational castes are prevalent in all sections of the population not only in India but in the whole world.

All these communities referred above and several other communities too that are still performing different occupations based upon their socio-cultural framework adopted a long time ago are facing health hazards both on account of their poverty as well as unsanitary habits and unhygienic practices. Among the occupational caste communities such as Nat, Kanjar, Kalabaz, Beria, Bhangi, Fakir, Dom, Nishad, Mallah, Darji, Lohar, Pasi, Sonar(or Swarnakar) and many other 'unclean castes' who are said to be related to particular caste occupations, it is also found that their women share considerable responsibilities to run the household work. They take care of children and other members of the family. However, generally, they do not pay proper attention to their own health due to their household responsibilities and also due to their reluctance to disclose their health problems.

Based on fieldwork among the Nats of Mirzapur, Upadhyaya (2000) has observed that the Nats of Mirzapur are a recently settled semi-nomadic community whose socio-cultural occupations are fakiri, acrobating, entertaining and many among the community are also engaged in ethno-medical practices. There are also many Fakirs among the Nats. While the 1931 census mentions them as a distinct caste, some of the earlier census reports do not record the Fakir as a distinct and separate caste. Besides begging the Fakirs are also traditional healers as seen among the 'Nats' of Mirzapur district. Some are also casual labourers and domestic servants (Ansari, 1960).

During another survey conducted among the different settlements of Nats of Mirzapur, Upadhyaya (2003) observed that family members, particularly the male seniors in the family, hardly bother about the health problems of their women because they are busy in their routines, and also that most of the families are nuclear rather than joint families.

The elderly Nat woman in the family acts as midwife whenever the birth of a child takes place. The elderly mother-in-law and sister-in-law also play this role in and outside the community where underprivileged sections such as Kewats, Mallahs, Chamars, etc. exist. They take all possible ante-delivery and post-delivery care for both mother and child, locally called *jachcha-bachcha*, particularly in North India. In the case of gastroenteritis and stomach-related diseases, the Nat women of gather in large numbers, and at least ten of them, during the evening, inhale ganja and tobacco through *hukka*. When asked why they did it, they replied that all gastric problems and stomach ailments are sorted out by doing so. They depend less upon allopathic medicines and all that, due to ignorance and their own way of living. Very nearly, the same situation prevails among other underprivileged communities as well.

The reproductive health status of the Nat women was also not satisfactory. In general, they did not seem to be in favour of family planning methods. The male heads of the household often remarked that there is no such code in their religion. But, when their women were asked whether they wanted to use such methods or not, they answered in the affirmative (in the case of Arjunpur and Hariharpur settlement of Mirzapur). Most women were in favour of using methods of birth control such as pills and copper-T etc. The reason is that an average Nat woman in her reproductive age (15-48 years) begets 10-11 children, of which three or four do not remain alive. Either they die in the womb itself or during post-delivery haemorrhage. This is because there is no regular ante-natal and post-natal check-up system among these women.

The condition of MCH centre, which is situated in village Khajuri, near the Nat settlements, is also very bad. During the time of fieldwork conducted in the month of June 1999, there was no arrangement for beds and contraceptive pills there. It looked deserted and doctors do not come to attend the patients. It is far away from the place where most Nats live. The only way to fulfil the health care requirements is from the Jholachchap doctors who are unqualified medical practitioners having diploma certificates from Bengal and Bihar. They choose to practice in such areas where health care facilities are non-existent or among poor who provide them scope for practice and also to make money.

Many women of the Nat community are found engaged in ethno-medical occupations and members of both the Nat community and other underprivileged groups and use these ethno-medical and primitive practices in diagnosing as well as curing diseases. The main occupation of the Nat women is to collect honey in gardens. They are sometimes active in surgery of small boils. Sometimes, they act as the traditional dentists among the underprivileged communities who do not avail of modern health facilities. They go to different places for tattooing purposes, since they are experts in it. Tattooing itself sometimes becomes a cure for the women suffering from arthritis, pain in the abdomen, and in the case of backache mostly occurring in pregnant women and those with irregular menstrual cycles.

According to the Nat belief and custom, it is necessary for every girl in the community before marriage to be tattooed. In the absence of the symbol of tattoo on their hand, no member in the *sasural* (bride's marital home) will accept water from her hands. In other words, she will be considered as 'unclean'. In this way, Nat women are mostly interested in traditional modes of treatment rather than depending upon the governmental health facilities as auxiliary nurse midwife, birth attendant, nurses etc. Where such beliefs, practices and customs prevail among the community, the members have the option to deal with such medical problems by not depending on the governmental health facilities. Doctors and other agents of the modern health care system have no definite role in their socio-cultural environment as seen in the case of scheduled caste Nat women of Mirzapur in UP. The Nat healers often perform *jadu*, *tona* and *totka* to cure the persons from evil eyes. They also apply mantra-tantra on the person, such as a pregnant woman for the easy delivery of child and on many other occasions as marriages and ceremonies. Nat women healers have a special position not only in the community but also outside the community.

The above findings of the study conducted by Upadhyaya (2003) in the Nat community corroborate the findings of other studies too. For instance, the findings of a household survey in Calcutta revealed that the families do not take proper care of women's health problems because of some important reasons. Largely women face two types of major difficulties in this regard. First, traditional medicine, which is generally cheaper and considered low status and less effective, is used more frequently by women than by men. Second, men accounted for increasingly larger proportions as the treatment cost per episode of diseases increased. Barring the possibilities that men contract preferentially diseases that cost more to treat, it is clear that the households are not willing to buy the same expensive care for the women that they do for the men.

It is by now a well-known fact that the negative effect of poverty on women's health is even more acute because of the existing gender bias against women. Gender bias in nutrition and health care in childhood, early marriages and conception, lack of voluntary check on the family size and poor state of prenatal and maternal health care services only intensify women's health problems. These all could be seen among the Nat community as well where women, due to gender bias, face many problems in the form of domestic violence when they return home after begging and do not get much food to eat. The outcome is often a quarrel between the husband and the wife, which results in beatings and damage to body and domestic utensils. This creates further mental tension and sometimes results in wife fleeing away with another companion. Normal women can sometimes bear the pain of domestic violence but it is very risky for the pregnant women.

It is also seen that nutritional imbalances for underprivileged women have a far-reaching impact on reproduction and the health of the infants they bear. Among such ethnic and cultural communities the lower status of women has a direct bearing on their access to food. While the custom of feeding males first is well known, it is less often realised that females end up with less nutrient food. Deprivation of food sometimes start in infancy where girl babies, as usually happens in the rural parts of Uttar Pradesh, are weaned earlier than boy babies. Parents may be unaware that their differential weaning practices have the effect of reducing the amount of high quality protein that girl infants receive. It is often a kind of nutritional deprivation that is always to be seen among the rural parts of UP where certain beliefs and customs still play such roles that seriously affect women's health.

The position of Nat women is not satisfactory in their society. That is why, they are neglected and deprived and do not enjoy the fruits of development. During the survey in Mirzapur, the researcher also participated in Nat Panchayat in the settlement of Arjunpur, which was traditional in nature and where a Muslim Maulavi was mediating on some quarrel between two parties. While writing down the conversations sitting with them, it struck him that there was no importance given to women in decision-making, nor were health and domestic issues their concern. Marginalisation, resulting in deprivation, also affects their health adversely. Similar is the situation with other nomadic communities such as Bedia, Kanjar and tribal women engaged in several clean and unclean occupations.

The rural scenario of UP is marked by numerous communities engaged in occupations that could be considered hazardous and injurious to their health. These are both traditional and non-traditional occupations. Traditional occupations like leather tanning that the Chamars do or oil pressing that Teli caste does are as much prone to occupational health injuries as the non-traditional occupations like *bidi*-making, quarrying, glass blowing and so on. In many of these occupations, women are engaged along with men and children with little or no protection.

Our foregoing analysis of rural women's health status in Uttar Pradesh suggests that there is need to reorient the state population policy programmes. Such programmes should go beyond demographic targets, contraceptive prevalence and female sterilisation to a more comprehensive focus on reproductive health needs and services. These should be particularly responsive to reproductive health needs in ways that are sensitive to the socio-cultural constraints that women and adolescent girls face in acquiring services and expressing health requirements. It is also necessary to ensure that the health policy for women is not over-obsessed with just the reproductive health needs of women as women do face numerous other health problems as well. A health policy for women should be sensitive to the constraining power of patriarchy that cuts across class and caste lines and make policies that are not merely gender-sensitive but make them sensitive to the power of patriarchy at all levels in all communities in ways that account for the structural dimensions of poverty and deprivation as well. This is a task that has not been paid serious attention to, but one that calls for initiatives from civil society organisations as well.

References

Ansari, Gaus (1960) "Muslim Caste in Uttar Pradesh: A Study of Culture Contact", Ethnographic and Folk Culture Society, UP, Lucknow.

Hasan, K.A. (1967) *The Cultural Frontier of Health in Village India*. Bombay: Manaktalas.

Mukhopadhyaya, Swapna and Savitri, R. (1998) *Poverty, Gender and Reproductive Choice*. New Delhi: Manohar Publications.

Upadhyaya, P.C. (2002) "Poverty and Health Condition of 'Nats' of Mirzapur", paper presented in the National Seminar on Labour and Poverty in Uttar Pradesh, organised by G.B. Pant Social Science Institute, Jhusi, November, Allahabad.

— (2003) "Health Status and Health Seeking Behaviour among Nats of Mirzapur", paper presented at the D.N. Majumdar Centenary Celebrations (2003-04), organised by Ethnographic and Folk Culture Society, February-March, Lucknow.

— (1999) "Women's Health Status in India: An Emerging Scenario", paper presented at the National Seminar on Changing Profile of Women with Special Reference to India: Fifty Years of Independence organised by Jagat Taran Degree College, September, Allahabad.

Vishwakarma, R.K. (1991) *Health Status of the Underprivileged*, a study sponsored by World Health Organisation, Vol. I.

5

Socio-Economic and Health Problems of the Urban Aged

A Case Study of Allahabad

R.M. Tripathi

Ageing of society has now become a worldwide phenomenon. This demographic problem with its far-reaching consequences has affected practically all walks of life. Ageing is something that happens to all of us. It is a natural and irreversible life process. The number of senior citizens and their ratio to the total population have been increasing rapidly in the both developed and developing countries. This is understandable. Advances in medical science, better nourishment, improved standards of public health have all contributed to increased longevity. The developed world has been taking effective measures to cope with the problem of looking after its growing numbers of senior citizens. The developing countries have so far failed to take sufficient notice of this problem. Plans to support the elderly are generally inadequate. For most old people in our society, long life is an adversity. They are often subjected to negative stereotypes. Many thousands of them continue to be neglected by society. The last years of their lives are full of hardships and loneliness.

The United Nations has declared 1999 as the International Year of Older Persons with an objective to prepare the world for a dramatic increase in elderly during the next century. According to the UN projections, by the year 2050, every third person on the earth will be aged 60 years and above. Similarly, by the year 2020, India will be among top ten countries globally with the largest population of the aged. The population aged 60+ is increasing rapidly in our country from 56 million in 1991 to 70 million in 1998 and expected to be 177 million by 2020.

Census reports emphasise the need to make provisions not only for the ageing population of today, but also for those of the future (Muttagi, 1980). This demands greater attention to the specific financial, physical, social and psychological problems of the elderly. It is necessary to direct policies and programmes not only towards managing on increasing population but also a growing elderly population in the coming years. Literature on the problems of elderly in India is very scant. These have not received high priority till recently. Bearing this in mind, this study was designed to examine the socio-economic and health problems of the elderly people in an urban community.

Objectives of the Study

The present study has made a detailed investigation into various dimensions of the elderly together with the implications of ageing population in a wider perspective in the urban settings of the city of Allahabad in Uttar Pradesh and to explain the part that social work can play in meeting these needs and problems.

The study is based on the following assumptions:

1. Analyse demographic structure of the urban aged population in terms of its growth dynamics.
2. Examine the socio-economic and educational status of the urban aged.
3. Study the health status of the aged.

4. Examine the day-to-day experiences of senior members of urban families regarding their rights to receive care and the responsibilities of the family members to provide that care.
5. Analyse the roles of the family, kin, neighbours and other members of the society involved.

Methodology

The study is mainly based on primary as well as secondary data collected by a research team. A structured questionnaire was prepared for the data collection. The interview schedule contained about 60 questions. The observational schedule was meant to enable the interviewer to record the observations and reactions to the conditions of the respondents.

The interview schedule covers almost every possible aspect of the life of an aged included in the scope of this study. It was designed with more care in order to avoid loaded and vague questions. Opinion questions and questions soliciting factual information were also included. The questions were phrased in such a way and listed in such an order that the investigator could establish and maintain rapport with the respondents. Questions were also included to serve as cross-check on other questions without giving the respondents any sense of duplication, thus providing a check against both error and attempted evasion. The interview schedule contained several types of question such as simple fact, multi-choice, open-end and funnel type. Questions on the readiness of the respondents to accept help as well as questions eliciting their suggestions were included.

The interview schedule was first pre-tested on some aged. This resulted in certain modifications in the schedule. The finalised schedule was personally administered by the investigator to 200 aged persons.

In some cases it was found necessary to call on time and again at the home of a respondent and obtain additional information or to clarify some of the particular points. Substitutions were not allowed under any circumstances. However, sometimes help had to be taken from other male members of the household, especially in the case of female respondents.

The secondary data have been obtained mainly from the Census Reports, District Gazetteers, District Census Hand Book (1991), District Statistical Bulletin (1991), District Directory, and other publications.

The data were processed and analysed for gaining insights into the relevant problems faced by the aged and for suggesting remedial measures for improving their financial, physical, sociological and psychological problems that are specific to these people.

Social and Economic Characteristics of the Aged

Old age, encompassing the later part of the life of an individual, is a period during which symptoms of physical deterioration begin to appear (Bali, 1995). It indicates the manifestation of physiological, social and psychological change. It makes a shift in an individual's position from active social participation to a state of marked decline in role playing and performance and from economic self-sufficiency to economic dependence in a majority of the cases (Muttagi, 1997).

This section is devoted to analyse the social and economic characteristics of the aged in an urban community. A study of the social status of the aged involves an analysis of their age and marital status, religion and caste, education levels and other factors. To understand the economic status of the aged, it is necessary to discuss the income of the individual and the income of the family he lives with (Nayar, 1992).

Social Characteristics

The aged population in the city of Allahabad, as shown by this study, covers a set of diverse groups, which differ from each other in a variety of ways. There are persons who have just turned 60 years of age and are likely to become very keen to earn and support their families by giving their full time in different economic activities. There are general, minority, SC and OBC caste groups seeking refuge in religious pursuits. There are single and married people, well-to-do as well as penniless individuals, depending upon others for their essential needs. There are also people who are healthy and look ahead with plenty of time for relaxation after a busy active life and others not so healthy and waiting as it were, for death to rescue them from their worldly miseries. These characteristics, which have a bearing on their social status, are discussed in this section.

Age and Marital Status

Table 1 shows the age and marital status of respondent aged persons. Accordingly, 73 per cent of the aged were in the age group of 60-69. The average age was worked out to be 64.5 years. The married aged constitute the largest group with 72.5 per cent, while 25 per cent were widowers or widows.

Table 1

Age and Marital Status

Age Groups	*Independent*		*Married*		*Unmarried*		*Widow/ widowers*		*Divorced/ deserted*		*Total*	
	M	*F*	*M*	*F*	*M*	*F*	*M*	*F*	*M*	*F*	*Total*	*%age*
60-64	-	-	50	07	01	-	05	10	-	-	73	36.5
65-69	-	01	49	01	02	-	15	05	-	-	73	36.5
70 and above	-	-	38	-	-	01	10	05	-	-	54	27.0
Total	-	01 (0.5)	137 (68.5)	08 (4.0)	03 (1.5)	01 (0.5)	30 (15.0)	20 (10.0)	-	-	200 (100)	100.0

Figures in parentheses show row percentages.

Similarly, 73 persons were in the age group 60-64, including 50 married men, 7 married women, 10 widows and 5 widowers. Predominance of married men against married women and of widows over widowers is found in the age group

65-69. This trend also appears in the married aged of higher age groups. This aspect of survival among the aged between men and women is an interesting phenomenon. The data also shows that the number of unmarried men are more than the women. It may also be noted that there are no divorcee or deserted in any age groups.

The incident of remarriage among the aged was not reported after separating from their spouses either because of death or desertion. None of the aged reported having more than one living marriage partner though quite a few went on remarrying or accepting partners for the fourth or fifth time.

Educational Profile of the Aged

Education is one of the most important determinants of a person's social status. It is a contributory factor for moving up the social ladder (James, 1995). A study of the educational accomplishments of the aged as depicted in Table 2 shows that illiteracy was very much pronounced among women (40 per cent). This could be due to lack of educational facilities as well as the attitude of the society towards female education. Among the male aged, only 5.88 per cent are illiterate.

Table 2

Educational Level

Educational Level	*Males*		*Females*		*Total*	
	No.	*Percentage*	*No.*	*Percentage*	*No.*	*Percentage*
Illiterate	10	5.88	12	40.00	22	11.0
Literate	13	7.65	05	16.66	18	9.0
Primary	21	12.35	06	20.00	27	13.5
High School	33	19.47	02	6.67	35	17.5
Intermediate	23	13.53	02	6.67	25	12.5
Graduate	40	23.53	01	3.33	41	20.5
Postgraduate	26	15.30	02	6.67	28	14.0
Technical	4	2.35	-	-	4	2.0
Total	170	100	30	100	200	100.0

The data also reveals that among the females, only 36.67 per cent had received formal education (primary to postgraduate) as against 84.12 per cent in the case of men. Secondly, majority of the men had received education from high school to intermediate, which was and still is minimum requirement for getting a white-collar job.

The table further illustrates that 11 per cent of the respondents were illiterate, whereas 13.5 per cent have studied up to primary level, 17.5 per cent up to high school, 12.5 per cent up to intermediate, 20.5 per cent up to graduation and 14 per cent up to postgraduation level. Only 2 per cent respondents were having technical education.

Religion and Caste

Table 3 shows the religion, caste and marital status of the aged. The majority of the respondents came from general caste category (63.5 per cent), followed by 23.5 per cent OBCs and 9 per cent SCs. Among the non-Hindus, a small group of 4 per cent belonged to minority (Muslim) group. The majority of the aged (about 72.5 per cent) enjoyed married status. Of the rest, who were single, the largest group was of those aged who were married but had lost their life partner.

Table 3

Religion and Caste according to Marital Status

Religion and Caste	*Single*	*Married*	*Un-married*	*Widow/ widowers*	*Deserted divorced*	*Total*	*Percent-age*
General	-	98	2	27 (21.26)	-	127	63.5
Minority	-	7	-	01 (12.5)	-	08	4.0
OBC	1	30	2	14 (29.79)	-	47	23.5
SC	-	10	-	08 (44.44)	-	18	9.0
Total	1 (0.5)	145 (72.5)	4 (2.0)	50 (25.0)	-	200 (100.0)	100

Figures in parentheses denote percentages.

The incident of widowhood was reported among the SCs to the extent of 44.44 per cent, among the OBCs 29.79 per cent, among the general castes 21.26 per cent and among Muslims 12.5 per cent. The known cause, i.e., non-acceptance of widow remarriage among Hindus as well as general caste, obviously accounted for the higher incidence of widowhood compared to its lower incidence among Muslims whose religious laws do not placc any hindrance against widow remarriage. However, the high incidence of widowhood among SCs is intriguing.

Living Arrangement

As shown in Table 4, about 13 per cent of the aged lived as wholly dependent upon others, and 25.5 per cent partially dependent. Nearly two-thirds of the aged were still the chief breadwinner in the family they lived in. The onus of supporting them was found either on their children or one or other relatives. Among the male aged, 64.12 per cent were chief breadwinner, 27.65 per cent were partially dependent, and only 7.06 per cent were wholly dependent upon others. In case of females 40 per cent were the chief breadwinner, 46.67 per cent were wholly dependent upon others and 13.33 per cent partially dependent. Dependency among the females was more

Table 4

Gender-wise Economic Status in the Family

Status in the family	*Males*		*Females*		*Total*	
	No.	*Percentage*	*No.*	*Percentage*	*No.*	*Percentage*
Chief breadwinner	109	64.12	12	40.00	121	60.5
Wholly dependent	12	7.06	14	46.67	26	13.0
Partially dependent	47	27.65	04	13.33	51	25.5
Others	02	1.17	-	-	02	1.0
Total	170	100.00	30	100.00	200	100.0

pronounced for the obvious reasons, viz., lack of education and unemployment. With the spread of education among women and availability of wider employment opportunities, this trends is likely to be reversed or one may say that the incidence of dependency among the women, which is directly correlated to their education and employment status, is likely to be reduced.

It is significant to note that as many as 86.5 per cent of the aged lived with their children or other relatives and only 13.5 per cent lived alone or with their spouse. Of the former group, 81.5 per cent lived with their children, including grandchildren, 2 per cent with their sons-in-law and 3 per cent with other relatives.

The study further shows that 6.5 per cent of those who lived alone, majority of them earned their livelihood own while the remaining 7 per cent who were living with their wives, the majority were the chief breadwinner. The majority of the women in 'living with children' group were dependent except for a few among them.

Table 5

Living Arrangements according to Gender

Living arrangement	*Males*	*Females*	*Total*	*Percentage*
Living alone	09	04	13	6.5
Living with husband/wife	12	2	14	7.0
Living with children	142	21	163	81.5
Living with married daughters (sons-in-law)	02	02	04	2.0
With relatives	05	01	06	3.0
Total	170	30	200	100.0

It is interesting to note that the aged, living with other relatives, mainly consisted men who were partially dependent, while in the case of those living with their sons-in-law, the majority were women who were wholly dependent.

In the discussion of living arrangements of the aged, an important aspect is the ownership of the living accommodation. The study shows that 78.5 per cent of the aged lived in homes owned by them and hardly 15 per cent in rented houses. The former includes aged couples whereas the later category includes both the aged who pay the rent out of their own income as well as those who are dependents and pay the rent. As regards the rest 4.5 per cent lived in rent-free houses and the remaining 2 per cent were found to be living on pavements. The last group, therefore, needs immediate proper living arrangements such as the one available in the homes for the aged.

Table 6

Type of Accommodation

Accommodation Type	*Number*	*Percentage*
Living in owned homes	157	78.5
Living in rented houses	30	15.0
Living in rent-free houses	09	4.5
Living on pavements	04	2.0
Total	200	100.0

Economic Characteristics

Income

Income and occupation are the other two very important and closely related determinants of the status of the aged (Bambawale, 1997). The present study reveals that 30 per cent of the respondents had an income of their own. Of the remaining 50 per cent reported to have different kinds of pensions as their source of income and 13 per cent had no income. Thus, the majority (over 47 per cent) of the aged fell in the middle income group with monthly income varying between Rs. 1,500 and Rs. 5,000.

Table 7

Income Pattern

Income Group	*No. of Cases*	*Percentage*
No income	26	13.0
Low income group (0-1500)	30	15.0
Middle income group (1500-5000)	95	47.5
Upper income group (15000 and above)	49	24.5
Total	200	100.0

Although the role of religion and caste for determining the social status has weakened (Singh, 1989) these days, their influence on the other determinants of social and economic status still remains strong. Whether religion and caste have any correlation with income can be observed from Table 8.

Table 8

Income according to Religion

Income Group	*General Caste*	*OBC*	*SC*	*Minorities*	*Total*
No income	17 (13.49)	6 (12.77)	3 (16.67)	-	26 (13.00)
Low income (0-1500)	11 (8.70)	11 (23.40)	7 (38.89)	1 (11.11)	30 (15.00)
Middle income (1500-5000)	65 (51.59)	21 (44.68)	4 (22.20)	5 (55.55)	95 (47.50)
Upper income (7500 and above)	33 (26.19)	9 (19.15)	4 (22.20)	3 (33.33)	49 (24.50)
Total	126 (100.00)	47 (100.00)	18 (100.00)	9 (100.00)	200 (100.00)

Figures in parentheses denote percentages.

It is quite evident from the table that religion and caste also have an effect on the economic status of the aged. Among the OBCs and SCs about 36 per cent and 55 per cent respectively were below the low income category. However, in case of general castes, the proportion of respondents in low income group was found only about 22 per cent. This substantiates the hypothesis that lower is the caste hierarchy, lower is the income level.

Sources of Income

The aged earn their income from different kinds of sources like self-employment, salaries and wages, property, interest on savings, pensions etc. The data gathered in this regard are presented in Table 9.

Table 9

Source of Income according to Income Group

Source of Income	*Income Groups*			*Total*	*%age*
	Low	*Middle*	*Upper*		
Salary and wages	14	6	3	23	10.18
Self-employment	5	11	7	23	10.18
Property	13	4	-	17	7.52
Interest on savings	12	10	1	23	10.18
Pensions	11	80	23	114	50.44
More than one source of income	12	9	5	26	11.50
Total	67	120	39	226	100.00
Pensioners	11	80	23	114	50.44
Central Government Service	2	20	8	30	13.27
UP Government Service	7	50	15	72	31.86
Old Age Pension	1	9	-	10	4.42
Freedom Fighters	1	1	-	2	0.9
Total	22	160	46	228	100.00

The table clearly shows that more than 50 per cent of the aged draw income from different kinds of pensions, while 10.18 per cent each from salary and wages, self-employment and interest on savings, and 7.52 per cent from property. The study also reveals that 31.86 per cent respondents were found drawing pensions from State Government, 13.27 per cent from Central Government, 4.42 per cent under the old age pension scheme of the Central Government and 0.90 per cent from the freedom fighters pension schemes. Besides, 11.50 per cent of the aged had more than one source of income, which included property and self-earnings, property and interest on savings, pension and salary, pension and self-earnings, veterans special pension from Central and State Governments. Thus, it can be seen from the above that different kinds of pension schemes formed the major source of income for the aged urban community of Allahabad city.

Health Status and Physical Handicaps

Old age in itself is not a disease. It is both a universal and a natural process (Bali, 1999). Every living being may have disabilities or weaknesses. With advancement in age these ailments come to the surface. They may be of recent origin or a carry-over from the past. The aged are normal people. They may become ill but they are not necessarily sick.

This section is devoted to analyse the incidence of disease and health problems and physical handicaps among the aged of Allahabad city. Apart from, a theoretical discussion about some of the common diseases in old age and their implications for the aged and their families, an attempt has also been made to find out the health needs of the elderly and the problems faced by them to meet these needs. Existing health services available to the elderly will be evaluated in terms of the special health needs of the elderly. A comparative study of the health services available to the aged in some of the countries will be made to ascertain the advisability of providing similar services to the aged in our country.

According to Phelps and Henderson (1952), "old age is a natural and normal condition. Its pathologies are the same as those that occur at any other age period, but they are intensified by illness, family disorganisation, unemployability, reduced income and dependency". Of all the problem of old age, the problems of health is a major unsolved problem because it is accentuated by an "increasing number of physical handicaps, more frequent and serious illness, more mental disturbances and a general reaction among the aged that ill-health is their major burden" (ibid).

Chronic and degenerative diseases and physical defects are major causes, which make the aged dependent, because they continue over a longer time and recovery is slower and less favourable than when they were younger in age. Long-term illness or incapacity poses major health problems for other people because the duration, more than the severity of the illness, has a direct bearing on the social functioning of a patient and his family as well as upon the provision that society must be prepared to make.

Health and Illness

Many thinkers equate old age with decline in sensory sharpness, with weakness or sickness and death. According to Goldforb (1960), "a common emotionally determined view of old age is that it is a period of illness, weakness, disability and helplessness about which little or nothing can be done". Goldforb and others deplore this view of old age as a stereotype of an aged person which "should be abandoned because of the obvious heterogeneity of chronologically old people". Indeed, our attitude of hopelessness about old age is resulting in our unjust neglect of old people except in certain sections of the community where due to their cultural heritage the aged still enjoy respect and reverence. This, however, is fast crumbling under modern living.

What is health and disease in relation to the aged? An antiquated definition of health is that it is "that state of being existing in the absence of disease". According to Stieglitz (1980), who considers this a negative and inadequate statement, "health is that state of being in which all the reserve capacities of the organism are at their maximum". He considers this an ideal state an abstraction, unattainable in its perfection, but yet approachable. According to him, there are no specific diseases of old age. "Any illness may occur at any age. But certain disorders increase in frequency after the peak of maturity. These disorders, while not limited to senescents, are nevertheless characteristically geriatric" (ibid). In these disorders are included several vascular problems, such as arteriosclerosis (hardening or thickening of the vessels), high blood pressure and heart diseases. Included also in the disorders of the later years are several metabolic disorders (chemical transformation), diabetes mellitus, the male and female climacteric (a critical crisis occurring at a period of life when vital forces begin to decline), gout, anaemia, obesity, arthritis (inflammation of the joints), and many types of cancer. Their causation is endogenous, i.e., they arise from within. Their causation is a series of superimposed insults comparable to various stresses and strains. The onset of beginning of these disorders is without symptoms, they are chronic, slow and progressive. They also increase an individual's vulnerability to other disorders (Turner, 1969).

In fact, people live in two environments: first, an external environment, which is full of social strive, conflict and competition, and is not always the same all the time; and secondly an internal environment, which is extraordinarily stable and varies very little chemically. If our temperature varies more than a degree or more than one per cent of the optimum, we are by no means healthy. The same is the case when the concentration of sugar in the blood rises above a certain level, or the glucose content of the blood falls below a certain level. It is similarly true also of other chemical constituents of the body. In other words, optimum interval environment varying from the desirable in any respect is tantamount to disease. The factors discussed above, viz., body temperature, pulse rate, blood pressure, chemical concentrations and the like, which are relatively constant, do not change with ageing. But, the ability to maintain the equilibrium of the so-called 'constants' diminishes with ageing. That makes all the difference.

The aged respond to habits rather than adjust habits to environment. They live by habits. This perhaps is a major cause of health problems for the aged. There is constant fear among the aged that a new symptom of disease may bring permanent incapacity and loss of independence.

Attitudes towards aged people's illness have been changing. According to Turner (1969), 'until around 1880 most doctors made little differentiation between ageing as a natural life process and disease, and they tended to overlook or neglect specific physical diseases or infections, which they saw as an inevitable and natural part of ageing. The ageing were not considered interesting or hopeful patients. In contrast to this, there are more recent medical opinions, such as Worcester's that "there are no diseases peculiar to old age and very few from which it is exempt" or Zeman's that "disease in the aged is characterised by multiplicity, chronicity and duplicity".

According to Phelps and Henderson (1982), "in addition to the risky economic status of the aged, the chief causes of dependency are the chronic and degenerative diseases and the physical defects". The elusive nature of the deterioration of the body caused by these diseases is characterised by the following facts, which were observed in this study:

1. Most elderly people have several of these illnesses or defects.
2. Often symptoms of the illness may be non-existent or very few that they are either not observed or ignored both by the individuals and the physicians.
3. Many individuals either regard themselves as in excellent condition or are satisfied with or are indifferent to their health in spite of their suffering from illness.
4. When pointedly enquired about physical ailments or handicaps most common among the aged they reported a lot that is wrong with them.
5. Most of the aged remain indifferent to what may be happening to the health either because the illness had not

disturbed them or the persons near them do not do enough to seek medical aid or because of lack of money.

Diseases reported as among the leading causes of death in the case of the general population are also the major disabling illnesses of old age. These are the diseases of the heart, cancer, diabetes, cerebral haemorrhage, pneumonia, tuberculosis, nutritional diseases and accidents.

The limitation of this study is that we could not go deep into the phenomenon of disease among the aged because (i) to do so would have necessitated a thorough study of medicine and its practice in order to arrive at a correct diagnosis of the maladies of illness, (ii) not a single aged person interviewed for this study had regular medical examination who could provide the investigator his or her detailed medical history, and (iii) this was beyond the scope of the present study. The responses to the questions on physical ailments and defects involved only their knowledge of the symptoms of any ailments or defect along with its effects on the body, the onset of a particular ailment or defect, the attention given to get it treated, the result of that treatment and other related aspects.

For example, an aged would say that he gets periodical pains in the joints which get worse in winter causing agony and preventing him from going out. But, he would not know that he is suffering from arthritis (inflammation of the joints) and rheumatism. He would simply dismiss the whole thing by dubbing it as '*Vai-badi*' (Ayurvedic name for such conditions) and wrapping the knees and ankles in woollen or cotton rags to keep them warm. It is the same with other complaints. The ignorance of the nature of the various illnesses one may suffer from and inadequate attention paid to remedy their underlying causes shown by an aged person holds good for the general fun of ailing and suffering people throughout the country. Even, a large number of medical practitioners aim only at symptomatic relief of their patients complaints.

Under the circumstances stated above responses of the aged to questions concerning their health have been tabulated in a manner as to give as nearly a true picture of the health problems and needs of the aged as could be possible.

Physical Ailments

For the purpose of the present study illness was defined as any condition, i.e., disease, impairment, symptom, or a group of related symptoms, which was reported by the aged as having bothered them.

Indigestion, constipation, anaemia, urinary troubles, blood pressure, skin diseases, pain in joints, reduced eyesight and power of hearing, and the diseases of the respiratory system with varying degrees of affliction were some of the conditions of physical ailments, which were observed among the respondents. Among these, those complaints which worried the aged more or caused concern are discussed in this section.

An attempt to assess the physical and mental health of the surveyed elderly, together with their preference in use of medical services, is made in Table 10. The subjective domain of physical health is viewed in terms of the general feelings and the medical domain of it accounts for chronic illnesses, as well as several other handicaps that the elderly have. The self-rating of the health status by elderly individuals is presented against their individual characteristic differential. Though such a biased assessment based on self-rating may be subjective or relative, it

Table 10

Perception of Health Status

Health Status	*Male*	*Female*	*Total*
Very healthy	59 (34.71)	8 (26.67)	67 (33.5)
Fairly alright	76 (44.71)	8 (26.67)	84 (42.0)
Unhealthy	35 (20.58)	14 (46.66)	49 (24.5)
Total	170 (85.0)	30 (15.0)	200 (100.0)

can still be considered as the rough assessment of health status as far as the elderly are concerned. So as to identify the health problems faced by the elderly, they were observed, whether they fell ill at any time during the last one week/month/year, together with any perennial health problems. This information is analysed with regard to sex of the respondent.

Table 10 presents the percentage distribution of the aged by self-assessment of health condition in the study area. It is quite evident from the table that the health condition of the males is better than females. It could be seen that 34.71 per cent male and 26.67 per cent female respondents rated their health as very good. Again, there were 44.71 per cent male and 26.67 per cent female elderly, who thought that their health was fairly alright, while 20.58 per cent male and 46.66 per cent female elderly considered themselves unhealthy.

Table 11

Chronic Illness or Disability among the Aged

Disease	*Male*	*Female*	*Total*	*Percentage*
Asthma	12	5	17	10.00
Heart disease	17	3	20	11.76
Muscular pain	17	8	25	14.71
HBP	21	2	23	13.53
Diabetes	18	1	19	11.18
Paralysis	3	-	3	1.76
Arthritis (Rheumatism)	17	9	26	15.29
Blindness	5	2	7	4.12
Kidney disease	4	1	5	2.94
Gastroenteritis	12	2	14	8.24
Depression	3	-	3	1.76
Others	7	1	8	4.71
Total	136	34	170	100.00

Table 11 shows the incidence of different physical ailments among the aged according to sex. While arthritis affected the maximum number of the aged, i.e., 15.29 per cent, followed by muscular pain (14.71 per cent), high blood pressure (13.53 per cent), diabetes (11.18 per cent), asthma (10 per cent), gastroenteritis (8.24 per cent) and so on.

Physical Disabilities

The phrase 'physically handicapped' includes the blind, the partially sighted, the deaf, the dumb, the hard of hearing, the cripple, the cardiac patient, the spastics, the epileptics, the tubercular, the diabetics and all persons who have either completely lost the use of or can make only a restricted use of one or more of their physical organs. For the purpose of this study, a person was considered blind who could not 'count the fingers of an outstretched hand held at a yards distance. Likewise, any person whose sense of hearing was non-functional for the ordinary purposes of life, was considered deaf and one whose sense of hearing was not functional but impaired to an extent that he experienced difficulty in communicating easily with others was considered 'hard of hearing'. A person was considered dumb if his power of speech was non-functional for the ordinary purposes of life and who could not express himself in an articulate language. A person who had lost the power of motion, sensation or function or any part of the body and was deprived of the power of action was considered a paralytic.

Keeping in view the above definitions of some physical disabilities, an attempt was made to study the extent of some disabilities among the aged in the study area. The study reveals that of all the physical handicaps, two were most common. One was cases of hard hearing and the other was cases of impaired or reduced eyesight. In between these were an insignificant number of aged suffering from blindness, deafness and paralytic and diabetes (see Table 11).

Table 11 shows the number of aged with different physical disabilities according to their sex. Diabetes affected 11.18 per cent, paralytic claimed 1.76 per cent and blindness 4.12 per cent. None was suffering from hard of hearing.

Health Services

The aged, like others, are free to receive free medical assistance at the general hospitals or dispensaries run by the government, the local bodies and other charitable organisations. If they can afford it, they are free to consult private doctors.

Nature of Treatment

Almost all the respondents (80.5 per cent), who suffered from major ailments, had gone for allopathic treatment. Only 11.0 per cent took homeopathic medicines while 4.5 per cent ayurvedic, and 2 per cent each tradition therapy and other treatment. There was a solitary instance of using herbal medicine for healing muscular pain. Although reliance upon the modern medicines is greatly marked among the respondents, yet case histories have revealed that the urban elderly also usually explore simple and less expensive methods as mode of treatment at the initial stage of their ailment. The data obtained in this regard are presented below in Table 12.

Table 12

Nature of Treatment

	Allo-pathic	*Homeo-pathic*	*Ayur-vedic*	*Unani*	*Tradition Therapy*	*Others*	*Total*
Male	135	18	9	-	4	4	170
Female	26	4	-	-	-	-	30
Total	161	22	9	-	4	4	200
	(80.5)	(11.0)	(4.5)	-	(2.0)	(2.0)	(100)

Figures in parentheses denote percentages.

Source of Treatment

Table 13 shows that more than half of the patients obtained treatment from private doctors, three-fourths from government hospitals, and the rest from other kinds of health centres. Women consulted private doctors and attended the health centres less than men possibly because of proximity and greater accessibility. Men seemed to be relatively more mobile and economically more capable to avail of the treatment from hospitals located at far-off places as compared to women whose movements are traditionally restricted.

Table 13

Source of Treatment

Source of Treatment	*Male*	*Female*	*Total*
Government hospital	43 (42.94)	18 (60.0)	91 (45.5)
Private hospital	93 (54.71)	12 (40.0)	105 (52.5)
Others	4 (2.35)	-	4 (2.0)
Total	170 (100)	30 (100)	200 (100)

Figures in parentheses denote percentages.

Arrangement of Treatment

It is usually held that old people are very much fussy about their health needs and personal services (Chakrabarti, 1998). This tendency becomes more apparent when they get major ailments. For the slightest lapse in health care and treatment, the patient may get upset and start making troubles, which naturally disturbs the family environment. This discontentment often creates a misunderstanding and generates tension (Khan, 1995). We, therefore, took the opinion of the elderly about the arrangement of treatment which was made available to them and, also the reasons furnished for their untoward reactions. At the outset, it may be made clear that we did not expect that everybody would be happy with the nature of arrangement of treatment. We also did not assume that all the respondents would hold adverse opinion about it. The survey confirmed our assumption. It is found, for instance, that half of the respondents had no complaints about the nature of arrangement that was made for their treatment.

Dissatisfaction thus prevailed mostly among the poor and economically dependent respondents. The male and the female respondents differ, respectively, in attributing the causes of their dissatisfaction towards the arrangement of treatment. Three-fourths of the dissatisfied males reported that poverty and inadequate health care facilities had forced them to remain as such, while half of the dissatisfied females said so. In fact, a sizeable proportion of the dissatisfied females blamed their family members for not making proper arrangements. However, blaming members of the family was less apparent among males. Could it be that the majority of the elderly males being the heads of households and controllers over resources, have none to complain against? Thus, from the above, it is evident that poverty and lack of health care facilities in the study area had left most of the elderly unhappy with regard to their personal health.

Health Care System

Caring for the elderly can be viewed from two perspectives: (1) the daily care, and (2) the nursing and care during illness. We shall examine both these perspectives here.

Besides the need of care during illness, the elderly may also seek help in managing their daily activities. For example, many infirm elderly find is difficult or impossible to manage such basic activities as walking outside, bathing, washing, wearing garments, getting around the house, getting in and out of bed and so on. To perform these personal basic activities they require daily care from others, primarily from the family members or nearby kins. To the question whether they would require any help in managing the foregoing activities, an overwhelming majority of the respondents replied in the negative suggesting thereby that only disabled and infirm elderly need daily care. The survey revealed that only 10.7 per cent respondents were feeling the need for daily care. Disease and old age seemed to have made them infirm. The proportion needing help with these basic activities is 6 per cent for those aged 60-69 and 15 per cent for those aged 70 and above. It is also found that more men than women need daily care presumably because the former as patriarch are habituated to receiving personal services throughout their life. On the other hand, because of their deep involvement in domestic chores, many female respondents can scarcely afford to have the occasion to think for their personal comfort. Unless one is totally invalid, no woman perhaps would seek daily care from others.

Since an overwhelming majority of the respondents were afflicted with one kind of illness or other, it is quit natural that they would have somebody to render nursing and care during ailments. We wanted to explore the issue in order to test the assertion that family in urban society still play the dominant role in care-giving to the old persons. Table 14 shows the persons from whom the respondents received nursing and care while they were ill. The table clearly demonstrates the decisive role of family in elderly care. An overwhelming proportion of respondents (78.5 per cent) did receive nursing from their family.

Table 14

Who Cares for the Elderly During Illness

	Male	*Female*	*Total(%)*
Family members	137	20	157 (78.5)
Neighbours	2	-	2 (1.0)
Relatives	6	1	7 (3.5)
None	2	2	4 (2.0)
Self	7	5	12 (6.0)
No answer	16	2	18 (9.0)
Total	170	30	200 (100.0)

A very small proportion of respondents (1 per cent) were nursed and cared for by their neighbours. Relatives also came to volunteer the tasks. Such respondents constitute 3.50 per cent of the total. The elderly who lived alone (mainly the widows) stated to have received medicare self.

Gender-wise, there is a distinct variation in the type of persons who provide nursing to the old persons. Men tend to depend more on their wives for nursing and care than women on their husbands. For, it is noticed that two-thirds of the elderly males were nursed and cared for by their spouses during illness whereas not even one-tenth of the elderly females received care from their consort. Two factors may explain this. First, the female respondents being mostly widowed, there was no scope for receiving such aids from the spouses. Second, even those who had partners could not expect due nursing from their respective husbands possibly because domestic tasks are considered to be less culturally normal for men than for women. Or may be men would otherwise be involved in economic pursuits relegating thereby the responsibility to other members of the family. However, when there is no such members in the family, or if utter negligence becomes apparent, then only a husband would take the role of an aid provider.

More than half of the total female respondents received nursing from their sons and daughters-in-law while they fell ill. The corresponding figure for males is distinctly low. For, barely one out of seven respondents got nursing from them. In the absence of spouse, a widow is mainly dependent upon her children for sustenance and care. It is quite natural, therefore, that the old widows would expect care from their sons and daughters-in-law. It may be worth-while to mention that the female respondents paid excessive importance to their sons in this respect undermining or even ignoring thereby the services rendered by the daughters-in-law. Personal observations as well as probing revealed that it was the daughter-in-law rather than son who actually did the major nursing to the elderly. This way of undermining their roles and showing in little or no appreciation for their services tends to embitter the relationship between mother-in-law and daughter-in-law.

References

Bali, Arun, P. (1999) *Understanding Greying People of India.*

Bali, P. (1995) "Role of the Family in Elderly Care", *Research and Development Journal* 2(1).

Bambawale, U. (1997) "Ageing and the Economic Factor in Later Life", in *Life in Turiligut Years* (ed.), Indrani Chakravarty, Kwality Book Company, Calcutta.

Becker Charles, S. (1969) "Physical Functioning of Older People", in C.S.W.E's, op cit, p. 13.

Chakrabarti, Prafulla (1998) *Health and Care of Elderly in The Eastern Anthropologist,* Vol. 51, No. 3, July-Sept, p. 256.

Goldforb, Alvin, J. (1960) "Emotional Functioning of Older People", in C.S.W.E's, op cit, p. 21.

Hasan, S.Z. (1960) Report of the Survey of the Incidence of Blindness and Prospects of the Survey of the Incidence of Blindness of Prospects of Employment of the Blind in the City of Lucknow. J.K. Institute Monograph No. 8. J.K. Institute of Sociology and Human Relations, Lucknow University, p. 2.

"Health Care for the Elderly", in *ICMR Bulletin No. 1.(26),* No. 5, May 1996, pp. 33-35.

James, K.S. (1995) "Demographic Transition and Education in Kerala", *Economic and Political Weekly*, 30(51), 3274-3276.

Khan, M.Z. (1995) "Service for the Elderly in India", *Research and Development Journal*, New Delhi, Helpage India.

Muttagi, P.K. (1997) *Ageing Issues and Old Age Care*, New Delhi: Classical Publishing Company.

Nayar, P.K.B. (1992) "Needs and Problems of the Aged: A Study in Kerala", Research Report, New Delhi, ICSSR.

Phelps, Harold A. and Henderon, Dowis (1952) *Contemporary Social Problems,* Prentice Hall Inc., New York, p. 217.

Singh, R.R. (1995) "Family Change and the Social Care of the Aged", in S. Vijaya Kumar (ed.), *Challenges Before the Elderly: An Indian Scenario*, New Delhi, M.D. Publication.

Singh, Yogendra (1995) "Changing Trends in the Indian Family and the Adjustment of the Aged", in *Research and Development Journal*, Vol. 3, No. 2, pp. 31-42.

Stieglitz, Edward J. (1980) "The Personal Challenge of Ageing" in *Biological Changes and Maintenance of Health*, Tibbittts, Clark and Donahul Wilma, p. 50.

Turner, Helen (1969) "Physical and Emotional Functioning of Older People", in *Implication for Social Works*, C.S.W.E., p. 39.

Vijaya Kumar, S. (1995) "Widows in Countryside: Problems and Prospects", Studies on Human Development in India Project of UNDP, Memio, Hyderabad, Council for Social Development.

6

Girls' as Real Stakeholders in Community School

Sunit Singh and Vanita Somvanshi

It has become a truism to say that the community participation is an essential component for the success of any development project. Nearly all the donor agencies, whether at international or national level, while approving any proposal, explicitly mention the clause as an essential condition to ensure the involvement of community members at every level of implementation of the project. The government departments are placing special emphasis on community participation. They also include strategies for eliciting community participation as an integral part of the programme. But, in spite of all these commitments and conditions, the involvement of community members in the projects has been a distant dream at the ground level. Various evaluation studies have found that there exists a wide gap between the intentions of planners at the helm of affairs and the grassroots functionaries responsible for programme implementation. In fact, the grassroots functionaries of government line departments are the victims of bureaucratic approach and are not convinced that community members have the required skills for successful implementation of the project. However, certain NGOs have shown greater enthusiasm and commitment in working with community in planning, implementation, monitoring and evaluation of the projects but they too lack skilled manpower at grassroots who could understand the dynamics of community participation and formulate appropriate strategies keeping in view the objective conditions in the field.

The Govind Ballabh Pant Social Science Institute, Allahabad (GBPSSI) is engaged in rural outreach activities at its four rural stations located in four different development blocks of Allahabad district. At all the rural stations it is actively involved in promoting community participation in various developmental projects. From research point of view the Institute is interested to study the processes and outcomes of outside intervention for encouraging participatory planning and local initiatives in the field of development planning.

The present paper is based on the processes and outcomes of the intervention activities organised by the GBPSSI at one of its rural stations, namely, Asepur, during last eight years. In mobilising the community, the Institute has played the role of a catalyst. A team of facilitators had a meeting with the then panchayat and other community leaders of the village to identify a common problem that could attract consensus of maximum number of members of the community. The village had no girls' school at the time when the experiment was initiated. Thus, the Institute facilitated opening of a community-initiated girls' junior high school, which is still continuing without any outside financial support since then. Currently, about 150 students are enrolled in the school. In this respect, community has been supportive since last eight years. However, the most striking feature of the experiment is that that the school has now been taken over by the students themselves, who also happen to be the product of the same school.

The major underpinnings of this paper deal with the following issues:

- The strategies that should be adopted for mobilising the community for development projects on sustainable basis.
- Once the process of mobilisation sets in, it attempts to understand how the local level organisations take over the project. These organisations can be in the form of existing government structures, for instance, village panchayats or newly emerged local group. If new group emerges from the grassroots level, then it explores the antecedents in the formation of such a group.
- Amidst divergent viewpoints and difference of opinions between community members, what techniques should be practised so as to reach appropriate consensus. It also deals with the nature of conflict, which emerges during group discussions and meetings and how they move towards its peaceful resolution.
- It ponders over how community members gradually become assertive and confident in actively participating in community development programmes. It analyses factors that motivate people to take entrepreneurial and innovative initiatives, including the capacity-building features. It also probes the strategies they adopt in dispensing their duties as change agents and thereby meeting the objectives of the project.

The paper is divided into seven sections: (i) objectives of the experiment, (ii) intervention approaches in the experiment, (iii) village profile, (iv) experimental processes, (v) strategies adopted in the experiment, (vi) experimental outcomes, and (vii) learnings derived from the experiment.

Objectives

The broad objective of the current experiment is to understand the strategies that are required to make such community-based experiments self-recurring and self-sustaining and to explore the factors, which underlie the success or failure of any experiment entailing community participation in rural areas. Therefore, in order to attain these broad objectives, a number of specific objectives have been formulated. These are:

(i) to understand how the local level organisations, either the existing or the emerged structures, take over the experiment towards sustainability;
(ii) to comprehend the functioning of these local level organisations in making the experiment self-sustaining, including the processes of conflict resolution and reaching consensus;
(iii) to delineate the strategies adopted by local level organisations in mobilising the community towards self-development and sustenance;
(iv) to enumerate the outcomes that the current experiment yielded in these eight years; and
(v) to share the lessons drawn for successful conduct of community-based programmes in future.

Intervention Approaches

The present community school is a resultant of multiple interrelated approaches, which became operational as progress was gradually made in setting up of the school. One of them is process approach. The basic premise of this approach is that there are no fixed procedures or guidelines for attaining the goals. It moves on as a part of the trial and error process. It entails flexibility in its mechanism. It is learning by doing and things take shape as one progresses ahead.

Another is agency approach, where stakeholders are seen as an agency, which is responsible for transforming the village and sufficing the community with a progressive outlook. In order to stimulate the community, presence and active involvement of such change agents is critical. They play an intervening or a mediating role between the facilitators and the passive society. Such agents adopt self-sustaining approach, which is equipped with a strong will, determination and an optimistic attitude. These attributes energise the stakeholders to move ahead with their goals even in the face of crisis and difficulties.

There is also convergence approach, where attempt is made not only to bring revolution in one arena but in related fields as well so as to diversify actions for achieving all-round development. This approach comprises diverse aspects like attaining educational milestones, skill development, commercial agriculture, awareness in the area of health and environment, and self-generated employment. Such an approach provides boost not only at structural and material levels but also at personal level by raising the consciousness of people towards progressive-optimistic outlook needed for achieving overall development in the concerned area.

Once evolved, they are not dependent on external organisations/agencies for realising their goals. They become empowered enough to handle their own problems, for example, for raising funds, resolving conflicts, convincing village leaders, removing administrative impasses, etc. In brief, they adopt the self-sustaining approach through active vigilance. The basic assumption is that capabilities for self-management among the community members evolved through practice rather than prescription. Therefore, it is important to vest in the community the responsibility of determining the demand and preparing local education development plans based on concrete empirical explorations (Govinda and Diwan, 2003). Thus, the success of any programme through community participation is reached only when the programme acquires the status of autonomy and self-sufficiency.

Village Profile

The village Asepur is situated in the central part of the Saidabad block in Allahabad district. It is one of the biggest villages in Saidabad block representing people of different castes. The village is surrounded by Badhya village in north, Dankeshra and Bizhawaniya villages in the east, Binda Chak Mukhim and

Saraydasu Urf Haripur villages in the south and Hirat Rameshwar village in the west (all belonging to Saidabad block). The village is at a distance of about 30 kms from the district headquarters on the Allahabad-Varanasi road. The village is well connected by roads and railways.

The whole of the village area is composed of Gangetic alluvium, the deposition of which began in the pleistnene period. The parent material is deposited by river Ganges transported from the central of outer Himalayas, which is mainly composed of meta sedimentary rocks.

Asepur village comes under the sub-tropical seasonal climate and is characterised by a long and hot summer, followed by a pleasant monsoon and cold seasons. The winter usually extends from mid-November to February and is followed by the summer, which continues, from March to the middle of June. The monsoon continues till September. The month of October and first half of November constitute the post-monsoon period. The rainfall is average.

Demography

The total population of the village is 2,460 (Census 2001). In the last decade (1991-2001) the population shows an increase of 19.82 per cent, more in case of males than females. However, the number of households has decreased from 334 in 1991 to 328 in 2001. The population density in the village is more than 2,009 inhabitants per square km. The sex ratio (906.98) is quite high, i.e., population is well balanced. Although in case of Scheduled Castes (SCs) and in the age group of 0-6 years, it is somewhat low. Moreover, the number of girls in the age group of 0-6 years has decreased at a considerably high rate than that of boys over the last decade. Muslim community dominates this village. Brahman, Kushwaha, Yadav and Harijan castes represent Hindus. There are no Scheduled Tribes (STs) in the area.

Table 1
Demography of the Village

Indicators	*2001*	*1991*	*% Change*
No. of households	328	334	-1.79
Population growth (in %)	2,460	2,053	19.82
Males	1,290	1,048	23.09
Females	1,170	1,005	16.42
Population of children (0-6 years)	427	464	-7.97
Boys	229	247	-7.29
Girls	198	217	-8.75
Population of SCs	641	546	17.40
Males	342	292	17.12
Females	299	254	17.72
Population of STs	-	-	-
Sex ratio	906.98	958.97	
0-6 years	864.63	878.54	
SCs	874.27	969.86	

Source: Census 2001.

Literacy

The literacy level of the village is shown in Table 2. Accordingly, the literacy rate among the males is almost the double that of females. But, the situation has improved a lot over the decade, especially in case of females, i.e., 15.7 per cent in 1991 to 43.3 per cent in 2001.

Table 2
Level of Literacy

(in %)

Indicator	*2001*	*1991*
Rate	63.60	37.76
Males	82.19	59.43
Females	43.31	15.74

Source: Census 1991 and 2001.

Occupation

The majority of the population is involved in agriculture related activities (56.6 per cent). In general, there has been decrease in the proportion of main workers from 1991 to 2001 in all the sectors, except in the area of agriculture labour. Proportion of cultivators shows a decrease of 38.5 per cent over the last decade (1991-2001). Conversely, there has been tremendous increase (61.9 per cent) in the percentage of agricultural labourers during the last decade. This is an alarming figure. Table 3 depicts these facts:

Table 3

Occupation of Main Workers

Occupation	*2001*	*1991*	*% Change*
Cultivators (as % of total main workers)	25.14	34.8	-38.46
Agricultural labourers (as % of total main workers)	31.42	16.54	61.9
Workers household industry (as % of total main workers)	13.68	16.06	-27.45
Other workers (as % of total main workers)	29.76	32.6	-22.22

Source: Census 2001.

Infrastructure

Medical Facilities

The village has only one sub-centre for providing the health facility, which is established by the government. But, there is no primary health centre (PHC) in the village. The nearest PHC is in Saidabad, which is at a distance of about 4 kms.

Educational Facilities

There are total five schools in the village. Among these, one is primary, two are junior high schools, one high school and one 'madarsa'. Interestingly, the community itself manages the high school.

Rural Station

A rural station has been set with the efforts of G.B. Pant Social Science Institute (GBPSSI). Arrangement for 150 books (English and Hindi) sports material (skipping rope, indoor/ outdoor games, etc) has been made. Besides, to evoke interest in computer literacy among the girl students, a computer has been installed.

Experimental Processes

This experiment is analogous to bringing up a handicap baby. Sincere efforts made in nurturing a baby in these eight years (1998-2005) have finally helped the child to see the light of the day. The experimental processes have been broken down into different phases. These different phases through which the experiment went through to take the current shape have been unfolded in this section.

The Initial Move

In the first phase, an attempt was made to awaken the dormant society about the relevance of community participation in the development of any village, town or city. This initial icebreaking is important so as to help people to brainstorm their ideas. Several rounds of meetings and discussions were held with village men so as to explore those aspects, which are critical for transforming the village. Number of issues like the necessity of proper roads, transportation, hospitals, panchayat bhawans, schools for girls, etc., came up. Of these, the necessity of opening girls' school through community initiative was taken up as it had maximum consensus because there was no school for girls in the village after fifth class, which forced them to dropout from school. Furthermore, a high level of community participation involving minimum amount of conflicts in opening girls' school could also be expected. Thus, the idea of opening a school for girls in the village came from the community itself.

In this regard, few representatives from GBPSSI visited Asepur village and held an initial dialogue with Pradhan and other learned men regarding opening of a junior high school for girls. They were sensitised about the need for promoting girls' education. A high-level campaigning about the probable benefits that could be attained by opening girls' school in village was carried out. Frequent meetings with different sections of people like local leaders, teachers, parents, children, youths and people from Harijan community were held. In order to bring them at a uniform level of understanding, it was essential to generate such awareness in different groups. Thus, in the initial phase, a 'big push' was required to mobilise the community group by taking the latter into confidence.

Doubts and Curiosities

The faith instilled in the people about the pious aim of the project stirred up further curiosities and doubts in people. They were often misguided by the ostensible intentions of the village elites. They had couple of queries relating to various issues like the procedure of appointment of teachers, selection of curriculum, admission of students, fee structure, availability of books and uniform, recognition of the school, rules to be observed in the running of the school, etc. They also wanted to know the nature of support GBPSSI would extend to this community initiative. However, an attempt was made at each level to satisfy their curiosities and clarify their doubts through several meetings and group discussions amongst community members.

For instance, it was clarified to them from the very beginning that GBPSSI will provide only technical, and not financial, help in the form of holding workshops for training the teachers, entering into partnership with other organisations, removing administrative bottlenecks, etc. It was community that also decided the appointment of local people as teachers in the school, adopting the curriculum of Uttar Pradesh Education Board, providing special package for skill development depending on their needs and requirements, providing physical space and other resources for the school, formulating rules for students as well as teachers regarding discipline, fee charged, uniform, etc. Emphasis was placed only to adopt the agency and self-sustenance approach. This helped people to break free from their obsolete thought processes and to conceive an alternative progressive viewpoint in the form of community school.

Resource Mobilisation

It was obvious that by simply infiltrating such viewpoints in the people was not enough to realise the goals. It required community members to build upon it and to put their ideas into practice in concrete terms. For mobilising resources, support was sought from four main sources: (i) community support in the form of voluntary labour, (ii) community support in the form of material aid, (iii) support from other organisations, and (iv) government/administrative support.

(i) Community Support in the Form of Voluntary Labour

One of the prerequisites of the experiment was to convince people to make non-material contribution in the form of voluntary labour along with material contributions. This was essential so as to instil in them the feeling that the project belongs to them and they are the direct beneficiaries. Voluntary labour was required for the construction of the boundary wall and school building.

(ii) Community Support in the Form of Material Aid

Funds for construction of school building were raised by making a list of few people who agreed to contribute between Rs. 51 and Rs. 2,000, making a total sum of Rs. 20,000. In addition, under the mission "donate for girls' education" school students through door-to-door visits, collected about 7 quintal wheat, which was later sold to collect money for the smooth running of the school. Thus, community members contributed their labour, time and money, as and when required.

(iii) Support from Other Organisations

Support was also extended to community school from outside organisations like GBPSSI that played the role of training and consultancy agency. It also entered into partnership with education department, Allahabad University, district administration, etc. It took lead in changing people's redundant frame of mind and replacing it with an alternative optimistic outlook. In all these years, this village has succeeded in asserting itself as a model village. It has been chosen as one of the four rural stations established with the support from GBPSSI. Representatives from GBPSSI often frequent visit the village and form an important part of their meetings. They also help in removing administrative bottlenecks that crop up in their way. For any consultations and clarifications community members also visit GBPSSI.

Holding periodic workshops at GBPSSI provided further boost to their mobilisation. This provided them with appropriate solutions needed for coping with problems experienced in managing the school. Experts in the field of education also briefed them about various strategies for making rural education in the context of community participation a success. Lately, to take the village in strides with modern cities, community school has been updated with 150 books (English and Hindi) and sports material (skipping rope, indoor/outdoor games, etc). Besides, to evoke interests in computer literacy among the girl students, a computer has been installed.

(iv) Government/Administrative Support

In a feudal social, political and administrative climate, commitment to individuals is given precedence over commitment to an idea or a goal. As a result, such projects tend to get into conflicts. This was experienced in the current project. While on one hand, the administration showed keen interest and assured full cooperation when needed, on the other hand, they expressed their helplessness in extending their support during times of need. Thus, for most of the time, they proved to be a source of disappointment rather respite. For instance, it was a herculean task convincing Chief Development Officer to release a grant of Rs. 50,000, which was announced by the then Education Minister for the construction of school building. Likewise, more than often police officers took the stand of Pradhan rather community members. Moreover, because of their busy schedule, they hardly got time to work out the problems faced in conducting the experiment. Thus, the role of administrator as a facilitator in the process was minimal.

School Management

Running and managing of community school involved setting up of number of different school-related features through active involvement of the community members. Such initiatives were also made in Lok Jumbish Project in Rajasthan (Ramachandran and Sethi, 2000). These were as under:

(i) Enrolment of Children

Cent per cent enrolment of children till 12 years of age in school was stressed so as to realise the mission of 'Education for All'. Door-to-door strategy was adopted for filling the admission forms. An attempt was made to make sure that admission forms for every non-school-going children in the village was filled. Even for children who were not present during door-to-door visits, provision was made to fill their forms on their behalf and submit it on time. Care was taken not to force people to fill the admission form for the community school. It depended on their genuineness and free will. A free and fair test was conducted under the guidance of representatives from GBPSSI and village leaders.

(ii) Appointment of Teachers

There were certain criteria for the appointment of teachers like education at least up to intermediate level, formal or informal teaching experience and inherent interest in the profession of teaching. Emphasis was laid on selecting local candidates so as to give break to young educated village youths and being conversant with local language and culture, a high level of commitment and easy rapport building was expected from them. Preference was for selecting female candidates. Males are selected only in absence of eligible female candidates. All through the interview, attempt was made to conduct unbiased proceedings. Each interviewee was treated with equal respect. Interference and pressure from outside was resisted. Selection was made on basis of their educational qualifications and aptitude for teaching.

(iii) Rules for School Management

In subsequent meetings, the community members framed number of rules to be observed by students, parents and teachers. Rules for students dealt with punctuality, daily class attendance, completing everyday assignments, observing discipline, coming to school in proper uniform and carrying relevant books. For teachers, it was stressed on punctuality, regular attendance, timely completion of prescribed syllabus, stressing on moral values and civic sense and adopting friendly strategies for dealing with students, parents and other co-teachers. Parents were expected to encourage and remove impediments in the way of their children's education as well as to exhibit patience in dealing with school problems. Rules were also framed in regard to fee charged from each student (Rs. 15 per month) and teacher's salary. The school provided delivery of books and uniform on basis of caution money. Arrangements for holding evening classes for children, who failed to attend morning classes, were also made. Thus, such developments would not have happened unless deliberate efforts were made at the grassroots level.

Surfacing of Conflicts

In the first few years a great deal of time and effort went into fine-tuning of techniques for community participation and mobilisation. However, this phase of community mobilisation was not smooth. It led to emergence of inevitable conflicts of varying degrees at one or the other point. Few cases illustrated below highlight the nature of conflicts and their resolutions:

(i) The construction of the boundary wall aligning the school campus was not even completed when it was dismantled by one of the village elites on account of owning the land on which it was constructed. This aroused frustration and anger in community members. However, this problem was resolved by the intervention of revenue officer (at village level) who rationally decided the ownership of land in favour of the community school.

(ii) It was also observed that conflicts often broke out amongst teachers as well as between teachers and school principal. It led to role confusions and small factions where one group always opposed the ideology adopted by another group. Intervention of representatives from GBPSSI was always sought to sort out the differences between them.

(iii) The government school, which was assumed to flourish under the influence of the community school, also posed a problems by misguiding village people about the dire consequences of the project.

(iv) A new panchayat, which was elected after few years, was not comfortable with the school norms. To defeat the efforts made by community members, it posed number of hurdles in the flawless running of the school. In order to carry out their selfish manifestations, they demanded that school should be shifted elsewhere as the land where school is being run belongs to the gram sabha, so panchayat bhawan should be constructed there rather school. Thus, their vested interests were putting hurdles in the construction of the school building. As a result, the school shed was broken and put on fire. Not only this, they aborted the efforts made by community members to reconstruct the building by threatening them with dreadful consequences if they continued with the same.

They manhandled and misbehaved with school authorities. They instilled apprehensions in village people that after few years GBPSSI will take over the school from the community.

Conflict Resolution

In order to deal with these conflicts to pave way for smooth running of the school, students, teachers and parents took the lead and came out on the streets to assert for their right to education. A number of peace marches, silent protests and rallies were taken out by students of the school in order to make the parents and the community as a whole aware about the disruptions caused in their daily studies. Teachers too shared a common vision with students to fight for the right to education. They made appeal to their parents and also to the community leaders to allow them to continue studying in the same school at the same place. For this, they also observed 12 hours' fast, i.e., from 7.00 a.m. to 7.00 p.m. Thus, parents and teachers joined hands with students to make the mission successful despite non-cooperation from various powerful vested interests.

Decision-Making

All along the way a democratic rather autocratic pattern of interaction was maintained so as to facilitate open and free exchange of ideas amongst members. Active participation of members was encouraged. After repeated discussions and decisions different members assigned themselves different roles through mutual consent. They volunteered to assume different responsibilities for smooth running of the school. This led to gradual emergence of local leadership in the community group. This local leadership initially constituted of people mainly from dominant sections of the society who more than often attempted to contaminate the devout aim of the project under some false pretext. Community members opposed the long-entrenched vested interests of these people. Thus, democratic set-up helped in taking decisions in favour of the majority, i.e., in the common interest of the community members. Community members arrived at the decisions on the basis of the wholesome agreement by the majority. Members with divergent viewpoint were also given an opportunity to clarify their views. However, later, they were convinced in favour of the majority decision.

Social and Cultural Mobilisation

The mobilisation, which was swayed by the community initiative, was not only in terms of making members recognise their rights of a citizen, awakening them to emergence of non-political institutions, democratic decision-making, utilising local resources, value of education, etc., but also in terms of breaking structural hierarchies in-built in our societal system. Such mobilisation broke the gender, religion, caste and class boundaries to converge under one umbrella to achieve a common goal. Various societal stratifications in the form of males, females, rich, poor, literate, illiterate, Hindus, Muslims, higher caste as well as lower caste people willingly participated in the experiment. Women and young girls of the village experienced the taste of empowerment in the process. Thus, heterogeneous boundaries of varying types gave way to form one homogeneous group.

Besides this, mobilisation was also in the form of encouraging them to take mutual decisions independently and to make self-arrangements for conducting formal and informal meetings or cultural functions, e.g., foundation day ceremony, Independence Day, essay competition, etc. Thus, participation of this sort envisaged different social and economic groups under one hegemonic notion of a community.

Organisation Building

This was not an easy process. The experience went a long way, when it finally succeeded in building its own organisation composed of community members. In initial phases, people with ostensible intentions became linked with the experiment. However, gradually, when their vested interests were revealed, then, they were cleverly detached from the process. Organisation finally constituted of those members who had devout aims for achieving overall community development in concrete terms. They were those members who remained in the experiment even in its difficult phases and who made material and non-material contributions while relentlessly participating in its very move. Building of such an organisation to a large extent was successful in Lok Jumbish Project in Rajasthan (Govinda, 2003).

Local Level Strategies

In order to meet these objectives, a number of strategies have been developed. The major strategies that were and are still being utilised have been elucidated below in this section:

Voluntary Labour

The main strategy adopted for this community participation is contribution of voluntary labour or *shramdaan* by community members. This strategy quashes the much-acclaimed notion that participation can be maximised only by distribution of money and power to the community. Though money is important but it has to couple with non-material aspects like self-interests and need for achievement, otherwise such experiments cannot sustain. In order to attain community goals, when people contribute their labour willingly, it gives birth to feeling of belongingness and hence, their devotion, commitment and sincerity for their work increases. Such a feeling acts as a catalyst to motivate and energise them to overcome all the hurdles that come their way. Thus, by contributing voluntary labour, they automatically get their power and authority to fight for their basic rights and achieve their goals. This was one of the major features in National Literacy Mission (Mathew, 2000).

Partnership Building

To make such experiments successful, it is important to enter into venture with the existing formal/informal or government/ non-government organisations. This suffices them with double advantage. Firstly, such partners act as facilitators. When these community organisations work in harmony with their partners, the latter cooperate with them to remove potential hurdles that may otherwise come in their way. Secondly, feedback received from them can help in improving the functioning of the community set-up. Thus, one can expect an empowered society where partnership with government or non-government institutions and their participation can proceed together in future. Such a strategy was adopted in a number of experiments like the Shiksha Karmi Project, the Bihar Education Project, the Lok Jumbish Project of Rajasthan, the Rajiv Gandhi Shiksha Mission of MP, and DREP societies in various states (Raina, 2003).

Local Resource Mobilisation

The strategy to utilise the local resources is based on the supposition that a change agent, especially in the field of education, can work effectively if he/she belongs to the same locality. Therefore, by using local resources, an attempt is made to build a system of local governance for primary education from the grassroots levels. Therefore, it is important for parents and community to recognise the availability of local facilities and utilise them (Ramachandran, 2003). Such a strategy propels such experiments towards self-dependency and sustenance. In the present context, it was important to identify available local resources and make their optimum use. By adopting such a strategy, the experiment not only attained the status of self-reliance and autonomy but also acted as a safeguard to protect the experiment against probable failures. Moreover, local resources, which were obsolete since ages, gradually gained value once their relevance was realised.

Convergence

The community school is treated not only as a centre of learning but also an altruistic conduit for promoting overall village development. It is envisioned as a point of convergence where children as well as adults are taught to learn along with spreading skill training in diverse areas. Apart from formal education, informal group discussions are also held on various issues like current political scenario, sports, health and hygiene, environment, culture and national and international agenda. Dance, drama, elocution, essay competition, etc., are held on special occasions like foundation day, Independence Day, etc. Thus, community school is conceived as a platform where not only educational but also vocational, social, cultural, economic and political issues are taken into cognisance (Saxena, 2003).

Vocational Training

School is patterned in a way that along with imparting formal education, its functional relevance is also highlighted. This functional relevance is in terms of training the students for vocational skills, like cutting, tailoring, embroidery, painting, knitting, mechanics, agriculture-related skills, animal husbandry, etc. These are life-sustaining skills that equip children with certainty of secure livelihood in future. It is an extra incentive for children who can be further encouraged to pursue their studies sincerely. It was another major features of National Literacy Mission (Mathew, 2000).

Democratic Decision-Making

This strategy offers equal opportunity to all people across class, caste, religion and gender to present their views (Govinda, 2003). Each member experiences liberty not only in floating his ideas freely but also in critically analysing the views presented by others. Decision was reached only through consensus after repeated discussions. Such a strategy slashes the age-old authoritarian style of working where decisions are biased and unjust.

Thus, it proved to be a productive and fruitful strategy as whole community was fully represented in such a democratic set-up.

Community Level Organisations

The elected bodies, like village panchayats, usually constitute influential people, mainly representing dominant sections of the society. They function on basis of their vested interests using centralised mechanism for planning and decision-making. Interests of the common men are always marginalised. Thus, in order to combat the mal-intentions of these people, an attempt in the current experiment is made to set up a community level organisation represented by stakeholders. Such organisations always flag the voice of common men and work for the welfare of the community. This organisation comprises of those people who volunteer to work for the benefit of the community and therefore is actively involved in all stages of its development. Thus, in community involvement, there emerges a situation where hierarchical relationships are minimised and genuine partnerships are maximised. It is most productive when handled as a joint exercise in communication and redistribution of power, responsibility and money (Popkewitz, 1979).

Women Leadership

For the success of such experiments, it is imperative to identify and cultivate leadership qualities in women. This was also followed in Lok Jumbish Project in Rajasthan (Ramachandran, 2003) and Total Literacy Campaign in Bhojpur district of Bihar (Kantha and Narain, 2003). It is important to instil in them the confidence that if they get actively involved in community development programmes, not only be exercising their rights as a responsible citizen but also make a positive impact in the implementation of these policies and programmes by their immense and value contributions. They are encouraged to balance household responsibilities and community responsibilities, i.e., they are motivated to adopt new roles of teachers and leaders while simultaneously playing the roles of wife and mother. This women leadership is evident in the present experiment from the fact that a local woman holds the current post of school principal in the present experiment.

Peaceful Methods of Conflict Resolution

As a democratic group consists of different types of people, surfacing of disagreements and divergence in discussions is natural. These conflicts and differences are resolved using peaceful methods. Physical and verbal confrontations at both individual and group levels are avoided. Tendency to form counter-groups and factions are always thwarted. Viewpoint of every member is given importance and the group hears it patiently.

Informal Dialogues/Discussions

It is penultimate to hold discussions and meetings with community members in an informal manner. This is essential not only in rapport building but also in making people comfortable so as to actively participate in the ongoing activities without any hitch. An attempt is made to create non-evaluative and non-threatening atmosphere during group discussions and meetings, so that people are optimally productive in their thought processes.

Outcomes

Eight years of intensive deliberations made in the area have borne major outcomes, both positive as well as negative. In a way, these outcomes appraise our performance during our tenure from a scratch to a scoop.

- Local level organisation has emerged in the form of women as real stakeholders for the development of community school.
- The target of cent per cent enrolment of girl children in the village has been achieved.

- Girls in these schools are passing out with flying colours. The past school record has shown that girls are doing equally well in school as in case of boys. This is evident from the fact that up till now 36 girls have cleared high school examination from this school (2000-2005), majority with second division marks. Six girls from the school are currently pursuing their graduation. This itself is setting a positive image in village regarding girls' education.
- Girls after acquiring education are not just limiting their knowledge to their own self but also are disseminating it others, who are deprived of this valuable asset. For instance, educated girls have taken the initiative to teach other children in schools. They have also stepped in the era of e-literacy where girls after being trained in computer use for about three weeks at GBPSSI are teaching other fellow students. In addition, they are also taking pains in providing basic education to adult members in the village. Apart from imparting formal education, they hold informal discussions to create awareness amongst the masses regarding health, hygiene, environment, culture, political turmoil, industrialisation, mechanisation, commercial farming, etc.
- Their educational robustness has increased their need for achievement. They now aim for gaining economic independence and financial security. Nature of their role models has undergone change. They not only include their female family members as their ideals in life but also females who have excelled in various fields at the national front, e.g., Kiran Bedi, Indira Gandhi, Kalpana Chawla, etc. In general, they are more influenced by the life of Kalpana Chawla as she hailed from a small village in Haryana. Therefore, they feel that they can also reach that zenith of dignity and status if deliberations are made in an appropriate direction.
- Education has upgraded the awareness of young girls and women about their health, hygiene and environment.

- Girls after attaining education have gained confidence and assertiveness in managing the school. As real stakeholders they are actively involved in school-related discussions and meetings. They exhibit determination and strong will in the running of the school. In no circumstances, they want the school to close down. They want it to continue, with or without structural or financial support. This is so because education has improved their quality of life, which may become worse if they are deprived of it.
- To sustain the school, these girls, who have always been confined to their families or neighbourhood, have taken out rallies and peace march, shouted slogans and made appeals to their parents and community people in favour of the right to education and raising funds. Additionally, they are also culturally active. Cultural activities are frequently held in the school like celebration of foundation day, Independence Day, annual function, dance, drama, folk song, essay competition, elocution, etc. This has instilled further confidence and self-reliance in them.
- There has also been change in the attitude of parents. Those parents, who never valued education and harboured no faith in its functional relevance, gradually realised its relevance and validity. They now extend this privilege not only to their sons but also to their daughters and hold equal aspirations for both of them.
- The education bug has not only spread amongst the children and their parents but the society as a whole. Society is undergoing fast transformation not only in the field of education but also in related fields like agriculture, health, environment, industrialisation, etc.
- In eight years time span, the community school has become self-sustaining. Through trial and error method it has learnt to solve its own administrative and study-related problems. It adopts peaceful way of resolving conflicts. It now relies less on outside community support for

overcoming its hindrances. It gets no financial assistance from outside the community but depends on fee paid by children and donations made by community members.

- The school has also been successful in entering into partnership with a number of organisations like village panchayats, education department, health department, local administration, GBPSSI, etc.
- Local resources like panchayat bhawan, barren land surrounding the school, local educated village youths, aged and other people willing to make voluntary contributions have been linked with the experiment. Voluntary contributions in the form of labour, money and time (i.e., attending meetings, giving suggestions and feedback, cooperation, etc.) have been forwarded as and when required.

Learnings

The outcomes highlighted as above form the basis of future learnings for both the community-based organisations and government and non-government agencies. These learnings draw our attention to mistakes made as well as the way in which developmental milestones were achieved in the experimental process. These form the guidelines for pursuing other community-based programmes in future:

- Building an informal relationship with community members is an integral part of any community participation. Until and unless such a relationship is developed, take off of any experiment is not possible. Such relationships play a critical role in bringing people from diverse social strata closer and united to stand for a common cause. It helps people in analysing their own basic needs and raising their consciousness to denounce their prescribed form of lifestyle so as to realise their actual needs. This informal mode adopted in the initial phases should be maintained throughout the conduct of the experiment.

- Minimum social support at local level is critical for effective implementation of any community project. This support can be in terms of a significant number of local people agreeing with the aims and objectives of the project, endorsement of influential people and easy accessibility to local resources. Hence, minimum amount of support at certain levels is essential for the success of any community-based programme.
- Local level strategies, like voluntary labour, partnership building, convergence and peaceful method of conflict resolution, are effective in mobilising the community for devout aim of such experiments.
- The democratic pattern of interaction adopted in the experiment provided equal platform to everyone to articulate their ideas freely. The subaltern view was given equal importance as the elite view. This helped in getting rich and diverse feedback from different strata of the society. Moreover, such a system worked as an internal check on the fellow members, i.e., each member had liberty to check another if they deviated from the norms. Therefore, democratic-egalitarian framework is worked out to achieve the aims of any community-based experiment in a realistic way.
- Female participation can be increased and their empowerment can further be strengthened if policies for development are partially biased in favour of females. This instils in females the confidence to assert for their rights and evolves in them high-level positive future aspirations. Moreover, when females are afforded treatment at par with their male counterparts, the probability of gender difference is automatically reduced.
- Implementation of the policies and programmes in rural areas is rarely followed by a systematic documentation. This creates problems in keeping track of the level of progress achieved in these schemes. Therefore, to make these schemes more functional and inclusive, it is

imperative that all the major and minor proceedings should be documented in written form.

- Support from outside organisation, as a facilitator is equally essential. For this, it is important to develop rapport and informal relationship with community members. They should be encouraged to be assertive in articulating their ideas and holding optimistic attitude. Continuous and close monitoring should be followed so that faith and confidence instilled in the people is not weakened but is further strengthened. It requires frequent personal supervision and active patient listening to the woes of community members. Community members should be given periodic feedback regarding the nature and level of contributions made by them during the entire conduct of the experiment, i.e., about their status of progress, achievements, mistakes, miscalculations and difficulties encountered.
- The administration has to play a pro-active role in sustaining the momentum. It needs to create a supportive environment comprising people with commitment and vision. If people are the most precious resource, demoralisation through administrative red tape, suspicion and disrespect has the potential to kill their initiative. Therefore, the role of administration should be made more functional and effective.

References

Govinda, R. and R. Diwan (2003), 'Introduction: Emerging Issues and Practices'. In R. Govinda and R. Diwan (eds.), *Community Participation and Empowerment in Primary Education*, New Delhi: Sage Publications.

Govinda, R. (2003), 'Dynamics of Decentralized Management in Primary Education: Policy and Practice in Rajasthan and Madhya

Pradesh'. In R. Govinda and R. Diwan (eds.), *Community Participation and Empowerment in Primary Education*, New Delhi: Sage Publications.

Kantha, V.K. and D. Narain (2003), 'Dynamics of Community Mobilization in a Fragmented Turbulent State'. In R. Govinda and R. Diwan (eds.), *Community Participation and Empowerment in Primary Education*, New Delhi: Sage Publications.

Mathew, A. (2000), 'Indian Engagement with Adult Education and Literacy', in *EFA Assessment* 2000, New Delhi: NIEPA and MHRD.

Popkewitz, Thomas S. (1979), 'School and Symbolic Uses of Community Participation'. In Carl A. Grant (ed.), *Community Participation in Education*, Toronto: Allyn and Bacon Inc.

Raina, V. (2003), 'Making Sense of Community Participation: Comparing School Education and Watershed Development'. In R. Govinda and R. Diwan (eds.), *Community Participation and Empowerment in Primary Education*, New Delhi: Sage Publications.

Ramachandran, V. and H. Sethi, (2000), 'Rajasthan Shiksha Karmi: An Overall Appraisal'. Desk Study Commissioned by Sida, Embassy of Sweden, New Delhi.

Ramachandran, V. (2003), 'Community Participation and Empowerment in Primary Education: Discussion of Experiences from Rajasthan'. In R. Govinda and R. Diwan (eds.), *Community Participation and Empowerment in Primary Education*, New Delhi: Sage Publications.

Saxena, S. (2003), 'Community Participation and Literacy: Beyond Semantics'. In R. Govinda and R. Diwan (eds.), *Community Participation and Empowerment in Primary Education*, New Delhi: Sage Publications.

7

Does Gender Bias Really Hold Against Girl Child Education?

An Analysis of the Perception of Urban Poor in Allahabad City

S.K. Pant

The processes of urbanisation and industrialisation have, no doubt, pushed the economy of the country into a higher pedestal of development. The country has also, in the process, heralded many unforeseen socio-economic angularities in the form of poverty, malnutrition, rural to urban process of migration, etc. (Swaminathan, 1996). These socio-economic angularities have also escalated as the rate of industrialisation and development has picked up in the ensuing plan periods thereby putting a greater amount of stress on the fragile urban resources.

The rural migrants, who later become part of urban poor, initially face a hostile environment in the cities and being unable to meet the high urban cost, are forced to move to those places which are bereft of basic essential and sanitary services and which are basically not fit for human habitations (Singh and Pothen, 1982). This, incidentally, also lays the genesis for the formation and proliferation of slums. The urban poor, on account of their poor literacy and vocational skill status, fail to get employment in the urban organised sector and are eventually drawn towards its urban informal sector. This sector, on account of its diversified nature, offers a variety of jobs and has been playing a significant and critical role in supporting and supplementing the urban economy. However, as the wage structure, service conditions and remuneration are very meagre, they fail to support their large families. So, in order to supplement their household income, they, at times, work at many places and often deploy their whole family. This also lays the foundation of the problem of schooling of their children in general and girl child in particular. Education, in the process, is thus relegated to lower position, as survival for them becomes the foremost thing (Singh and D'Souza, 1980; Singh and Kishore, 1993; Bhattacharya, 1996; Reddy and Reddy, 1992).

The processes of urbanisation and industrialisation have also adversely affected the age-old traditional family structure in the urban areas to a great extent. The emphasis these days is increasingly being placed on working of both the husband and wife, their dependence on the urban poor migrant class is steadily increasing which is unlikely to get diminished in the near foreseeable future. Thus, it could be said that the urban poor migrant class is likely to play an increasingly important role in sustaining the urban economy and would become a force to reckon with.

While the male workers do various kinds of odd jobs, which include working as hawkers, vendors, mechanics in auto or cycle repair shops and helpers in roadside *dhabas*, restaurants, etc. The females either work independently or with urban households where they do various kinds of activities like cleaning of utensils, washing clothes or even cooking and many a time looking after the younger siblings of the urban families. It is their interaction with urban families that exposes them to a whole set of new urban values and culture, which they had not encountered in their earlier life.

It is expected that this exposure, on a regular and sustained basis, is likely to usher change in their perception and thinking on account of which they may start to send their children in general and girl child in particular to schools. It is against this backdrop that an attempt has been made to study to what extent the perception of urban poor households changes as a result of their interaction and exposure to urban households. An attempt has also been made to see whether the gender bias is practised among the urban poor classes in the schooling of their children.

Study Area and Magnitude of Slum Population

Allahabad is the fifth largest city in Uttar Pradesh. The decadal growth rate of 34 per cent (from 6,42,420 in 1981 to 8,58,213 in 1991) perhaps makes it one of the most rapidly growing cities in the state and tenth in the country as a whole. This rapid growth in population has also been partly on account of immigration from rural areas and the high fertility rate which was estimated to be 4.2 children per women in the city, which was exceptionally high as compared with the national fertility average of 3.4 children per women (Bose, 1996).

In Allahabad, according to the Municipal Corporation statistics, an estimated population of 2 lakh lived in 125 authorised slums in 1993. However, with the number of authorised slums going to 185, the slum population also registered an increase and was estimated to be 3.34 lakh in 2000, thereby recording a whopping 67 per cent increase in seven years' time period. Thus, the proportion of slum dwellers living in authorised slums comes close to 38 per cent of the city's current projected population.

For the purpose of the present study, these slums were classified into three categories as large, medium and small . The classification was based on their demographic size. While small slums were identified as those where the inhabiting population less than 2,500, medium size of slums were those where the size of population varied between 2,500 and 4,999 and the large slums housed the population of 5,000 and above.

Table 1
Classification of Slums

Category	*Number*
Small	148 (80.0)
Medium	32 (17.3)
Large	5 (2.7)
Total	185 (100.0)

Note: Figures in parentheses denote percentage.

Source: DUDA, Allahabad, 2002.

The perusal of the distribution of slums shows that smaller slums had an overwhelming majority, accounting for 80 per cent of the total whereas the share of medium and large slums was worked out to be about 17 per cent and 3 per cent respectively. Further, the District Urban Development Authority (DUDA) also classifies these slums as A, B and C in terms of facilities they possess. While the 'A' category corresponds to those slums which are yet to be provided basic infrastructural facilities like link roads, health services, drinking water, sanitation etc., the 'B' category slums are those where these services have been partially provided and 'C' category of slums are those slums where these services have been provided to the point of saturation. Therefore, according to this classification, there were about 66 slums belonging to 'C' category, 52 slums were from 'B' category and remaining 62 slums figured in the 'A' category. In tabular form it could be presented as under:

Table 2
Classification of Slums

Category	*Number*
A	62 (33.5)
B	57 (30.8)
C	66 (35.7)
Total	185 (100.0)

Note: Figures in parentheses denote percentage.

Source: DUDA, Allahabad, 2000.

In view of the time and resource constraint, it was decided to restrict the size of sample to two hundred households only, to be selected from the two slums. These slums were randomly picked. Further, in these sample slums, the households were classified on the basis of their nature of work. The first group consisted of those set of households, who were working or had the opportunity to work with the urban families, while the second group consisted of those households who were not associated with urban families. The comparison of these two groups, on the cross-sectional framework, would provide an opportunity to study and analyse their perception towards urban issues and values.

In the course of collection of data, five types of schedules, viz., school schedules, student schedules, household schedules, programme functionary schedules and village schedules were prepared. These schedules were deliberately kept open ended to enable the respondents to react and express their views freely.

The two slums, namely, Alopibagh and Mehdauri, were randomly selected from the list provided by DUDA. Incidentally, both of these slums belonged to the small category. In Alopibagh, about 1,550 households resided whereas Mehdauri accommodated a total of 1,936 households.

Though both the slums were of smaller size, however, they differed markedly in their nature, resources and period of existence. While Alopibagh slum was an older slum, which was located well inside the city, Mehdauri slum, on the other hand, was earlier a village, which later got accommodated to the city as it expanded. Mehdauri lies on the northern outskirts of the city close the Ganges, while Alopibagh is situated just east of the city.

One hundred families each from each of the two slums were randomly selected.

Analysis of the Data

Before analysing the perception of urban poor households towards the education and educating their children, an attempt has also been made to study the educational profile of the households. The education level has been scaled into eight distinct categories, viz., illiterate, literate, below primary, up to middle, up to high school, up to graduation, graduation and above and technical/professional qualification. Further, households were also broadly classified on the basis of the castes.

The study of caste- and gender-wise educational level of households in Alopibagh slum shows that of the total of 699 persons, over 65 per cent were illiterate, about 2 per cent were literate, around 18 per cent had acquired literacy upto primary or middle, while another 7 per cent had studied upto high school. The sample also contained around 0.1 per cent of the households that also possessed technical skills. The caste-wise analysis reveals that the incidence of illiteracy was higher (over 73 per cent) among OBC households while its proportion was about 65 per cent in SCs.

Likewise, the study of literacy profile of the sample households in Mehdauri slum show that of the total of 611 persons, the proportion of illiterates was about 61 per cent, which was lesser than that of Alopibagh slum. Similarly, in other categories of literates, the proportion of literates was much higher than that of Alopibagh. However, the study of inter-caste literacy pattern shows that, here too, the highest incidence of illiteracy was found among OBC population, followed by the Muslims and the SCs. Likewise, the proportion of literates was also higher in SC population while it was least in OBCs.

The study further shows that the sample contained an overwhelming proportion (over 63 per cent) of illiterates, while the proportion of persons technically qualified was least (0.2 per cent). It also shows that as one moves from lower classes to higher classes, the proportion of population acquiring higher level of literacy subsequently falls (see Table 3).

The perception of people is also influenced by many other supplementary factors like the enrolment level of students, state of educational institution, the resources it possess and the quality of teaching it offers. An attempt has also been made to study these.

Caste-wise Enrolment Pattern

Though Alopibagh slum did not have any schooling facilities within its own periphery, Mehdauri slum did have one, which was being managed by the missionaries. Therefore, for studying the enrolment pattern of students, two primary schools that were operating in the periphery of Alopibagh slum and were managed by the District Education Board were purposely chosen with the premise that these schools would draw their clientele largely from the slum areas. However, these schools also contained some proportion of students from other habitations that were located in their vicinity. Thus, the total number of schools selected in the two sample slums was three. The information regarding the enrolment of students was obtained from the records of these schools.

The perusal of the enrolment pattern of the students, in the total sample, shows that in all a total of 567 students were enrolled in these schools, of which over 21 per cent belonged to class I, 31 per cent to class II, over 17 per cent to class III, over 19 per cent to class IV and about 10 per cent to class V. It could

Table 3

Caste-wise Classification of Enrolled Children in Sample Schools

Classes	Alopibagh School No. 1 and School No. 2				Mehdauri School No. 3				Total All the Three Schools				
	SC	OBC	Others	Total	SC	OBC	Muslims	Total	SC	OBC	Muslims	Others	Total
1st	68 (25.2)	23 (34.3)	15 (18.1)	106 (25.2)	6 (15.4)	6 (15.0)	6 (8.8)	18 (12.2)	74 (23.9)	29 (27.1)	6 (8.8)	15 (18.1)	124 (21.9)
2nd	77 (28.5)	19 (28.4)	18 (21.7)	114 (27.1)	22 (56.4)	10 (25.0)	30 (44.1)	62 (42.2)	99 (20.0)	29 (27.1)	30 (44.1)	18 (21.7)	176 (31.0)
3rd	45 (16.7)	13 (19.4)	18 (21.7)	76 (18.1)	3 (7.7)	3 (7.5)	17 (25.0)	23 (15.6)	48 (15.5)	16 (14.9)	17 (25.0)	18 (21.7)	99 (17.5)
4th	63 (23.3)	-	16 (19.3)	79 (18.8)	6 (15.4)	16 (40.0)	9 (13.2)	31 (21.1)	69 (22.3)	16 (14.9)	9 (13.2)	16 (19.3)	110 (19.4)
5th	17 (6.3)	12 (17.9)	16 (19.3)	45 (10.7)	2 (5.1)	5 (12.5)	6 (8.8)	13 (8.8)	19 (6.1)	17 (16.0)	6 (8.8)	16 (19.3)	58 (10.2)
Total	270 (100.0)	67 (100.0)	83 (100.0)	420 (100.0)	39 (100.0)	40 (100.0)	68 (100.0)	147 (100.0)	309 (100.0)	107 (100.0)	68 (100.0)	83 (100.0)	567 (100.0)

Note: Figures in parentheses denote column percentage.

Source:. School registers of the sample schools.

be seen that from the time the student got enrolled in class I to the time he finally passed out in class V, the overall dropout rate was an astonishing 17 per cent.

The caste-wise enrolment pattern further shows that there has been a gradual decline in the level of enrolment as one move from class I to class V. The two caste groups where the dropout level was higher were SCs and OBCs where about 17 per cent and 11 per cent of the students respectively dropped by the time they completed primary level education. However, the enrolment level in 'others' category that largely comprised the Muslim households remained by and large stable.

The comparison of enrolment pattern of students in the two slums reveals that though the intake capacity of schools in Alopibagh slum was more (420 students) than that of Mehdauri slum (147 students), their overall dropout rate was over 14 per cent against 3.4 per cent witnessed in Mehdauri slum. The two caste groups that experienced this fall were the SCs (over 10 per cent) and the OBCs (with 2.5 per cent), while the dropout rate in the Muslims was nil.

Thus, the analysis clearly brings to light that the dropout rate of the students in SC category, for both the slums, was exceptionally high which may be on account of the fact that education has yet to find a place among their households. Secondly, the school at Mehdauri slum was being managed more efficiently than the schools at Alopibagh slum (see Table 4.)

Gender-wise Enrolment Pattern

Like caste, gender is also an important aspect of studying the enrolment pattern of the students. The study of enrolment pattern of student on the basis of their gender shows that though the overall dropout rate of students in schools for the whole sample was about 12 per cent, it was exceptionally high (around 14 per cent) for boys and about 10 per cent for girls. The study also brings to the fore another interesting yet important dimension, i.e., if we observe the enrolment of

Table 4

Class- and Gender-wise Distribution of Enrolled Children in Sample Schools

Classes	Alopibagh Slum School No. 1 and School No. 2			Mehdauri Slum School No. 3			Total Slum All Three Schools		
	Boys	Girls	Total	Boys	Girls	Total	Boys	Girls	Total
1st	55 (27.4)	51 (23.3)	106 (25.2)	12 (14.8)	6 (9.1)	18 (12.2)	67 (23.8)	57 (20.0)	124 (21.9)
2nd	50 (24.9)	64 (29.2)	114 (27.1)	33 (40.7)	29 (43.9)	62 (42.2)	83 (29.4)	93 (32.6)	176 (31.0)
3rd	31 (15.4)	45 (20.5)	76 (18.1)	11 (13.6)	12 (18.2)	23 (15.6)	42 (14.9)	57 (20.0)	99 (17.5)
4th	44 (21.9)	35 (16.0)	79 (18.8)	18 (22.2)	13 (19.7)	31 (21.1)	62 (22.0)	48 (16.8)	110 (9.4)
5th	21 (10.4)	24 (11.0)	45 (10.7)	7 (8.6)	6 (9.1)	13 (8.8)	28 (9.9)	30 (10.5)	58 (10.2)
Total	201 (100.0)	219 (100.0)	420 (100.0)	81 (100.0)	66 (100.0)	147 (100.0)	282 (100.0)	285 (100.0)	567 (100.0)

Note: Figures in parentheses denote column percentage.

Source: Field data.

students from class I onwards upto say class III or class IV, we find the dropout rate to be quite marginal, however, in class V the dropout rate suddenly shoots up. The gender-wise comparison shows that the decline in the case of boys has been of much higher order than in case of the girls. The high dropout rate among the boys may be attributed to the following two factors: (a) their role in supporting and supplementing the household income, and secondly, the inability of the households to appreciate the importance of education. The study also shows that, on the enrolment front, the girls were marginally ahead of the boys. However, there is a note of caution, which must be exercised before making a generalisation that the total strength of girls and boys between the age of 6 and 14 years was 129 and 170 respectively. Even if we assume that all children of the slums were attending school, which is a too far-fetched proposition, then also the strength shown in the school register was much higher than the strength of the slum children, which implies that the schools were also attracting students from the other localities.

The study also shows that if we compare the enrolment pattern of students in the two samples slums, the level of dropout rate in Alopibagh slum was more than four times than what was observed in the Mehdauri slum. What was quite interesting to note is that while the dropout rate for girls in Alopibagh was over 12 per cent, it was quite marginal in Mehdauri, which may largely be on account of the fact that the schools in Mehdauri was being better managed (see Table 4).

Involvement of Households in Child's Education

The study of the involvement pattern of sample households in the education of their children forms a crucial component in the study of educational profile of the region. If the involvement of the household is stated to be high, it is clearly manifested in other aspects of education, i.e., in the form of high enrolment of their children, high level of attendance in school and correspondingly low dropout rate etc.

For studying the involvement pattern of urban poor households in the education of their 10 children, children from each of the school in the two slums were randomly selected. Thus, the sample contained a total of 30 children from the three schools. They were administered a set of questionnaire that reflected the involvement level of their parents in their studies.

The questions that the children were asked were whether their parents had made arrangements for their tuition at home, whether the school had given homework on regular basis, whether it was checked at home by their parents or senior members of the family and did their parent ever write to school regarding the homework or the school ever complained to their parents about it. The perusal of the responses presented a very disappointing picture as over 96 per cent of the children stated that no arrangement of tuition was being made by their parents, over 56 per cent complained that no homework was being given by the school and even a higher proportion (over 65 per cent) confessed that their parents did not bother to check their homework at home or ever gave suggestions from their side regarding homework to the school authorities.

Likewise, the comparison of students' responses in the two slums provides an interesting yet contrasting picture. In Alopibagh slum, a majority of the children (from 80 per cent to 100 per cent) from both the schools stated complete absence of any sort of involvement of parents whether it was for arranging of tuition to checking of homework or even writing suggestions to the school authorities. However, in Mehdauri slum, with the exception of arrangement of tuition, the parents were involved in almost every activity, which may be on account of the fact that the school was being managed efficiently and often involved the parents into its working. The inability of the parents to arrange for the tuition could partly be on account of their poor economic condition.

Further, the lack of involvement of parents in Alopibagh could also be on account of the strategic location of the place that offered potential for a variety of petty employment

Table 5

Parents Involvement in Child's Education at Home

Level of Involvement	*Alopibagh*				*Mehdauri*		*Total Sample*	
	School No. 1		*School No. 2*		*School No. 3*		*All Three Schools*	
	Yes	*No*	*Yes*	*No*	*Yes*	*No*	*Yes*	*No*
Have made arrangement of tuition at home	-	10 (100.0)	-	10 (100.0)	1 (10.0)	9 (90.0)	1 (3.33)	29 (96.7)
Whether school gives the homework	1 (10.0)	9 (90.0)	2 (20.0)	8 (80.0)	10 (100.0)	-	13 (43.3)	17 (56.7)
Whether it is checked at home by parents	-	10 (100.0)	-	10 (100.0)	10 (100.0)	-	10 (33.3)	20 (66.7)
Do you ever get suggestion about homework	-	10 (100.0)	-	10 (100.0)	10 (100.0)	-	10 (33.3)	20 (66.7)
Total respondents	10 (100.0)		10 (100.0)		10 (100.0)		30 (100.0)	

Note: Figures in parentheses denote column percentage.

Source: Field data.

opportunities where children could be deployed, poor organisation and management of the schools and the inability of the parents to recognise and accept education as an important instrument of change (see Table 5).

Distribution of Resources in Sample Schools

The enrolment level of the students in the school, to a large extent, is also guided by the fact that how much resources or facilities the school has to offer to its students. It is generally observed that in the absence of some of the basic facilities like blackboard, reading and writing material, playing kit, display chart, mats for all children, drinking water facility, toilet for girls, etc., often discourages the parents to send their children to school, whereas if the school offers these facilities the parents are encouraged to send their children. The study also makes an attempt to study the resource pattern in the sample schools. The resources identified, ranged from availability of blackboard, chalk, duster, books, globe, maps, display charts, playing kit, ball etc. to drinking water facility, playground and toilet for girls. Further, the validation of these resources was done at the two levels – by undertaking physical verification and also by randomly schooling 10 students from each of these schools and validating the fact from them.

The facilities have further been scaled in three distinct categories as poorly equipped, moderately equipped and fully equipped. The poorly equipped facilities denote their complete absence, fully equipped refers to their 100 per cent availability, whereas moderate level falls between these two categories. The perusal of responses shows that the schools were poorly equipped in matters of possessing globe, display chart, playing kit, dustbins, playground and toilet facilities for girls, moderately equipped in the field of providing books, blackboard, chalk, duster and fully equipped in matters of having school bell, mats for all students and drinking water facility.

Table 6

Distribution of Facilities/Resources in Sample Schools

Resources	*Alopibagh*				*Mehdauri*		*Total Sample*	
	School No. 1		*School No. 2*		*School No. 3*		*All Three Schools*	
	Yes	*No*	*Yes*	*No*	*Yes*	*No*	*Yes*	*No*
Blackboard	10 (100.0)	-	-	10 (100.0)	10 (100.0)	-	20 (66.7)	10 (33.3)
Chalk	4 (40.0)	6 (60.0)	-	10 (100.0)	10 (100.0)	-	14 (46.7)	16 (53.3)
Duster	4 (40.0)	6 (60.0)	-	10 (100.0)	10 (100.0)	-	14 (46.7)	16 (53.3)
Books for reading	4 (40.0)	6 (60.0)	-	10 (100.0)	10 (100.0)	-	14 (46.7)	16 (53.3)
Globe	-	10 (100.0)	-	10 (100.0)	-	10 (100.0)	-	30 (100.0)
Map	-	10 (100.0)	-	10 (100.0)	-	10 (100.0)	-	30 (100.0)
Display chart	-	10 (100.0)	-	10 (100.0)	-	10 (100.0)	-	30 (100.0)
Playing kit	-	10 (100.0)	-	10 (100.0)	-	10 (100.0)	-	30 (100.0)

Contd...

Contd...

School bell	10 (100.0)	-	10 (00.0)	-	10 (100.0)	-	30 (100.0)	-
Mats for all students	10 (100.0)	-	10 (100.0)	-	10 (100.0)	-	30 (100.0)	-
Drinking water facility	10 (100.0)	-	10 (100.0)	-	-	10 (100.0)	10 (33.3)	20 (66.7)
Dustbin	-	10 (100.0)	-	10 (100.0)	-	10 (100.0)	-	20 (66.7)
Playground	-	10 (100.0)	-	10 (100.0)	-	10 (100.0)	-	30 (100.0)
Toilet for girls	-	10 (100.0)	-	10 (100.0)	-	10 (100.0)	-	30 (100.0)
Total respondents	10 (100.0)		10 (100.0)		10 (100.0)		30 (100.0)	

Note: Figures in parentheses denote column percentage.

Source: Field data.

The comparison of facilities, in the two sample slums, shows that the school at Mehdauri slum was marginally better equipped than the two schools at Alopibagh, though it also lacked in many aspects. However, whatever facilities or resources it had, their level was 100 per cent. The study also shows that the school at Alopibagh, though managed by District Education Board, lacked in most of the resources and with the exception of school bell, mats for students and drinking water facilities, in the majority of cases it was poorly equipped (see Table 6).

Households' Perceptions

Benefits of Education

The study of the perception of households on the benefits accruing from education helps in analysing the performance of educational institutions in the right perspectives. It is believed that if there an overwhelming consensus or even positive acceptance amongst the households on the benefits of education, then the education scenario of the concerned place or region brightens up.

The perusal of the perception of sample households shows that over 47 per cent of them had accepted that education helped in getting jobs or in becoming self-dependent. About 38 per cent of the households stated that education helped them to guard against cheating and fraud, and thus making them socially more conscious. Similarly, over 12 per cent of the households agreed that education helped them while travelling or in writing letters. However, the sample also contained about 7 per cent of the households who did not agree that education was helpful to them in any way.

The study of inter-caste perception for the whole sample shows that the proportion of SC households (over 51 per cent), who agreed with the view that education was helpful in getting jobs or in becoming self-dependent, was much higher than the proportion of OBC households (about 36 per cent), while the proportion of OBC households (over 41 per cent) was higher than the SC category households (36 per cent) in subscribing to the view that education was helpful in guarding against cheating or fraud. Similarly, over 15 per cent of the households from SC also agreed that education was helpful while travelling or in reading and writing. In the case of Muslims, the study demonstrates that there was an overwhelming consensus on the role of education in helping in getting jobs or in becoming self-dependent and about 50 per cent of them also agreed that education helped them to guard against cheating or fraud while an equal number of the households felt that education had an important role while travelling or in letter writing. However, there were about 17 per cent of the OBC households who also considered education to be futile.

The study of the perception of the households in the two slums shows that while about 42 per cent of the households in Alopibagh agreed that education helped in preventing against cheating or fraud, its proportion was a little subdued at 33 per cent in Mehdauri slum. However, there were over 56 per cent of the households in Mehdauri who supported the view that education was helpful in getting jobs or in becoming self-dependent while its proportion dwindled to 38 per cent in Alopibagh. The study also shows that there were over 20 per cent of the households in Mehdauri slum who accepted the fact that education was helpful while travelling or in letter writing. What came as a pleasant surprise was that none of the households in Mehdauri slum subscribed to the view that education's role was futile in promoting socio-economic activities, though about 14 per cent of the households in Alopibagh slum were critical of its role.

Thus, the inter-caste study of the responses reveals that the households in both the slums, by and large, agreed on two views about education, the first being that education was helpful in guarding against cheating or fraud and the second in becoming self-dependent. Further, another 23 per cent of the households in Mehdauri slum also shared the view that

Table 7

Perception of Households on Benefits of Education

Responses	*Alopibagh*			*Mehdauri*				*Total Sample*			
	SC	OBC	Total	SC	OBC	Muslims	Total	SC	OBC	Muslims	Total
Guards against cheating/socially more aware of fraudulence	28 (41.8)	15 (42.9)	43 (42.2)	26 (31.7)	7 (38.9)	1 (50.0)	34 (33.3)	54 (36.2)	22 (41.5)	1 (50.0)	77 (37.7)
Helps to develop right perspectives	9 (13.4)	5 (14.3)	14 (13.7)	12 (14.6)	-	-	12 (11.8)	21 (14.1)	5 (9.4)	-	26 (12.7)
Helps getting jobs/making self-dependent	28 (41.8)	11 (31.4)	39 (38.2)	48 (58.5)	8 (44.4)	2 (100.0)	58 (56.9)	76 (51.0)	19 (35.8)	2 (100.0)	97 (47.5)
Helps in business	9 (13.4)	-	9 (8.8)	3 (3.7)	3 (16.7)	-	6 (5.9)	12 (8.1)	3 (5.7)	-	15 (7.4)
Helps to understand mathematics	6 (8.5)	1 (2.9)	7 (6.9)	-	-	-	-	6 (4.0)	1 (1.9)	-	7 (3.4)
Helps in reading and writing	1 (1.5)	5 (14.3)	6 (6.9)	-	-	-	-	1 (0.7)	5 (9.4)	-	6 (2.9)
Helps in travelling, letter writing	4 (6.0)	-	4 (3.9)	19 (23.2)	1 (5.6)	1 (50.0)	21 (20.6)	23 (15.4)	1 (1.9)	1 (50.0)	25 (12.3)
Education is always rewarding	3 (4.5)	-	3 (2.9)	1 (1.2)	1 (5.6)	-	2 (1.9)	4 (2.7)	1 (1.9)	-	5 (2.5)

Contd...

Contd...

Helps in developing country	2 (3.0)	-	2 (1.9)	2 (2.4)	-	-	2 (1.9)	4 (2.7)	-	-	4 (2.0)
No benefits	5 (7.5)	9 (25.7)	14 (13.7)	-	-	-	-	5 (3.4)	9 (17.0)	-	14 (6.9)
No responses	1 (1.5)	-	1 (0.9)	2 (2.4)	-	-	2 (1.9)	3 (2.0)	-	-	3 (1.5)
Total respondents	67 (100.0)	35 (100.0)	102 (100.0)	82 (100.0)	18 (100.0)	2 (100.0)	102 (100.0)	149 (100.0)	53 (100.0)	2 (100.0)	204 (100.0)

Note: Figures in parentheses denotes column percentage.

Source: Field data.

education was helpful in travels or in letter writing while its proportion was quite insignificant (about 4 per cent) in Alopibagh slum. Similarly, over 25 per cent of the OBC households in Alopibagh were also critical of education's role (see Table 7).

Role of NGOs/Governmental Organisations for Promoting Schools

The study amply demonstrated that the performance of educational institutions, in the sample, has been quite disappointing as has been witnessed by their high dropout rates. It also shows that how poorly these institutions were equipped in the matter of providing reading and learning materials to the students. All these events make these institutions a very unattractive and uninspiring site that discourages the households to send their wards to study. Hence, it was felt necessary to pose the question to the sample households on what they feel about the current state of education and how could it be made more attractive so that the households are tempted to send their children to seek enrolment there.

The study reveals that over 34 per cent of the households felt that for promoting schooling among urban poor, provision of economic assistance and free education needs to be given to the children, whereas another 27 per cent of them felt that books and copies should be distributed among the children free of cost. Similarly, over 37 per cent of the households pleaded exemption of fees and about 16 per cent observed that provision of dress for students should be made by the school.

Similarly, the analysis of inter-caste perception shows that a majority of the households from all castes, whether it be SC or OBC or Muslims, had agreed on three major causes: (a) economic assistance needs to be provided to school children, (b) there should be free distribution of books and copies, and (c) provision of exemption of fees for the urban poor children. The study of the perception of households in the two slums shows an interesting state on prioritising the issues. While a

Table 8

Perception of Households in Role of NGOs/Governmental Organisations for Promoting Schooling Children

Responses	*Alopibagh*			*Mehdauri*				*Total Sample*			
	SC	*OBC*	*Total*	*SC*	*OBC*	*Muslims*	*Total*	*SC*	*OBC*	*Muslims*	*Total*
Provision for dresses	13 (9.4)	1 (2.9)	14 (13.7)	11 (13.4)	7 (38.9)	1 (50.0)	19 (18.6)	24 (16.1)	8 (15.1)	1 (50.0)	33 (16.2)
Provision for exemption of fees	18 (26.9)	3 (8.6)	21 (20.6)	14 (17.1)	9 (50.0)	1 (50.0)	24 (23.5)	32 (21.5)	12 (22.6)	1 (50.0)	45 (22.1)
Provision for medicines	2 (3.0)	-	2 (2.0)	2 (2.4)	3 (16.7)	1 (50.0)	6 (5.9)	4 (2.7)	3 (5.7)	1 (50.0)	8 (3.9)
Provision for refreshment	4 (6.0)	5 (14.3)	9 (8.8)	3 (3.7)	7 (38.9)	2 (100.0)	12 (11.8)	7 (4.7)	12 (22.6)	2 (100.0)	21 (10.3)
Economic assistance and free education to poor children	25 (37.3)	8 (22.9)	33 (32.4)	21 (25.6)	15 (83.3)	2 (100.0)	38 (37.3)	46 (30.9)	23 (43.9)	2 (100.0)	71 (34.8)
Provision of books and copies	21 (31.3)	3 (8.6)	24 (23.5)	17 (20.7)	15 (83.3)	-	32 (31.4)	38 (25.5)	18 (34.0)	-	56 (27.5)
Provision of scholarship	7 (10.4)	-	7 (6.9)	6 (7.3)	18 (100.0)	2 (100.0)	26 (25.5)	13 (8.7)	18 (34.0)	2 (100.0)	33 (16.2)
Location of school be in their locality	8 (11.9)	1 (2.9)	9 (8.8)	3 (3.7)	5 (27.8)	2 (100.0)	10 (9.8)	11 (7.4)	6 (11.3)	2 (100.0)	19 (9.3)

Contd...

Contd...

Education be vocation oriented	1 (1.5)	3 (8.6)	4 (3.9)	3 (3.7)	1 (5.6)	-	4 (3.9)	4 (2.7)	4 (7.5)	-	8 (3.9)
Regular inspection of all facilities provided to schools	15 (22.4)	17 (48.6)	32 (31.4)	9 (11.0)	3 (16.7)	-	12 (11.8)	24 (16.1)	20 (37.7)	-	44 (21.6)
Banning of donations	1 (1.5)	-	1 (1.0)	2 (2.4)	1 (5.6)	-	3 (2.9)	3 (2.0)	1 (1.9)	-	4 (2.0)
No response	1 (1.5)	-	1 (1.0)	2 (2.4)	-	-	2 (2.8)	3 (2.0)	-	-	3 (1.5)
Total respondents	67 (100.0)	35 (100.0)	102 (100.0)	82 (100.0)	18 (100.0)	2 (100.0)	102 (100.0)	149 (100.0)	53 (100.0)	2 (100.0)	204 (100.0)

Note: Figures in parentheses denote column percentage.

Source: Field data.

majority of households (over 32 per cent in Alopibagh slum and over 37 per cent in Mehdauri slum) were unanimous that economic assistance, along with free education, needs to be provided to the children of urban poor, 30 per cent of the households from Alopibagh slum also insisted on regular inspection of all facilities that were being provided to the school while 30 per cent of the households from Mehdauri slum felt that the distribution of books and copies was an important issue that needs to be addressed on urgent footing.

The inter-caste analysis of the perception of the sample households also endorses the above mentioned trends to a large extent, except with some minor variation in scaling their priorities. For example, about 37 per cent of SC households in Alopibagh slum felt that provision for economic assistance and free education needs to be offered to the children, its proportion was worked out to be 23 per cent in the OBC households in the same slum. Likewise, an overwhelming majority of the OBC households (83 per cent) in Mehdauri slum supported the view to provide economic assistance to the children while only about 26 per cent of the SC households subscribed to this view (see Table 8).

Gender Equality

The study of the perception of households on the gender equality holds an important place in defining the role of females in the socio-economic milieu in which they operate. It also helps in identifying the forces that promote or retard the process of development of female's education. It is assumed that if the households do not observe any gender discrimination, the females in the society get opportunity to progress both socially as well as economically. An attempt has, therefore, been made to study the perception of sample households on the issue of gender equality.

The study shows that out of a total of 204 households, only 16 households, accounting to nearly 8 per cent of a total, were quite emphatic and vocal in explaining the importance

Table 9

Perception of Households on Gender Equality

Responses	Alopibagh			Mehdauri				Total Sample			
	SC	OBC	Total	SC	OBC	Muslims	Total	SC	OBC	Muslims	Total
Son is responsible for lineage/clan	-	-	-	1 (14.3)	-	-	1 (14.3)	1 (6.7)	-	-	1 (6.3)
Son can earn wage anywhere	-	-	-	1 (14.3)	-	-	1 (14.3)	1 (6.7)	-	-	1 (6.3)
Son can live independently	-	-	-	1 (14.3)	-	-	1 (14.3)	1 (6.7)	-	-	1 (6.3)
Son cannot be compared	2 (25.0)	-	2 (25.0)	1 (14.3)	-	-	1 (14.3)	3 (20.0)	-	-	3 (18.8)
Son bears families responsibilities	1 (12.5)	-	1 (12.5)	1 (14.3)	-	-	1 (14.3)	2 (13.3)	-	-	2 (12.5)
Son earns	1 (12.5)	-	1 (12.5)	2 (28.6)	1 (100.0)	-	3 (21.7)	3 (20.0)	1 (100.0)	-	4 (25.0)
Daughter leaves parents' house	1 (12.5)	-	1 (12.5)	-	-	-	-	1 (6.7)	-	-	1 (6.3)
Son is involved in final rites	2 (25.0)	-	2 (25.0)	-	-	-	-	2 (13.3)	-	-	2 (12.5)
No response	1 (12.5)	-	1 (12.5)	-	-	-	-	1 (6.7)	-	-	1 (6.3)
Total	8 (100.0)	-	8 (100.0)	7 (100.0)	1 (100.0)	-	7 (100.0)	15 (100.0)	1 (100.0)	-	16 (100.0)

Note: Figures in parentheses denote column percentage.

Source: Field data.

and superiority of males in the society. Thus, they could be called the households that hold gender discriminating view however, a majority of the households believed in gender equality. Thus, it could be safely stated that the girls' schooling did not suffer on account of gender discrimination but due to the prevalence of some other but equally compelling factors.

The perusal of the responses of the 16 households who observed gender discrimination, reveals that about 25 per cent of them believed that the sons held an important place in the family because they could earn, another 19 per cent also felt that a son's place could not be taken up by the daughter in our society because he has been ordained the right to perform the final rites in the family. Likewise, other views, in lesser proportions, expressed by the households, were that the son was held responsible for propagation of clan, could go and earn anywhere, and could live independently, whereas the daughters were destined to finally leave their parents' home etc. The study further shows that these discriminatory views were emanating largely from the households belonging to the SC community.

The study of the response pattern of the households, in the two slums, shows that while the view, that son was a bread earner and the girl was not, was highly dominant in Mehdauri, in Alopibagh, the households believed that the son's role was incomparable and his involvement in performing the final rites was necessary (see Table 9).

Reasons for the Discontinuation of Girl Child's Education

The study has clearly shown that the overall dropout rate in the sample schools has been quite high, the situation could have been more alarming because the two of the three schools selected also have enrolment of students from the other localities. It has also been analysed that gender discrimination, by and large, was not being followed by sample households and, therefore, could not be stated to be an important factor for the girl child dropout from the school. An attempt has, therefore, been made to study the perception of sample households on why they have not been interested in getting their girl child educated beyond the primary level.

The analysis of the responses reveals a variety of factors responsible for the girl child's discontinuation of studies. However, for simplification, four to five prominent responses have been summarised. Accordingly, about 28 per cent of the households, in the total sample, have cited poverty and other economic handicaps as the main reason, over 21 per cent felt that the general environment of the area was not good, over 20 per cent voiced their concern about the problems encountered in getting them married at a later or older age while 17 per cent of the households believed in traditional values that encouraged girl child's early marriage.

Similarly, the analysis of the responses of the households, belonging to different castes, shows that there was an element of unanimity in most of the issues. However, their priority and magnitude, at times, varied marginally; still there was an overwhelming consensus in accepting that poverty and other economic handicaps were largely responsible for girl child's discontinuation of education. While over 20 per cent of the SC households stated the problems faced in getting their child married at a later stage, for over 28 per cent of the OBC households, it was the non-availability of school in the vicinity. The Muslim households also feared that girls often faced the problem of intimidation or misbehaviour from the people. It could be seen that over 19 per cent of the SC households, on account of their traditional belief and conservative outlook, preferred early marriage of their girl child.

The study of the data obtained from the two slums demonstrates that while over 29 per cent of the households in Alopibagh did not send their girl child to school beyond the primary level on account of their traditional outlook and preferred an early marriage, in Mehdauri slum, their proportion was hardly 5 per cent. Likewise, over 27 per cent of the households in Alopibagh observed deterioration in the

Table 10

Reasons for Discontinuation of Girl Education

Responses	Alopibagh			Mehdauri				Total Sample			
	SC	OBC	Total	SC	OBC	Muslims	Total	SC	OBC	Muslims	Total
General environment of the area not good	14 (20.9)	14 (40.0)	28 (27.5)	15 (18.3)	-	1 (50.0)	16 (15.7)	29 (19.5)	14 (26.4)	1 (50.0)	44 (21.6)
School not located in the vicinity	12 (17.9)	13 (37.1)	25 (24.5)	9 (11.8)	2 (11.1)	-	11 (10.8)	21 (14.1)	15 (28.3)	-	36 (17.6)
Conservative norms/ illiteracy preference for early marriage	24 (35.8)	6 (17.1)	30 (29.4)	5 (6.1)	-	-	5 (4.9)	29 (19.5)	6 (11.3)	-	35 (17.2)
Belief in discrimination or bias against girls	3 (4.5)	-	3 (2.9)	-	-	-	-	3 (2.1)	-	-	3 (1.5)
Poverty and other economic handicaps	11 (16.4)	7 (48.6)	18 (17.6)	30 (30.6)	8 (44.4)	1 (50.0)	39 (38.2)	41 (27.5)	15 (28.3)	1 (50.0)	57 (27.9)
More demand for dowry if girl is more educated	3 (4.5)	1 (2.9)	4 (3.9)	5 (6.1)	2 (11.1)	-	7 (6.9)	8 (5.4)	3 (5.7)	-	11 (5.4)
No scope of education in getting service	2 (2.9)	1 (2.9)	3 (2.9)	1 (1.2)	-	-	1 (0.9)	3 (2.0)	1 (1.9)	-	4 (2.0)
Preference for domestic work, family responsibility	4 (5.9)	4 (11.4)	8 (7.8)	5 (6.1)	-	-	5 (4.9)	9 (6.0)	4 (7.5)	-	13 (6.4)

Contd...

Contd...

Problems in getting married at older age	8 (11.9)	3 (8.6)	11 (10.8)	22 (26.8)	8 (44.4)	1 (50.0)	31 (30.4)	30 (20.1)	11 (20.8)	1 (50.0)	42 (20.6)
People misbehave with girls	6 (8.9)	3 (8.6)	9 (1.8)	15 (18.3)	-	1 (50.0)	16 (15.7)	21 (14.1)	3 (5.7)	1 (50.0)	25 (12.3)
Not responded	2 (2.9)	1 (2.9)	3 (2.9)	2 (2.0)	-	-	2 (1.9)	4 (2.7)	1 (1.9)	-	5 (2.5)
Total	67 (100.0)	35 (100.0)	102 (100.0)	82 (100.0)	18 (100.0)	2 (100.0)	102 (100.0)	149 (100.0)	53 (100.0)	2 (100.0)	204 (100.0)

Note: Figures in parentheses denote column percentage.

Source: Field data.

general environment as the other key factor whereas about 16 per cent of the households in Mehdauri slum endorsed this view. Similarly, over 24 per cent of the households in Alopibagh slum felt that the non-availability of schooling facility in the locality was another factor that limited the scope of girl child's schooling while in Mehdauri about 11 per cent accepted this view. The factors prominently emerging in Mehdauri slum for girl child's failure to study higher included poverty and other economic handicaps (38 per cent), problem of getting the girl child married at older age (30 per cent) and general deterioration of environment (15 per cent).

Thus, it can be inferred that the three major factors that were militating against the scope of girl child education were poverty and other economic handicaps, conservative norms and general deterioration in the environment (see Table 10).

Conclusion and Suggestions

The sample in the present study contained an overwhelming proportion of SC households (over 72 per cent), while the proportion of OBC and Muslims was reported to be 26 per cent and 2.6 per cent respectively. The average size of household was much bigger in Alopibagh slum than in Mehdauri slum.

The analysis of literacy status shows that the sample comprised over 63 per cent of the households as illiterates, where the proportion of females was conspicuously higher (over 70 per cent). Similarly, the incidence of illiteracy in the OBC households was higher than in the SC households in both the sample slums.

The study of enrolment pattern of students reveals that the dropout rate among the SC students in the sample was much higher than the students of OBC households. Further, the study also shows that the dropout rate of students in Alopibagh was much higher that the students of Mehdauri.

On the gender-wise enrolment pattern, the study shows that the dropout rate among the girls was less than the boys though their enrolment level was also marginally lower than that of the boys. However, these observations need to be accepted with a bit of caution because these schools also contained students from other localities that were located in the proximity. These students belonged to different socio-economic backgrounds and therefore, the outcome of the results of the study could both be applied on them without undertaking a comprehensive study of their socio-economic status.

The analysis also reveals that the involvement of parents in the education of their children in Alopibagh slum was negligible while it was of an exceptional order in Mehdauri slum. The plausible reason could be traced to the fact that the school in Mehdauri slum was not only better managed but it also involved the parents of the students in its working. The study of the resource pattern in the school shows that the schools of both the slums were poorly equipped in terms of teaching and learning materials and also in other basic curricular activities.

The analysis further demonstrates that the households in both the slums, by and large, accepted the relevance of education in day-to-day life. However, a small proportion of households, largely from the SC category was also critical of its relevance. On the question of how education could be promoted among urban poor households, a majority of the households from all caste groups were unanimous in suggesting that the government should provide economic assistance besides insisting on regular inspection of the facilities in the school.

Another finding of the study was that a majority of the households in both the slums observed gender equality. Thus, it could be safely concluded that gender discrimination could not be held as a factor that militated against the scope of girl child's education. The factors that were acting against the scope of development were prevalence of traditional values and outlook, deterioration in the general environment, lack of schooling facilities near their localities, poverty and other economic handicaps and problems confronted by the parents is getting their daughters married at a later stage etc.

On the basis of analysis, it could be said that the educational institutions have not been able to discharge their functions effectively and unless some concrete steps are not taken for the development and expansion of education, the universalisation of education would always remain a distance dream. Therefore, it is suggested that:

(i) There should be a qualitative improvement in education. The school should be equipped with necessary infrastructure, reading and learning materials. Regular inspection of these facilities by higher authorities would streamline their functioning and would also instil an element of accountability and restore confidence among the students, teachers and parents.

(ii) All incentive schemes that are currently in vogue be stopped as they are doing more harm than good both to the students and teachers alike. In place of incentive schemes, the students should be provided dress material, copies, books etc. The modalities could be worked out by separate groups involving teachers, parents and higher authorities of education department.

(iii) The study also found that most of the schools were functioning in dilapidated buildings. It is, therefore, suggested, that all such buildings be brought down because their mere sight brings fears to the heart and most of the parents also felt quite apprehensive about them. Further, it has also been observed that in most of the cases, where the buildings had collapsed, the proportion of schools operated by the District Education Board was fairly high. Moreover, such buildings do not provide healthy environment to interact.

(iv) Similarly, for promoting female's education, the literacy programmes targetting this group should be launched, from time to time. The help of some professional groups like the NGOs should be taken who could sensitise the women.

(v) The government's literacy programme may be extended to cover the habitation where these households reside and the female members, particularly the girls, should be encouraged to join these literary programmes.

(vi) Efforts need to be made to put a check on deterioration of environment in and around their areas and for this besides encouraging the local people to form self-help group, the local administration may be approached to provide security in the area.

References

Aldrich, Brain, Sandhu, Ravinder, C. (1995), *Housing the Urban Poor, Policy and Practices in Developing Countries*, Vistaar Publication, New Delhi.

Annual Plan (2000-01), Government of India, Planning Commission, New Delhi.

Aziz, Abdul (1984), *Urban Poor and Urban Informal Sector*, Ashish Publishing House, New Delhi.

Bapat, Meera and Crook, Negel (1979), "Housing and Slums in Poona Reconsidered: The Possible Alternatives", *Economic and Political Weekly*, August 18, Bombay.

Bhattacharya, Ardhendu (1996), "Problems of Slums and Possible Solutions", *Nagarlok*, Vol. XXVIII, No. 3, July-September, New Delhi.

Bhattacharya, Mohit and Kundu, Nitai (1998), "The Rag Pickers: A Study of Urban Poverty", *Nagarlok*, Vol. XXX, No. 3, July-September, New Delhi.

Bose, Ashish (1996), *Indian Basic Demographic Statistics*, B.R. Publishing Cooperation, Delhi.

Bulani, H.U. (1989), "Some Lessons Learnt from Various Studies in Hyderabad Slum Improvement Project", *Nagarlok*, Vol. XXI, No. 1, January-March, New Delhi.

Dandekar, V.M. and Rath, N. (1970), *Poverty in India*, Indian School of Political Economy, Pune.

Das, Biswaroop (1996), "Growth Trends, Physical Profile and City Dwelling Characteristic of Slums in an Industrial City - The Case of Surat", *Nagarlok*, Vol. XXVIII, No. 2, April-June, New Delhi.

District Census Handbook (1981), "Part XVI - A Village and Town Directory, District Allahabad".

Dubey, V.P., Kalla, H.L. Duggal, Dindu, Kaur, Ravindra and Vardhan, Ranjay (1999), "Socio-Economic Profile of Slum Dwellers", *Man and Development*, Vol. XXI, No. 3, September, Chandigarh.

Gustav, Ranis and John, C.H. Fei (1961), "A Theory of Economic Development", *The American Economic Development*, September, U.S.A.

Kailash (2000), "Slum And Environmental Sanitation in Madhya Pradesh", *Indian Social Science Review*, 2(1), Sage Publications, New Delhi.

Kansal, S.M. (1988), "Measurement of Poverty in Indian An Evaluation". Paper presented at the Second Seminar on Social Statistics, 4-6 February, Central Statistical Organisation, New Delhi.

Kumar, Mahendra, Singh, S. and Gill, S.S. (1998), "Facets of Primary Education in Rural Punjab: An Appraisal", *Manpower Journal*, Vol. XXXIV, No. 2, July-September, New Delhi.

Kundu, A. (1993), *In the Name of the Urban Poor*, Sage Publications, New Delhi.

Lewis, W.A. (1954), *Economic Development with Unlimited Supplies of Labour*, Manchester School, London.

Majumdar, M. and Vaidyanathan, A. (1994), "Access to Education in India: Retrospect and Prospect", *Journal of Educational Planning and Administration*, 7(4), New Delhi.

Majumdar, T.K. (1998), "Squatters Responses to Government Policies and Programmes", *Young India*, January 20, New Delhi.

Majumder, M. and Vaidyanathan, A. (1994), "Access to Education in India: Retrospects and Prospects", *Journal of Educational Planning and Administration*, Vol. 7(4), October, New Delhi.

Mehta, A.C. (1995), *Education for All*, Kanishka Publishers and Distributors, Delhi.

Meshram, D.S. and Quiyum, Abdul (1995), "Urban Poor in India: Approach to Better Life", *Nagarlok*, Vol. XXVII, No. 4, October-December, New Delhi.

Pande, B.N. (1955), *Allahabad Retrospects and Prospects*, Municipal Press, Allahabad.

Papola, T.S. (1984), *Rural Pc verty Issues and Options*, edited by Bajaj, J.L. and Shatri, C., Print House (India), Lucknow.

Pillai, P.G. (1992), "Akshar Keralam Total Literacy Programme in Kerala: A Case Study", *Journal of Educational Planning and Administration*, Vol. 6(3), New Delhi.

Planning Commission (1985), Seventh Five-Year Plan, New Delhi.

Pothen, K.P. and Singh, S.D. (1982). *Slum Children of India*, Deep and Deep Publication, New Delhi.

Prabhu, Seetha (1998), "Social Sector in Economic Development", *Journal of Social and Economic Development*, Vol. 1, No.2, July-December, Bangalore.

Prashad, C. (1991), "Perception of Urban Poor on Anti-Poverty Programme: An Empirical Study", *Nagarlok*, Vol. 23, January-March, New Delhi.

Pugh, Cedric (1990), *Housing and Urbanisation A Study of India*, Sage Publications, New Delhi.

Radha Krishan, R et al. (1988), *Determinants of Labour Force Participation and Living Standards*, Centre for Economic and Social Studies, Hyderabad.

Rahi, A.L. (1996), *Adult Education Policies and Programme*, The Associated Publishers, Ambala.

Ranis, Gustav and Fei, John, C.H. (1961), "A Theory of Economic Development", *The American Economic Review*, September.

Roy, Maitraya Bardhan (1995), "The Calcutta Slums: A Shift in Public Policy Intervention", *Nagarlok*, Vol. XXVII, No. 2, April-June, New Delhi.

Shankar, P. Uma (2000), "Housing Urban Poor: Problems and Prospects", *Nagarlok*, Vol. XXXII, January-March, New Delhi.

Singh, Andrea Manefar and deSouza, Alfred (1980), *The Urban Poor, Slums and Pavement Dwellers in Major Cities of India*, Manohar, New Delhi.

Singh, L.R. (1984), "Slums of Allahabad", Project Report No. 74, G.B. Pant Social Science Institute, Allahabad.

Singh, U.B. and Kishore, Kumkum (1993), "Socio-Economic Status of Indore Slums", *Nagarlok*, Vol. XXV , No. 1, January-March, New Delhi.

Smith, David Drakkis (1987), *The Third World City*, New York, Methuen.

Spodak, Howard (1983), "Squatter Settlements in Urban India: Self-Help and Government Policies", *Economic and Political Weekly*, September 3-10, Bombay.

Sridharan, N. (1995), 'Indian Slums: Problems, Policies and Issues", in *Housing the Urban: Policy and Practice in Developing Countries* by Brian S. Aldrich and Ravindra S. Sandhu (eds.), Vistaar Publication, New Delhi.

Statistical Bulletin (1998), Allahabad, Department of Economics and Statistics, Government of Uttar Pradesh, Allahabad.

Swaminathan, D. (1996), "Inaugural Address", National Seminar on Rural Water Supply and Sanitation, sponsored by Rajiv Gandhi National Drinking Water Mission, New Delhi and organised by Centre for Development Studies, Thiruvananthapuram, June 20-22.

Swamy, M.C.K. (1990), "Development of Urban Poor: A Policy in Shambles", *Nagarlok*, Vol. 22, No. 1, January-March, New Delhi.

Tewari, H.R. (1999), "The Myth About Slum Dwellers Economic Life", *Indian Journal of Regional Science*, Vol. XXXI, No. 2, Calcutta.

Todaru, Michael P. (1967), "A Model of Labour Migration and Urban Unemployment in Less Developed Countries", *The American Economic Review*, March, U.S.A.

Visaria, P., Gumber, A. and Visaria, L. (1993), "Literacy and Primary Education in India, 1980-81 to 1991: Differentials and Determinants", *Journal of Educational Planning and Administration*, New Delhi.

8

Socio-Cultural Lag and Sectoral Underdevelopment in Uttar Pradesh

A.R. Mishra

The word 'lag' means not keeping pace. This paper attempts to identify the slow pace of development of Uttar Pradesh in socio-cultural field from 15th century onwards. It was the period marked by a kind of renaissance through the spread of the message of the Bhakti movement. Its teachings erected foundation stone not only for ontological development of the individual self but also of social equality. Many developed states of today derived the required force for progress from it. However, in Uttar Pradesh, this could not happen. This was the beginning of its backwardness. The forces opposed to the 'Nirguna' mode of Bhakti continued to exercise their dominance. The present paper analyses this process in Uttar Pradesh in a nutshell. The source of inspiration for undertaking such an analysis was Muktibodh's essays on Bhakti movement. The states in the southern part of India could not covered for the purpose of comparison due to non-availability of required literature Tables used in this paper have been produced from B.B. Misra's book, *The Indian Middle Class*.

Burdened with the growing onus of progress and petrified by absence of committed and stable leadership added with rigid social structure, too obdurate and amorphous to allow transformative measures to succeed, Uttar Pradesh has come to depict an enervating picture of its developmental scenario and social achievements. In terms of women's life expectancy, impact of developmental schemes, agrarian reforms, literacy achievements, corruption, violence and criminalisation of institutions, undernutrition of a major portion of its population, caste factionalism, state apathy, increase in the number 'of landless labourers, the recurrent phenomenon of low payment of wages, and atrocities against the marginalised sections of society, Uttar Pradesh reveals a dismal picture. Any empiric-rational analysis of these factors refuses to optimistic and fructiferous factors, indicating an early solution. The question pertaining to such a collocation of negative factors, eliding the echoes of hope, needs to be searched in history of the area and not only in statistical comparisons!

Past has often been described as a source of surcease from the weariness of the present but it is also a storehouse of strengths and weaknesses of a society, an informative canopy that shows multi-coloured linings of achievements and losses is a silent recordkeeper of symphonic and cacophonic currents of society. It does not provide a mechanism of immediate resuscitation but it gives an insight to understand, evaluate and modify the given more comprehensively. Uttar Pradesh has been the area sprouting new visions of social transformations through iconoclastic philosophical upheavals from ancient times to 15th century, challenging all forms of supremacy which the self-proclaimed leaders of axiological world brought. It was the light of Uttar Pradesh that became the light of Asia propounding theories of liberation – both ontological and sociological. Ironically it is Uttar Pradesh of today that nakedly reveals obstructions to ascendance at a higher level of development. A major cause of it lies in its loss of what it produced and this process starts with 15th century and continues till date.

This contrast is the product of centuries old travail of the soul of a majority of its population.

Bhakti Movement

There are no dearth of interpretations regarding the etiology of the Bhakti movement in India but what is surprising is the immensity of its intellectual influence both in quantitative and qualitative terms and its impact cutting across human and spatial boundaries. Grierson, the well-known orientalist, takes this event as a lightening in the sky thus concluding it as accidental and contingent. It has been also described as a protest against Islam that was trying to encapsulate all aspects of human life. As the coming of Islam in the 7th century India and popularisation of this movement belong to the same period, this conclusion has its own analytical base. The other version of the emergence of this movement is related to the resurrection of the elements that were lying hibernated and waiting for the appropriate movement to appear on the surface. With Buddhism at its perigee and Islam at its nascency, the Upanishadic contents manifested in local forms and idioms. As it contained perennial wisdom within a new framework, it was widely received in the form of Bhakti.

The Bhakti movement originated in Tamil Nadu and the poems of the Alwar saints are contained in the book called *Divya Prabandh*. It is argued that by 6th century AD, the influence of Buddhism and Jainism waned due to excruciating effects of renunciation and asceticism. Acceptance of the worldly life, with exclusive emphasis on heart as the fountain of wisdom, had salubrious psychological receptivity among the masses. Alwars travelled through villages and hamlets inhabited by marginalised castes, forests where tribals lived, and spreaded the succulent and supple message of ontological unity and sociological integration. They confronted Brahminism and negated both state and wealth power. Above all the powers was the power of God who loved worldly powerlessness. To valuate the enormities of influence that this movement had, many sociological studies yet remain to be undertaken but the fact is that after the Vedic period India had for the first time female philosophers like Aandal (Tamil Nadu), Akkmandevi (Karnataka), Laldadd (Kashmir) and Meera (Rajasthan). It was the only movement that unified the whole of India from east to west and north to south. In Uttar Pradesh, this was brought by Ramanand, born in Allahabad, and Kabir was the doyen among his twelve disciplines although others like Ravidas, Peepa, Sena were equally competent but none had the roar of the lion as the Kabir had. Kabir became both the culmination of the Bhakti movement as well as source of many other future sects. But now it was not Uttar Pradesh but other parts of the country where Bhakti movement provided cementing forces helpful in new social formations and the two most important regions were Maharashtra and Punjab. How the departure of Kabir and his philosophy was ruinous for Uttar Pradesh will be discussed later but this period was a defining time in the history of Uttar Pradesh because by then it stopped consuming what it had produced.

Social Translation of Bhakti

Maharashtra is said to have produced various kinds of mystical personalities, viz., intellectualistic (Jnandev), democratic (Namdev), synthetic (Eknath), personalistic (Tukaram) and activistic (Ramdev) but all of them attacked the divisive tendencies in the society and were parts of the Bhakti movement. An alembicated mixture of rationalism, compassion, social activism and cultural synthesis is visible in the formation of state power under the leadership of Shivaji in 17th century. Bhakt Ram Das was the cultural dimension of Shivaji's leadership. Without existence of the term 'social justice' in that period the change in the pattern of land holding and economic transactions fructified in an unimagined social fermentation. Shivaji successfully fought three states ruled by Muslim rulers, five states ruled by French, English and Dutch imperial powers, various dynasties of More, Sawant,

Nimbalkar, Ghatke and Shinde besides feudaltories within the state and the provinces of the Mughal empire.

Shivaji stopped the land grant system and made cash payment for services to the state. The land that was granted earlier to landlords, who acted as intermediaries between the state and the farmers, was seized by Shivaji. He anticipated the significance of naval bases and subsequently established four of these for defence and trade with Arab countries. Introduction of 'Chautha' system by him was aimed to collect revenue for protection of the subjects. Manufacture of canons was given utter priority by him. His love for Hinduism never allowed him to go against Muslims as is evidenced by his attitude towards Muslim religious places, women and the nature of group of his close associates. The 17th century state formed by Shivaji declined at a later period but this translation of humanism into practice was a task unthought of in India since many centuries. Thus, Maharashtra was transformed into a vibrant territory and this set in motion the formation of a distinctive nationality, the spiritual force behind which was Ram Das.

The history of protest, subversion and formation continued in Maharashtra and after an interval of almost seventy years, the Britishers captured Western Indian, in 1818 but spirit of the Bhakti movement and Shivaji again resurrected in the new situations. In 1848, the Students Literary and Scientific Society was founded to disseminate and popularise modern knowledge. The year 1849 saw the birth of Paramhans Mandali that crusaded against the caste system and when it got dissolved on account of stiff opposition by upper castes, Prarthana Samaj was established during Keshub Chandra Sen's visit to Bombay in 1864. A replica of Brahma Samaj in Bengal had four objectives, namely, annihilation of caste system, widow remarriage, popularisation of female education and stoppage of child marriage besides aiming at unity of all religions. Many branches of Prarthana Samaj were opened throughout Maharashtra to popularise these messages with M.G. Ranade as the propelling force. Gokhale was a disciple of Ranade. The other two great personalities of Maharashtra during this period were Agarkar and Tilak. Agarkar's strong Hinduism prevented him from undertaking socially transformative activities but the fire in Tilak was unextinguishable. He adopted Marathi language in his articulation. Tilak undertook whirlwind tour of almost all the villages in Maharashtra, teaching the lessons of fearlessness. He published newspapers in Marathi. In fact, what is known as political mobilisation in modern language, Tilak was the first to use it in Maharashtra.

In Maharashtra, two other dimensions of social movement deserve attention, i.e., women education and dalit movement. Ramabai founded Sharda Sadan for women's welfare, although it could not succeed as many prominent leaders had certain apprehensions about its objectives. The spirit of the Bhakti movement was kept alive by Ranade. In 1873, Jotiba Phule founded Satyashodak Samaj (Truth Seeking Society), which was the first organisation instituted by a lower caste that laid the foundation stone for dalit mobilisation and, this platform was used by Ambedkar in later 19th and 20th centuries. Phule also has the credit of starting a girls' school at Poona in 1851. Besides, Vishnu Shastri Pundit founded the Widow Remarriage Movement in Maharashtra and Gopal Hari Deshmukh advocated reorganisation of Indian society on rational humanist values. This then was the socio-cultural scenario of Maharashtra when Congress under Gandhi became an all-India organisation. In Uttar Pradesh, during this period, one finds consolidation and expansion of taluqedars and zamindars.

Hinduism and Christianity: Renaissance in Bengal

The term 'renaissance' in general sense can be viewed as a phenomenon of change in perspective that is caused by contact with new cultures. So it happened in the West but with patterns and trends differing in character. Similarly, the nature of renaissance in Bengal has its own text and contexts. The colonial civilising mission, besides having economic designs, carved out a cultural mechanism to be implemented through the superiority of Christianity. After the battle of Plassey and establishment of capital at Calcutta, the debate between the protagonists of two religions commenced, including its sociological implications, and it was Raja Ram Mohan Roy who took the lead in this dialogicality. He founded Atmiya Sabha in 1816 in Calcutta for religious discourse and also established Vedanta College, besides Calcutta Unitarian Society which is said to be the English version of Atmiya Sabha and which was joined by Britishers also. Being dissatisfied with his achievements, he later founded Brahma Samaj based on the philosophical components of the Upanishads. He translated four Vedas and five Upanishads in Bengali and after his death in 1833, Devendra Nath Tagore's Tattvadodhini Sabha merged with it. Keshab Chandra Sen also joined Brahma Samaj in 1857. But whereas Devendra Nath wanted to inform Christians of the subtle contents of Hinduism, Keshab desired to push Hinduism toward Christianity. By the year 1866, Brahma Samaj was split. Adi Brahma Samaj became the name of Tagore's organisation. Keshab Chandra Sen's Brahmo Samaj again split up and his organisation was now known as Nav Vidhan (New Dispensation). The conflict between Tagore and Sen was also a clash between Hinduism and Christianity that ended with Vivekananda's famous speech at the Chicago Religious Parliament and thereafter wherein he condemned the frivolity of Christianity for its pretentious humanism and ostentatious superiority. However, in between the period between Ram Mohan Roy and Vivekananda, Bengal witnessed various socio-cultural reform movements with many educational institutions both for males and females being instituted with Ishwar Chandra Vidyasagar as the leading figure. This was also the period when Hindu social reforms were enthusiastically initiated. In the 19th century, Bengal was ahead of all parts of the country in terms of educational status and social reform movements. As per the report of Lieutenant Governor of Bengal in 1855, there were 515 publishers producing Bengali literature. Besides, there were 46 Bengali presses printing 252 books and pamphlets amounting to Rs. 4,18,275. A total of 19 newspapers and periodicals were being published and their circulation within a period of ten years increased from Rs. 8,100 to Rs. 2,00,000. The speech of Vivekananda in Chicago symbolises the regained confidence of India and also its underlying strength although Bengal did not represent the whole of India. To quote:

> We look about us and we see England, the most prosperous Christian nation in the world, with her foot on the neck of 250,000,000 Asiatics. We look back into history and see that the prosperity of Christian Europe began with Spain. Spain's prosperity began with the invasion of Mexico. Christianity wins its prosperity by cutting the throats of its fellowmen.

The Practical Bhakti: Religious and Social Transformations in Punjab

Babur and Guru Nanak were contemporaries. Nanak is reported to have reprimanded Babur, who earlier lost many battles against Uzbeks, for his violent acts against weak Hindus. His regard for Kabir is a well-known fact. Being the most popular personality of his times in Punjab, he succeeded in founding a community that was neither Hindu nor Muslim. He wrote neither in Sanskrit nor Persian but in the language of the masses. There used to be a common kitchen and all helped in collection of ration and cooking of food. His philosophy of God beyond time and space and yet helpful to those in time and space brought human beings of different communities to form a different society. His message of work, worship and charity injected new spirit and formed the quintessence of later Sikhism. After Nanak, his successor Angad perfected Gurumukhi language, started *langars* at various places that became an instrument of negation of the taboos of caste and creed.

Till the third quarter of the 16th century, Sikhism flourished providing succour to the people deprived since centuries from religious solace and social space. By now, this religion had a language, a tradition of gurus, various institutions reprobating deprivation and approbating communal mode of existence. Through donations and labour, religion contributed to the pace of urbanisation with Amritsar acquiring sacred status for the new religion. An anthology of the sacred writings was compiled by the year 1604, reflecting the full bloom of the religion rooted in the Bhakti tradition. But, the beginning the 17th century saw a confrontation between Sikhism and Islam that added militaristic dimension to it.

In Hargovind, Sikhism had a Guru with two swords for two separate enemies, viz., the inner and the outer. This symbolism infused a new psychology among Sikhs. The crusade against the world had to be as strong as the crusade against the carnal passions within. Sikhs were no more a community of metaphysical seekers only but also the pioneers against tyranny. This culture of optimism came to be so deep rooted in the new community that for centuries to come, they fought with various kinds of enemies and successfully defeated them. The last Guru, Govind Singh further ignited this spirit through his inspirational writings. He transformed the Sikhs into a militant Khalsa. It is said that the steel provided by Nanak was transformed into sword by Guru Govind Singh and the whole process took hundred years, i.e., 17th century to 18th century.

The beginning of the 18th century witnessed transformations in Punjab that could hardly have been anticipated. Banda Bairagi, a disciple of Guru Govind Singh, awakened the slumbering peasantry to take up arms against the zamindars. What Shivaji had accomplished in Maharashtra, Banda Bairagi did it in Punjab. Big zamindars were executed and their lands were seized and distributed among small peasants. Small landholdings were now owned by Sikh and Hindu peasants of Malwa and Jallandhar. His pious intentions and civalrous acts not only invited many to embrace Sikhism but it infused a new kind of identity that allowed the Sikh community to survive against repeated onslaughts during Afghan invasions (1738-1769). Banda Bairagi coined two terms – Begh (cauldron in the Guru's langer) and Tegh (the sword of the Khalsa) and it became the future mark of the community besides five Ks, popularised by Guru Govind Singh. After Banda Bairagi, Punjab remained under jatheders (group leaders) and in 18th century emerged the great leader Ranjit Singh who with great vision modernised the army. The origin of Nirankaris and the Arya Samaj movement made the Sikh community move towards the British. However, the 19th century on one side witnessed consolidation of the state power and on the other emergence of various religious movements after the death of Ranjit Singh in 1839. Four significant movements, viz., the Nirankari movement, the movements of Radhaswamis, Namdharis and Arya Samaj, besides activities undertaken by different Christian missionary organisations, viz., American Presbyterian Mission, Church Missionary Society, Society for the Propagation of the Gospel, the Salvation Army, Methodists, and several other Roman Catholic orders, had deep-rooted impact in Punjab, especially in the fields of education and journalism. The towering personality of Arya Samaj leader Swami Dayanand Saraswati pushed the Sikhs to organise the Singh Sabhas which laid emphasis on revival of the teachings of the gurus, protection of religious life from impurities and launch campaign against illiteracy. In 1892, with the foundation of the Khalsa College at Amritsar, great strides were made in the field of education. An Oriental College, a University Library, Museum, School of Arts, Science Institute and a Medical College were opened. Besides, a number of magazines, newspapers and journals, such as Gurumukhi Akhbar, 1850, Lahore; Sakabi Subodhini, Amritsar, 1875; Akal Prakash, Amritsar, 1876; Khalsa Prakash, Amritsar, 1884; Sri Gurumeet Prakash, Rawalpindi, 1885; Punjab Darpan,

Amritsar, 1885, Khalsa Akhbar, Lahore, 1886; Vidyarak, Lahore, 1886; and Khalsa Samachar, 1899, published from the different parts of Punjab, played vital role in disseminating not only modern knowledge and relevant themes but also conscientised the audience in the lessons of self-assertion and progress.

Social Development of Uttar Pradesh: The Burden of the Past

The history of Uttar Pradesh from 16th to 19th centuries marks the end of Halcyon days and reveals contrasts and contradictions in variegated colours unlike many other states in India wherein new socio-cultural patterns were emerging from the space created through struggle among opposites. On the contrary, most of UP's geographical area remained an operational amphitheatre for reteogressive forces. During the Akbar's reign, i.e., 16th century, the present Uttar Pradesh was divided into three *subas*, namely, Allahabad, Agra and Avadh and the economic relationship between the dominant communities also helped in cultural synthesis. The 16th century Uttar Pradesh has been described as the nodal place of renaissance in the Hindi belt and it is the period marked by the poetry of Surdas and Tulsidas, music of Tansen, architecture of Fatehpur Sikri, and of course attempt by Akbar to find a new religion encompassing the virtues of all the religions of the world besides development of learning centres at Agra and Jaunpur. Hita Hari Vansha and Swami Haridas established two Vaishnavite sects during this period. Money economy developed with flourishing of markets as a result of the increase in the purchasing power of people and consequently the trade also flourished during their respective periods.

However, this period also witnessed dismissal of many egalitarian tones and appearance of orthodox social philosophies. The Ramanandi Sampradya that militated vigourously against caste and gender discrimination was shifted to Rajasthan by Anantanand, a disciple of Ramanand. The philosophy of Kabir migrated to Punjab where Nanak translated the messages of 'Nirguna' into social reality. In Maharashtra, by 17th century Shivaji, under spiritual guidance of Ramdas, established a state, which was more egalitarian than many modern states of Europe during that period. In Rajasthan, Meera accepted Ravidas, a Chamar by caste as her guru and declared herself to have been emancipated from the suffocating burden of all social norms and customs of course. It is in this century when Kumbhandas said:

> What have the saints to do with Sikri
> In travelling the shoe shall go ragged
> And the name of Ram
> Into oblivion.

These lines undoubtedly speak of the progressive spirit of the saints who were indifferent to the state power with their faith in a single transcendal authority. But is it not also an escape from the sociological point of view, a shift from the earlier position of the Nirguna saints who confronted social and state power, enthusing the weak and the marginalised to negate social differences superimposed over them by the ruling class. The Bhakti movement was also a social movement and had links with the weds and woes of the people afflicted from injuries of deprivation. Kabir confronted Ibrahim Lodhi, Meera confronted Rana and Nanak confronted Babur. The question now is to explain this social inertia at a place where the greatest iconoclast Kabir was born and died and where many other Nirguna saints like Pattu Das and Jagjivan Das disseminated the most revolutionary thought of the period. In this context, the view of Gajanan Madhav Muktibodh deserves mention:

> Akbar was the first ruler, who after calculating the immediate social reality, openly welcomed the Hindu feudals. In and around Delhi and Uttar Pradesh, the Hindu feudals could not

> exist as separate entities from the Muslim feudals. In that age of plunder and exploitation, the socio-economic condition of the ordinary man was deplorable. The revolutionary reformatory voice of the lowly born Nirguna saints expressed the necessity of formation of a humane society and articulated people's anguish against the existing social condition. The cultural layers of the consciousness of the downtrodden bloomed in Nirguna form. This had multiple elements against the prevailing feudalism... (At a later stage) The Saguna bhakti, imbued with emotional mode of individual self-identification, militated against the Nirguna philosophy. This (Saguna) sect had sufficient members belonging to the aristocratic class and they succeeded in changing the course of the movement covertly (tr. A.R. Mishra).

Muktibodh further states:

> These Saguna poets with metaphors of beauty and beautiful confronted sedulously the Nirguna philosophy and succeeded in erecting a system of saguna. Only a single step was required to resurrect the *varna* system. This was accomplished by the irrepressible personality of Tulsidas. Thus, the Bhakti movement which was initially in the hands of the deprived and the marginalised castes was appropriated by Brahminism and turned against social reform and reconstruction, making the puranic sectarianism victorious. In this the feudals belonging to both the communities (Hindu and Muslim) in and around Delhi and Uttar Pradesh were united (tr. A.R. Mishra).

The change in the literary canopy of the area is the reflection of the retrogression of social forces and birth of a new ideology. Literature, the potent medium of awakening the masses, developed in 17th and 18th centuries an organic relationship with the ruling class instead of the marginalised class as will be evidenced by facts presented below in a tabular form:

Relationship between Literary Personalities and Courts in Hindi Belt

Name of the Poets	*Affiliated Courts*
Keshavdas	Orcha
Senapati	Many Courts
Bihari	Jaipur
Dev	Many Courts
Bhusan	Chitrakoot
Padmakar	Sugara, Sitara, Jaipur and Gwalior
Gang	Fatehpur Sikri

These poets, although not a member of the feudal force, directed their creativity to serve the honour and lascivious tastes of the ruling class and helped in proliferating a culture of passive acceptance among the deprived masses. The entire effort of the ruling class was directed to keep the masses under terrible psychological hold pauperising them of the very notion of protest. This was the period when Shivaji was building a new state in Maharashtra, the Sikh gurus were integrating the society and assuaging the feelings of the injured in Punjab, when social reform movements were making headway in Bengal and English education was being popularised in South India with the spread of Christianity, and influence of Vaishnavite movement was tearing asunder many reactionary conventions inherited from the past. Hazari Prasad Dwivedi says that it was a literature concerned with eroticism, ornamentation of language and description of nature of heroes and heroines. It was not a literature of intoxication with love for others but a means of relief from burden.

The weakening of the central authority in India allowed many marauding groups to invade Uttar Pradesh either to conquer its territories or to plunder its wealth. It became a hunting ground for Marathas, Sikhs, Gujjars and of course Ahmad Shah Abdali. The Britishers, with their acquiline glance on this region, started their operation since 1775. The area ceded to Britishers or conquered from Marathas formed North-Western Provinces besides Avadh consisting of the largest area and Baranas which too was ceded to Britishers at a later stage. The administrative shake up in Uttar Pradesh, especially in the Avadh region, started after 1857 Mutiny and a three-tier system was implemented in 1859 comprising taluqdars, zamindars and pattadars, besides occupancy tenants, tenants-at-will and agricultural labourers. The wretched section of the area survived on a new class of moneylenders. The Britishers attempted to introduce modern institutions in the regions of Uttar Pradesh also although their underlying design of vertical integration of the privileged class from the Indian society cannot be ruled out. Amazing was the lack of receptivity among the ruling class of modern education and instruments of social upliftment. The year 1861 saw the formation of the British Association of Avadh and the taluqdari system was declared to be 'indigenous and cherished' institution of India. The Avadh region had 270 taluqdars besides zamindars. Meanwhile, two colleges, namely, Canning College and Colvin Taluqdars College were established in Lucknow. In Bengal, the coming of the Britishers had aroused enthusiasm for rational argumentation and understanding through contesting the given. As regards the 'garden of India', pictures of the absence of urge for modern learning can be gleaned from the figures of students attending the two schools founded for rational and scientific education to the children of the dominant sections of society.

Social Category	*Students in 1868*
Taluqdars	24
Petty zamindars	27
Government servants	291
Private servants	128
Professional men	55
Traders	42

A part of the report published by the Directorate of Public Instructions in the same year says:

> It is very much to be regretted that more of the class which ought to be the most enlightened and most anxious to understand the wishes and objects of government do not attend school...

If this is the situation in Avadh, the educational scenario among the middle class of North-Western Provinces, which included more than 17 districts, was equally dismal as depicted by Harishchandra Magazine, published on 15th October 1873. It says:

> Few institutions of a public character such as Aligarh, Allahabad and Benaras Institutes, Moradabad associations and other associations of minor character, which are established under the auspices of the few educated middle class men, do not prove that the middle class has made any considerable progress towards civilization... The people of North-Western Provinces are conservative and are quite against the innovations of anything whether of social, moral or intellectual reform and hence the progress is slow. Bengal is ahead and is actively progressing, being divested of conservatism. We should not however urge over north-west middle class to speedy progress which may bring reaction but shall patiently and gradually aid them to march cautiously and deliberately towards the attainment of that position in which the classmen of civilized nation are nowadays placed.

The class considered to bear the responsibility of social transformation not only spurned education but refused even to attend the meetings of various organisations of which they were members. They were equally incredulous of use of improved technology in agriculture. When India reached 20th century and the cause of social mobilisation vested with the Congress, the picture was equally deplorable in 1921 as compared to other states. Of 192 colleges and 57,125 students in different states, Uttar Pradesh with more colleges as compared to Bombay and Madras, was having less number of students.

States	*Total Colleges*	*Total Students*
Madras	61	10,491
Bengal	46	21,595
Bombay	17	7,424
Uttar Pradesh	42	7,128
Punjab	26	10,787

Similar deplorable condition continued to prevail in the post-independence period also. Leading in population but lacking in educational facilities is the scene presented by the table below that depicts the situation in 1949-50:

Proportion of College Students to Population

Province	*Population*	*No. of Schools to Every 1,00,000 Population*
Madras	57.01	88
Bombay	35.95	137
West Bengal	24.81	272
Punjab	12.64	157
Uttar Pradesh	63.21	52
Bihar	40.22	58
Kerala	18.35	367

Thus, one finds that after the first quarter of the 16th century, there was no social movement in Uttar Pradesh. Nirguna philosophy was translated into social reality in Punjab and Maharashtra. Kabir's most favourite disciple Dharmdas settled in Madhya Pradesh. The philosophy of Kabir and Vajrasuchi Upanishad formed the basis of Jotiba Phule's movement. Shivaji fought the indigenous feudals in Maharashtra and Banda Bairagi in Punjab. Ishwar Chandra

Vidyasagar fought the values of feudalism and Vivekananda attacked institutionalised Hinduism in its accreted form. In South India, anti-Brahmin movement provided a new space for traditional oppressed masses. In Kerala, Narayan Guru succeeded but Uttar Pradesh failed to march with the ongoing progress in other parts of the country.

In Bengal, the first school was opened in 1814 and thereafter within a short span of 16 years, i.e., by 1830, many schools were opened on demand by the public. In between 1855 and 1885, with the efforts of Ishwar Chandra Vidyasagar, Bengal had 20 Model Bengali Schools and 35 schools for girls in rural areas with an enrolment of 1,300 girls. Thus, seed sown by Bethune flowered under Vidyasagar's leadership. The zamindars of Bengal donated generously for girl education. In Maharashtra Jotiba Phule played a nodal role in girl education and in Punjab similar role was played by Lala Deo Raj. In Uttar Pradesh, the situation was deplorable as at the end of the 19th century one finds a declining trend in female education as is depicted by the table below:

Period	*No. of Schools*	*No. of Girl Students*
1870-71	640	13853
1875-76	400	9,000
1880-81	160	3,757

For this, the responsibility is said to lie on the rich class that did not allow their educated female members to teach in the schools and moreover this class itself was not properly educated. In other parts of the country a conflict between religion and egalitarian culture emerged and ignited the society for production of effective leadership and appropriate direction of social transformation.

It can be argued that how a region, educationally so backward, socially so retrogressive and culturally so inert, becomes the leading force during the freedom movement. One reason may be that in the absence of any alternative mobilising force, Uttar Pradesh was a no man's land eagerly waiting for political leadership. But, a greater rationale is visible when one analyses the professional background of Uttar Pradesh leadership. Motilal Nehru, Jawaharlal Nehru, Madan Mohan Malviya, Govind Ballabh Pant, Ram Manohar Lohia, Narendra Deo all belonged to legal profession. During the period 1891-1900, this profession was most lucrative as is understandable from the following table:

Period	*Number of Lawyers*			
	Calcutta	*Bombay*	*Madras*	*UP*
1850-1870	50	27	19	34
1871-1880	94	101	63	89
1881-1890	105	124	164	121
1891-1900	212	298	231	335

During the period 1891-1900, Uttar Pradesh produced maximum number of lawyers and their relationship with zamindars facilitated their acceptance in rural areas also. As the legal profession was conducted only in English, Uttar Pradesh did not had a leader who could proliferate messages in Hindi. Ram Mohan Roy, Vidyasagar, Tagore used Bengali language in their communication and so was the case with Tilak and even Gandhi or Rajagopalachari who kept on writing in both English and vernacular languages. Uttar Pradesh was the only state where leadership denied Hindi an effective medium of communication. Thus, majority of Hindi-speaking population was deprived of a singular linguistic character. The ignorance of majority of population in Uttar Pradesh made them uncritical recipients of messages, which allowed the tyrannical rule of the zamindars to continue. A question from Gobbin's book, *The Garden of India* was used by Irwin to describe the condition of people in this region, which throws a light on the state of affairs:

> The Chamar, Lodhi, Kurmi, and all inferior castes are the prey of all, caught at every hour of the day or night, made use of as beasts of burden, beaten and abused, treated as if incapable of feeling pain or humiliation, never remunerated, but of often deprived of the scanty clothing they may possess.

Conclusion

In Uttar Pradesh, static culture continued to grow with greater strength after the eclipse of Nirguna Bhakti Movement. Of the total SC population in India, Uttar Pradesh alone had 23 per cent in 1921. The Brahminical class had some lines to its memory from *Ram Charit Manas*, which was quoted for every inaction and action. Nirala in his novel *Devi* has sketched this tendency of the society in Uttar Pradesh. Similar indifference was visible in Muslim community and also the Congress leadership which attempted to stifle every peasant movement against the exploitation by zamindars. The rich class was immune from changes in other parts of the country whereas in other states magazines were being published reflecting identity in terms of their rationality, e.g., Punjabi (Lajpatrai), Maratha (Tilak), Bengali (Bipin Chandra), whereas Uttar Pradesh remained caught in the quagmire of caste publications, i.e., Brahmin Sarvasva, Kstriyahitkari, Vaishyahitkari and Kyastha Samachar. On the achievement of independence, the desire to wipe out every tear from every eye was implemented on a homogeneous pattern without undertaking a differential amount of the tears and smiles in different regions of the country.

Contemporary politics in Uttar Pradesh successfully perceived the dormant and unutilised mobilisation resources in the Nirguna Bhaktas, potentially their literature and also the nature of consciousness amidst a large section of society that was anxious to see its dream realised. The lag in history was exploited by the dalit leadership in construction of a myth of liberation. This again resurrects the question of development of Uttar Pradesh in modern designed direction as myths have their own humdrum notion, "full of sound and fury, signifying nothing". Inverting Schopenhauer, it can be said that ruling political parties in Uttar Pradesh have a 'will' that is always satisfied although it never attains.

References

Dwivedi, Hazari Prasad, *Granthavali*, Vol. 3, Rajkamal, New Delhi, 1999.

Frykenberg, Robert Eric (ed.), *Land Control and Social Structure Indian History*, Manohar, New Delhi, 1979.

Majumder, R.C., *The History and Culture of the Indian People*, Vol. X, Bhartiya Vidya Bhawan, Bombay, 1980.

Misra, B.B., *The Indian Middle Class*, Oxford University Press, 1978.

Muktibodh, Gajanan Madhav in Muktibodh Rachnavali (ed.), *Nemi Chand Jain*, Vol. V, Rajkamal, New Delhi, 1998.

Sharma, Ram Vilas, *Bhartiya Sanskrit Aur Uttar Pradesh*, Vol. II, Kitabghar, New Delhi, 2001.

Talvar, Veer Bharat, *Rassakashi*, Saranath Prakashan, New Delhi, 2002.

9

Migration, Memory and Social Adjustment

The Narration of Pain

Badri Narayan Tiwari

If you start your journey from Delhi, as your train passes through Uttar Pradesh in North India, the lush green fields of the Ganga River Valley will appear in front of your eyes. As the train moves further, just after crossing Mirzapur in the Ganga River Valley, you will hear a voice crying, "*Kaho! kahan ja tar, arraah ki patna ki kalkutta!*"

These words are spoken in the Bhojpuri language by Bhojpuri people. It was from this region that a large number of 'Bhojpuris' were taken by the colonial masters to work as indentured labourers in the plantations of countries like Mauritius, Fiji, Trinidad and Surinam. The people who were left behind referred to these migrant labourers as 'Bidesia'. The departure of these migrants caused untold grief and sorrow, both to the persons who were left behind as well as to the persons who were leaving the country for foreign shores. This grief and sorrow gave birth to a distinct folklore culture, which emerged as an expression of the pain and anguish at the separation of the migrants from their families. Bidesia folk culture is the name given to this folk cultural tradition. This folk tradition is represented in many forms like *nautanki* (musical theatre), dramas, folk songs and folk paintings. It is a complete folk culture or holistic folklore tradition, which developed as an outcome of the vacuum caused by the departure of the migrant Bhojpuris.

In Hindi, the word 'Videshi' refers to the natives of foreign countries, but the Bhojpuri word 'Bidesia' refers to those Bhojpuris who have left their native place and have now become residents of the other countries. The word 'Bidesia' is derived from the Hindi word 'Videshi'. 'Videsh' means foreign country, which is called 'a muluk' in Bhojpuri. The Hindi word 'Videshi' is often used for the British, but in Bhojpuri language another word 'Firangiya' is used to refer to the British. 'Videshi' is hardly ever used for them. 'Bidesia' in Bhojpuri means a person who has gone to a foreign country, or a Bhojpuri who is a resident of a foreign country. Thus, the term 'Bidesia' is in one sense used as an affectionate term for non-resident Bhojpuris and in another sense, refers to the folk tradition which was composed in memory of those non-resident Bhojpuris. Because of the multiple meanings of the term 'Bidesia', it has now become a metaphor rather than a word with a single meaning.

Bhojpuri Region and Language

Bhojpuri area is not a political unit but a cultural entity. This area comprises of the eastern part of Uttar Pradesh and the western part of Bihar. The Bhojpuri culture has spread nationally and internationally due to large-scale migration from this region. On the north, it reaches across the Ganges and even beyond the Nepal frontier, upto the lower ranges of the Himalayas from Champaran to Basti. On the south, it crosses the Sone river and covers the great plateau of Chotanagpur, where it finds itself in contact with Bengali of Manbhum, with Oriya of Singhbhumi and scattered tribal languages of Chotanagpur plateau. The area covered by Bhojpuri is some fifty thousand squares miles. According to the census, the number of people speaking Bhojpuri came to be 78,42,722. In addition, it is used beyond the shores of India mainly in the lands of Mauritius, Fiji, Surinam, British Guyana, Uganda and some parts of Burma and Nepal. It is spoken by no less than forty to fifty millions of people. More than 15 per cent of the total Indian population speaks Bhojpuri.

Bhojpuri is the name of the language (dialect) spoken by the Bhojpuri people. It is named after a village 'Bhojpur', which is situated in the district of Bhojpur and was formally called Shahabad in the state of Bihar (Singh, 1958:6) in the medieval time. Buxar, where the battle of Buxar took place during the colonial time, is very near to this village. This village was the capital city of the Bhoja king who was a scion of the great kind Bhojraj of Ujjaini. Their family ruled here for some centuries, but due to the onslaught of Muslims they lost their kingdom. The modern representative of this royal family is the present Maharaja of Dumraon.

In 1745, the ruling dynasty of Bhojpur was divided into three branches. The elder brother Horilshah settled in Mathila (Dumaraon), Sujanshah and his son Udant Singh in Jagdishpur and Buddh Singh in Buxar. Kuaur Singh, a great chivalrous hero of the 1857 mutiny, belonged to the Udant Singh family.

In the 17th and 18th centuries, Bhojpur and Buxar were the recruitment centres of sepoys. The Mughals and Britishers both recruited sepoys from this region. The sepoys coming from this area were named Buxaria or Purbiha and their language was called Purubi by others. Hopson-Jobson Dictionary (p. 724) prepared by Colonel Henry Yule and A.C. Burnel, states that in northern India, Purubi means the areas of Avadh, Banaras and Bihar. The inhabitants of these areas are called Purubi. The sepoys of the Mughal and colonial armies, mill workers of Kolkata, the coolies of the tea gardens of Assam and the milk sellers of Bombay transmitted Bhojpuri to the other regions.

Bhojpuri language has four main dialects. Standard Bhojpuri is spoken mainly in the districts of Ballia and Gazipur in Uttar Pradesh and Bhojpur and Rohtas districts of Bihar. Western Bhojpuri is spoken in the district of Varanasi. This dialect is also known as Banarasi Boli. Madhishi is the dialect that is spoken in between the Maithili language of Tihat and Bhojpuri dialect of Gorakhpur. Tharu dialect is used by the people of the Tharu tribe living in the districts of Gonda, Baharaich in Uttar Pradesh and Champaran in Bihar (Upadhyaya, 1989:3).

The Story of Migration

A massive emigration took place from the Bhojpuri region in the 19th century and early 20th century to European colonies that were in need of manpower on their plantations, after the abolishment of slavery (see Table 1). In India, economic depression was taking place all over the country due to the decline of weaving industries caused by the Industrial Revolution in England, and by the extreme population pressure on agriculture and cultivable lands (Legene, 2001). The sepoys who were brave warriors belonging to the Bhojpuri area and had been recruited for the British colonial army, with the support of their people, revolted. The revolt was suppressed and the English punished the entire region with extreme brutality. In this context, the rural population all over India faced socio-economic hardships. The English introduced a system of indentured labour in the Bhojpuri region, which resulted in a mass emigration to European colonies in other parts of the world (The Census of India Report, 1931). Although this emigration took place under strict agreements and regulations set by the British government and governments of other European colonial powers, the treatment given to these labourers initially was often no better than that given to the slaves.

The system of indentured labour met with growing criticism in the early decades of the 20th century. The main point of criticism concerned the stigmatisation of India by the existence of the system of indentured labour. As a result, the emigration of contract collies stopped in 1915 (Defence of India Act) and was prohibited in 1922 (Emigration Act) after severe protests from the Indian communities abroad. Table 1 below shows the countries and the years when the migrations took place:

Table 1

Countries and First Year of Emigration of Indentured Labourers from India

Countries	*Year*
Mauritius	1843
Australia	1837
British Guyana	1844/45
Jamaica and Trinidad	1844/45
Natzal (South Africa)	1860
Surinam	1873
Fiji	1879

Source: De Kerk, 1953.

Some 4,49,220 Bhojpuri emigrants left India between 1843 and 1921 for Mauritius, of whom 1,65,282 returned. Most of them had migrated from Arrah district (Bhojpur) of Bihar (Trivedi, 1921). About overseas emigration, the 1951 census says: "The total number born in the Uttar Pradesh that sailed from Calcutta to various British colonies between 1901 and 1910 was 1,28,513. Of this number, 66,860 were from the East Plain." The Census of India, 1931 reported that out of a total of 555 registered emigrants from the United Provinces (now called Uttar Pradesh), who sailed from Calcutta, Bombay and Karachi between 1921 and 1931, as many as 202 belonged to the Gorakhpur district, which falls in the Bhojpuri area.

Emigration from the Bhojpuri region to Surinam has been sub-divided into six periods as shown in the following table:

Table 2
Emigration to Surinam

Year	*Particulars*
1873-1895	The period of forced labour on the plantation estates.
1895-1916	The colonisation period, in which immigration continued but Bhojpuri emigrants whose contract had expired became independent small farmers.
1916-1940	Settlement of the Hindustanis, enlargement of the cultivated areas in Surinam.
1940-1960	Entering other socio-economic domains in Surinamese society.
1960-1975	Further emancipation of the Hindustanis within Surinamese society, both in political, economic and socio-cultural respects.
1975 further	Massive emigration by Hindustanis from Surinam to Netherlands after Surinamese independence.

Some 34,000 Bhojpuri emigrants left India between 1873 and 1961 for Surinam, of whom approximately 11,000 returned; today, some 1,50,000 Hindustanis live in Surinam and 1,50,000 in Netherlands (Legene, 2001).

Multiple Migration

There is another form of migration from Bhojpuri region that is internal. This emigration has been going on for quite a long time now. The report of the United Provinces Banking Enquiry Committee of 1929-30 says: "Twenty years ago it was commonly said that there was not a single family in Banaras division which had not at least one member in the provinces of Bengal, Assam and other states." The Banaras division consists of the districts of Banaras, Ghazipur, Ballia, Jaunpur and Mirzapur. The first three of these fall completely in Bhojpuri region and the last two are partially included in it (Indra Deva, 1989: 236).

The emigration was generally of semi-permanent nature, in which the young men who left in search of employment often left their wives, children and other family members at home. They maintained contact through letters, paid occasional visits to them and in many cases, hoped to come back and settle in the village again.

Again, where emigration outside the province was considerable as in the Eastern Plain, since males pre-dominated among such emigrants and they were mostly married and at the working ages, the proportion of married males at all ages decreased, the decrease being more noticeable at the working ages (The Census of India Report, 1931). The eastern plain of Uttar Pradesh referred to above, forms the western part of the Bhojpuri-speaking area.

The emigrants from the Bhojpuri area went both to nearby and far off places. They went to metropolitan cities such as Calcutta, Bombay, Gauhati and Dibrugarh as jute mill workers, tea garden workers, in shoe making industries and as milk sellers. In the internal migration within Uttar Pradesh, the eastern plain lost in balance 2,00,489 persons – a loss higher than that of any other natural division (Census, 1951).

The villagers went to Calcutta to earn their living as coolies (Gopal and Jha, 1982: 253). Even cities almost 400 miles away attracted villagers who were in need of new sources of livelihood. Obviously, the introduction of steam ships and railways facilitated this long distance cross-country mobility; at the same time, it promoted short distance migration, i.e., from the village to the urban centre. Also, the new system of transportation enabled the urban migrant to keep intact his rural elite status (Buckland, 1863: 36). The coolies of Calcutta did not always belong to the lower castes for which manual labour was not taboo according to caste rules. The members of upper castes would avail of the anonymity of a large city, considerably far from their village home where chances of their recognition were negligible, to adopt a profession not sanctioned by caste rules.

In the last quarter of the 19th century, the mines in South Bihar attracted Bhojpuri migrants. Initially, the labour force consisted of local tribals but soon the demand for additional workers arose; there was a rush of labourers from all over Bihar plains. Gradually, the Bhuiyas, the Rajwara, the Gops, the Lodhs, the Pasis, the Kurmis, the Nonias and the Beldars came to settle as miners. They came from southern Bengal and western districts of Bihar. In addition, there was a small number of Muslims, locally known as Mees or Jalhas, employed in the collieries. Numerically, the Kurmis held the first place, then were the Koerias, the Goalas, the Khariwars, the Telis, the Dhanuks, the Gamjas, the Bedias, the Santhals, and the Kols. In 1894, James Grundy, the first Inspector of Mines of India, recorded the names of as many as 49 castes, sub-castes and tribes working in the Giridih coalfields (Sinha, 1974: 164).

Among the castes enumerated above, one can identify the primary agricultural castes, the Kurmis, the Koeris, and the Goalas and artisans cates such as Julahas (weavers), Telis (oil pressures), Nonias or Nunias (salt petre manufactures), Pasis (the tooddy trapers), Beldars (house builders) etc. Of course, the lure of higher wages might have partially caused this displacement of workforce but essentially this development has to be explained in terms of the failure of caste occupations to provide adequate means of livelihood, coupled with the over-saturation of the agricultural sector. In absence of any new capacity for capital investment, this segment of the population had no option but to become manual labourers where neither skill nor capital investment was needed.

Those who did not go to work in mines, immigrated to foreign countries or went to tea plantations in Assam and to jute mills in and around Calcutta. They also worked as coolies, domestic servants or peons. The migration was facilitated, no doubt, by the construction of railway lines in the region during this period which made long distance travel quick and safe.

A glance of the migration figures show that people were moving out in search of new economic opportunities. Hunter (1877) points out that the government had four recruiting centres in the districts at Patna, Danapur, Barh and Behar. The following table shows the number of Bhojpuris who emigrated:

Table 3
Emigrated Bhojpuris

1868-70	879
1870-71	850
1873-74	2800

Source: Hunter, 1877.

The majority of 879 emigrants belonged to the labouring classes (Hunter, 1877:19). However, we have no idea as to how many left through private agencies were more successful in luring men to foreign countries than government officials were. Considering the miserable hand-to-mouth existence of a large portion of the people of Bihar, their industrious habits and willingness to take service in other parts of India, and also the number of men who came back with really large sums of money from the West India colonies, it is very strange that recruiting depots, during all the year they had been at work, should have so little hold on the surplus population (Hunter, 1877: 40).

A study shows that in Bihar society rural people were forced to give up caste professions and turn to agriculture. When the land-man ratio became adverse, they became manual labourers and moved to areas both inside and outside the state in search of jobs (Buckland, 1863: 765-66).

After an initial spurt in overseas migration, the overseas migration rate from Bihar started decreasing day by day. In 1882, the government formulated Bihar to Burma emigration scheme. The scheme failed after a year and only 70 men and four women availed of it. This was the mother of worries for colonial surveyors and policy makers.

It is interesting to note that Calcutta and Bombay were not only the destination points for the migrants of the Bhojpuri region, but due to the depots situated there for recruitment of indentured labourers and the presence of the sea ports, they sailed to various overseas British colonies from there.

Emotional Loss and Folk Tradition

For the Bhojpuri people, this migration was a heavy emotional loss. Before they realised, many tender relationships were torn apart: a wife from her husband, a sister from her brother, a father's old age support who was an apple of his mother's eye. All were leaving for foreign shores and there was no way to hold them back. The social, economic, political and historical manifestations of colonial imperialism were compelling them for this 'migration', which was a kind of forced migration for the Bhojpuris.

Indian society, like other social groups, has been going through the process of migration from the very beginning. In the Vedic period, many Brahminical groups settled in different parts of the country under the fold of the various branches of the Vedas. Thereafter, they moved to distant far-off places to earn their livelihood. If a family belonging to a different Vedic sect was found among a particular Vedic sect, it was easy to believe that it had migrated from elsewhere. The phenomenon of migration in ancient Indian society can be evidenced from a study of the Sutras, Smritis, essays and the various kinds of rites and rituals, religious traditions and the fasts that are undergone on different religious festivals. Today, the Indian social set-up has become more complex and the ancient Vedic sects have almost been erased from memory. This is the reason why it is now difficult to recognise the original place from where the migrating families came and settled.

But, the migration during the colonial period was different because it entailed the danger of separation from dear ones to far-off places, and the snapping of many tender relationships. In the migrations that took place in the ancient periods, in spite of the movement involving geographical expansion, people were linked to each other through inter-caste marriages. For example, the Brahmins of Bansgaon near Gorakhpur are spread across large areas of Bihar and Uttar Pradesh but they are still linked to each other in different ways. The migrations which took place in the present era was more 'visible', since middlemen used to carry away jeep loads of Bhojpuri people before sending them off by ship to distant shores. This migration was therefore emotionally painful both for the migrants and also for the people who were left behind. Migration, since the time when Lord Krishna left Mathura, has been emotionally painful for all cultures and this pain has been manifested in many folk traditions.

Bhojpuri folk tradition had tried its best to stop this migration. This may have been there as on why overseas travel by ship was banned in Bhojpuri culture. But, in spite of their best efforts, the migration did not stop. As a result, both externally and internally, the pain of loss and separation became an important aspect of Bhojpuri society. This was revealed in the various facets of Bhojpuri folk traditions, whether they were 'Ganga Geet', 'Poorvi Lok Sangeet' or 'Bidesia Songs', or 'Nautaṇki'. Not only this, a new folk style called 'Bidesia Folk Tradition' emerged out of this phenomenon. Although this process of migration was painful for both the migrants and their family members, this study is concentrated only on the folk culture of the concerned social group that was expressed through their folk art and culture.

In the Bidesia folk culture, the migrants are referred to as 'Bidesia', 'Pardesi', 'Batohia' etc., which contain elements of both affection and complaint for leaving behind the loved ones. These three terms of address represent three different kinds of folk tradition:

1. In the 'Bidesia' culture, the chances of return of these migrants were very less. When the migrant left his 'an muluk' or native place, he snapped all ties with his loved ones. Even communication by mail was not carried out.
2. In the 'Pardesi' culture, the migrant is forced to leave his native place in order to earn a living, but communication ties with his family members are not cut off. But, the pain involved in this 'semi-permanent migration' comes through in the Bhojpuri folk songs. A 'Pardesi' may be

called 'Bidesia' in complaining tones, but a 'Bidesia' is very seldom called 'Pardesia'.

3. In the 'Batohia' culture, the migrant comes back as a traveller to his native place and communication ties are restored.

The Bhojpuri and Buxar soldiers, who were part of the Mughal and Bengal Armies, were referred to as 'Buxariha' and 'Poorviha' respectively. These soldiers spent their free time in composing and singing songs to express their sadness at being separated from their loved ones. The folk songs were given the name of 'Poorvi folk music'. Colonel Yule described this folk art in the following manner: "in the Poorvi folk songs, the pain of separation is expressed from the side of the wife, although the composers are males". In these 'Poorvi' folk songs, the word 'Pardesia' has been frequently used to refer to migrants. Later, this folk art became the main art of the jute mill owners of Kolkata, the labourers of Assam tea gardens and the milk sellers of Bombay.

Even before it appeared in Poorvi folk music, the word 'Pardesi' has been found in the Nirgun songs. In the spiritual discourse, the worldly phenomenon of migration has been used as a spiritual symbol, as the 'atma' or soul gets transferred to or 'migrates' to the other world. The body is referred to as the 'wife', the soul as the 'husband' and the pain of separation is expressed in these songs. Therefore, the use of the metaphor 'Pardesi' is quite natural here.

Calcutta as a Metaphor in Migration Oral Tradition

Bhojpuri migrants spread all over the world as a result of colonial exploitation of India. This migration happened in various phases. The groups of these indentured labourers reached Mauritius for the first time in 1834, Trinidad in 1945, South Africa 1864, Guyana in 1870, Surinam in 1873 and Fiji in 1879. Most of these migrants were from the Bhojpuri area.

In Mauritius, the maximum number of Hindus (near about 1,12,000) are of Bihari origin. They are called as 'Calcuttia', although among them, Bengalis are very nominal. Most of the Biharis belonged to Arrah district, who escaped British oppression just after the dèfeat of Babu Kuar Singh of Jadishpur Arrah.

There is an interesting dichotomy that Bhojpuri migrants were being called 'Calcuttia' in their destination point, but in their homeland Calcutta is perceived as a much-hated place. In Bhojpuri folk narratives, Calcutta is described as an illusive place, which causes pain and separation. There was a depot situated in Calcutta where migrants were brought together by Aarakati (agent) of colonial masters and dispatched to various countries, viz., Mauritius, Fiji, Trinidad and Guyana. Calcutta is also identified as 'Purabi Desh' in Bhojpuri folklores. The metaphors of Hooghly, Purub and Calcutta multiply the 'Bidesia' effect among the people of their homeland.

The lore lyrics very frequently show a woman remembering her husband who has gone to Calcutta or to the eastern country (Purab Des) in search of employment. References to Calcutta, where Bhojpuri young men go in large numbers, occur over and over again in these songs. The symbol of Calcutta evokes tragic memory in Bhojpuri folk consciousness. One very popular song, composed by Rasik Kavi of Shahabad in the 19th century, is as follow:

Piya Mor Gaile Rama, Hugli Saharawa Se lie aile na
Ek Bangalin Re
Sawatiyase, liere aile na.

(My husband has gone to Hooghly and has brought a Bengali woman as my co-wife).

Similarly, the phrase, *Kalkati Balam* (the lover, who lives in Calcutta or more literally, 'the Calcuttized lover') occurs frequently.

Mention of Calcutta as the city that attracts Bhojpuri emigrants and migrants occurs most abundantly in *jhumurs*, but is found in Purbi songs as well. Thus, a Purbi song opens with the following lines:

> I was sleeping O Nandi, and I saw a dream,
> From Calcutta my husband has come.

Calcutta as a symbol in the Bhojpuri collective memory is different from Calcutta as a real entity. In various Purbi songs, the metaphor of Calcutta and Purub (east) is synonymous, but some songs make a clear distinction between the east and Calcutta. For instance, in a Kanhar song, we find:

> Who of our people will go the east or the like
> And who of our people will go to Calcutta?
> My Debar will go to the east and the like
> My husband will go to the Calcutta.

In spite of very thin differences in perception between the east and Calcutta in the Bhojpuri folk consciousness, both evoke similar pathos among folk psyche. A folk song composed by Jagar Deo of Shahabad district in the 19th century is mentionable here:

> Swami Mora Gaile Ho Purab Ke Deswa se Deire Gaile Na
> Ek Sugana Khelona Se Dei Gaile Na

> (My husband has gone to Purab land and has left me a parrot to play with)

The Hooghly 'Calcutta' and 'Purab' are mentioned as the symbol of 'Bides' in the Bhojpuri folk songs. The concepts of 'Des' and 'Vides' are not identical to the concept of being 'similar' in folk consciousness. In folk consciousness 'Des' is the 'geographical region' which makes a space in folk consciousness as a consequence of its cognitive experience, i.e., by observing, listening, knowing and acknowledging. Other than 'Des' every other geographical region is called 'Bidesh'. On the other hand, colonialists and elites both describe 'Des' as a meta structure and perceive it as a 'unified territory'. In the

19th century, because the means of transport and information system were not developed, 'Des' was very small for them. Also, Calcutta was the gate for the Bhojpuris to enter Bides. Probably, this was another reason in folk consciousness to call it 'Bides'.

Des, Door Des and Bides

Bhojpuri oral tradition, the small part of which is compiled now, when studied and analysed makes it clear that the concept of 'Apna Des' and 'Door Des' were popular in Bhojpuri folk culture. There was also a concept of 'Agarmpur', which could not be approached in the Bhojpuri folklores. In a way, it is used for 'Parlok'.

In the Nirguns of Kabir also, 'Videsh' is used to mean 'Doosra Lok'.

Sainyaaji Vides Gayeele Ram

My husband has gone to Vides (foreign land), O Ram

The transcendental meaning of this new entrant word in Bhojpuri folk culture got transformed to its 'worldly' meaning, which then got converted into the word 'Bidesia' to signify people having gone from their native places. It is quite interesting that in the Bhojpuri folk culture the words 'Phirangi' and 'Angrezi' were used for the English. Seldom was the word 'Bidesia' used for them. Probably, for the first time, around 1860, the word 'Bidesia' was used in Bhojpuri folk songs by Beni Ram in the context of migration. This was the period of migration of people from Bhojpuri region to different countries. Pandit Beni Ram began composing folk songs just before Bharatendu Harishchandra. Bharatenduji has mentioned Beni Ram in his article on 'Kajli Chhand' which appeared in his book, *Hindi Bhasha*. A folklore composed by Pandit Beni Ram is mentioned below:

Kaahe Mori Sudhi Bisraye Re Videsiya
Tadapi Tadapi Din Rain Ganwayo Ri Videsiya

(Why have you stopped thinking about me, O Bidesia? I am spending my days and nights suffering, O Bidesia).

It was also during this period that Bhojpuri folk songs full of agony and complaint are seen expressed in the folk songs composed by Beechu Kavi from Benaras:

Liya Ke Gawanawa Rajau Chhod Le Bhavanava
Sooni Kar Gayele Sejaria
Piya Videsia Bhayi Le Na

(You brought me home after marriage, but you soon left me. My bed is empty, as my beloved is now a Bidesia).

Batohia Folk Songs

In Bidesia folk songs, the word 'Bidesia' has three different meanings:

1. It is an identity given to the migrants by the people of their homeland.
2. It is a form of address used by the people of the homeland to express their sorrow at the separation of their loved ones.
3. Sometimes, the word acquires an ambiguous meaning, in which both the 'self' and the 'other' are a part of one metaphor, representing both the emigrant and the emigree.

It seems to appear that the migrants have accepted the identity granted to them by the people of their homeland. That is the reason why they refer to themselves as Bidesia when they express their pain in the Bidesia folk songs and in the other folklores based on Bidesia tunes.

The history of migration, which emerges from a study of Bidesia folk culture, shows that there was a tradition of 'Pardesi' in the Bhojpuri society. The Bidesia form evolved from this tradition. In Bhojpuri folk songs, the word 'Pardesia' has been used simultaneously with the word 'Bidesia' as a form of address. But 'Pardesia' has been used to those migrants who are hopeful to returning to the homeland. It should be remembered that almost half of the overseas migrants did return home.

The word 'Batohia', meaning 'traveller', was used to refer to the migrants who went to foreign lands as tourists. The hopes in the minds of the Bhojpuri society, of the returning of those migrants who had gone to Surinam, Fiji, Trinidad, Mauritius, was very minimal. But, they had some hope that the migrants might return as tourists and be united with the soil, culture, environment and the people of their native land. The desire to be reunited with the migrants in this form caused the people of the homeland also to refer to them as 'Batohi' or 'traveller'.

> In the Bidesia folk culture, the word 'batohi' also carries two meanings. Invitation to migrants to return to their native lands even as tourists.

Batohia is the name of the migrant traveller who will narrate the pain and sorrow of the people of the homeland to their loved ones who are now permanent migrants.

Along with Bidesia folk songs, the Batohia folk songs also became quite popular. Babu Raghubir Narain, who was born in 1884 in the Naya Gaon in the Saran district, composed Batohi folk songs around 1910. Along with the Bhojpuri region, these songs were also popular among the Bhojpuri migrants in South Africa, Mauritius, Surinam and Trinidad (Singh, 1955: 216). In these folk songs, the migrants were requested to come and visit their native land India, at least once. Some lines from a Batohi folk song are given below:

> Sundar subhumi bhaiya bharat ke deswa se more pran base himkhoh se batohiya
> Ek dwar ghere rama him kotwalwa se, teen dwar sindhu gharhrav re botohiya
> Jahu Jahu bhaiya re batohi re hind dekhi aau, jahwa kuhuki koilari bole re batohiya

Jau Jau bhaiya re batohi hind dekhi aau jahan rishi charon ved gawe re batohiya
Seeta ke vimal jas ram jas krishna jas more bap dada ke kahabi re baotohiya

(The land of my country is so rich and fertile that my heart is ensnared in the beautiful mountains of the Himalayas. On one side, the lofty Himalayas stand guard like a sentinel, while on the other three sides, the waves of the deep seas keep guard, O Batohia. O Batohiya, come and visit this beautiful land where the koel sings so sweetly. O Batohia, come and visit this beautiful land where the saints recite the four Vedas. Come and hear the story of the pure Sita, of the glory of Rama and Krishna and the story of our fathers and brothers, O Batohia).

In the above lines, there is an attempt to rekindle the memories of the land of India in the minds of the migrants who were very attached to it.

The Batohi symbols and the lyrics became so popular, that later in 1916, when Bhikhari Thakur composed the Bidesia folk theatres, the 'Batohi' was an important character in them. The Batohi is supposed to be a person who travels to and fro between the native lands and the destination points of the migrants. He is created as a kind of messenger. The uneducated Bhojpuri women, who have never even visited a city, communicate their sorrow to their loved ones through the Batohi. Bhikhari Thakur has himself also composed many folk songs on the Batohi tune in his Bidesia folk theatre. The unfulfilled Bhojpuri women describe their husbands as a Batohi and request him to search for their husbands. The following lines show this:

Kariya na gor bate, lama nahi hauan nate
Majhial jaban, saam sundar batohia
Ghuti pale dhoti kor, nakua suga ke thor
Sir par topi, chhati chakar batohia

Awela asadh maas, lagela adhik aas
Barsatwa mein piya ghare rahitan batohia

(My beloved is neither dark, nor fair. He is neither tall, nor short. He is of middle height and is dark and handsome, O Batohia. His dhoti is upto his knees and his nose is like the beak of a parrot. He wears a cap on his head and his chest is broad. When the month of Asadh comes, I feel hopeful that he will come in the rainy season).

Conclusion

Bhojpuri folk culture has a special tradition that reflects the history of emotions of both the emigrants and the emigrees who are left behind in the homeland. This tradition has been given the name 'Bidesia Folk Cultural Tradition'. Although the word 'Bidesia' referred to those migrants who left their motherland to work in foreign lands, it later acquired a metaphorical meaning as a form of address used by the people of the homeland to express their sorrow at the separation of their loved ones. Sometimes, the word also acquired an ambiguous meaning in which both the 'self' and the 'other' became a part of one metaphor, representing both the migrant and the loved ones who had been left behind.

Although the Bidesia folk tradition has a separate form, but it is also identified in other folk songs like poorvi, kajri, jhumar, biraha etc. All these folk songs express the pain of the loved ones who have been left behind due to adverse economic circumstances. In today's context, where there is a danger of extinction of oral folk tradition, it is important to collect, document and analyse these oral traditions. Alongside it is important to relate them with other archival and secondary sources and develop a story of Bhojpuri overseas migration. It is interesting to note that these Bhojpuri folk songs are popular not only in the homeland of the migrants, but also in their destination points like Mauritius, Surinam, Trinidad, Fiji and Netherlands. These folk traditions are an important component of the cultural bags of the migrants. A study of these traditions will not only help in discovering the roots of the present-day non-resident Bhojpuris, but will also be an important element of their common cultural heritage.

References

The folk songs that have been documented here have been collected from both oral and written sources. Written sources like anthologies of folklores, popular booklets and journals have been used, alongside we have also recorded the songs of original Bhojpuri folk singers in different places of the Bhojpur district of Bihar. Due to the lack of technical support like audio and video recording facilities, we had to rely on field diaries and notes to record the folk songs.

Buckland, C.E. (1863), *Bengal Under Lieutenant Governors*, Delhi.

de Kerk, C.J.M. (1953), *De Immigratie der Hindostanen in Suriname*, Amsterdam (Urbi et Orbi).

Dwivedi, B.P. (2000), *Bhikhari Thakur*, Allahabad.

Gopal S. and Jha Hetukar (1983), Caste and Profession: A Case Study of Rural Bihar in the First Decade of the Twentieth Century, *Man in India*, 63:3, Ranchi.

Hunter, W.W. (1877) *A Statistical Account of Bengal*, London.

Indra Deva, (1989), *Folk Culture and Peasant Society in India*, Jaipur.

Kamata, Kamlesh (1999), Pravasi Hindi Lokgeeton Men Vedana Ke Swar, *Manav*, 22:1, Lucknow.

Legene, S. (2001), *Unpublished report on Museum of Ethnography, G.B. Pant Social Science Institute*, Allahabad.

Shurvir (1986), Purkhan Ki Yaad Mein Sarnami 3, magazine published from Hague, The Netherlands.

Singh, Durga Shankar Prasad (1958), *Bhojpuri Ke Kavi Aur Kavya*, Patna.

Singh, N.P. (1988) *Bhojpuri Sammelan Patrika*, Patna.

Sinha, P.B. (1975), *Development of Mineral Industry in Bihar*, Muzaffarpur.

Trivedi, R. (1921), *Maurishus Mein Bharatiya*.

Upadhyaya, H.S. (1989), *Bhojpuri Folk Songs from Balia*, Varanasi.

Contributors

Bhaskar Majumder, Reader, G.B. Pant Social Science Institute, Allahabad.

Bimal Kumar, Research Associate, G.B. Pant Social Science Institute, Allahabad.

K.N. Bhatt, Research Associate, G.B. Pant Social Science Institute, Allahabad.

P.C. Upadhyaya, Research Fellow, G.B. Pant Social Science Institute, Allahabad.

U. Kalpagam, Professor, G.B. Pant Social Science Institute, Allahabad.

R.M. Tripathi, Research Associate, G.B. Pant Social Science Institute, Allahabad.

Sunit Singh, Research Associate, G.B. Pant Social Science Institute, Allahabad.

Vanita Somvanshi, Research Officer, G.B. Pant Social Science Institute, Allahabad.

S.K. Pant, Reader, G.B. Pant Social Science Institute, Allahabad.

A.R. Mishra, Research Associate, G.B. Pant Social Science Institute, Allahabad.

Badri Narayan Tiwari, Research Associate, G.B. Pant Social Science Institute, Allahabad.